W9-AWJ-690

SUSQUEHANNA TOWNSHIP MIDDLE SCHOOL
801 WOOD ST.
HARRISBURG, PA 17109

PACEMAKER®

Basic
English

Third Edition

GLOBE FEARON

Pearson Learning Group

REVIEWERS

We thank the following educators who provided valuable comments and suggestions during the development of this book:

Patricia Berdan, Will Rogers Middle School, Fair Oaks, California
Nina Berler, William Annin Middle School, Basking Ridge, New Jersey
Grace Burkhart, Center for Applied Linguistics, Washington, District of Columbia
Dr. Dennis J. Carroll, Susan Wagner High School, Staten Island, New York
Jacqueline M. Kiraithe-Córdova, Department of Foreign Language and Literature, California State University, Fullerton, California
Carol Donahue, Neptune Middle School, Neptune, New Jersey
Christie Dorn, Indio High School, Indio, California
Ann Hilborn, Lee High School, Houston, Texas
Stephani Jones, Farmingdale High School, Farmingdale, New York
Barbara Loga, Bellevue High School, Bellevue, Michigan
Patsy Mills, Bellaire High School, Bellaire, Texas
Mary Moore, Frost Curriculum Center, Warren, Michigan
Anika Simmons, North Star Academy Charter School, Newark, New Jersey
Mildred Teague, Wallkill Valley Regional High School, Hamburg, New Jersey

Subject Area Consultants: Paul Gallaher, Florida Department of Education – Bureau of Instructional Support and Community Services, Tallahassee, Florida; Marcia Krefetz-Levine, Brookdale Community College, Lincroft, New Jersey; Paula Young, Orange County Public Schools, Orlando, Florida
Pacemaker Curriculum Advisor: Stephen C. Larsen, formerly of The University of Texas at Austin

Executive Editor: Eleanor Ripp; *Senior Editor:* Karen McCollum; *Editor:* Ayanna Taylor; *Production Editor:* Travis Bailey; *Designers:* Susan Brorein, Jennifer Visco, Evelyn Bauer (cover); *Editorial Assistants:* Amy Greenberg, Kathy Bentzen, Wanda Rockwell; *Market Manager:* Katie Kehoe-Erezuma; *Editorial Developer:* Pinnacle Education Associates; *Electronic Composition:* Burmar Technical Corp., Phyllis Rosinsky, Linda Bierniak

About the Cover: English skills help people communicate effectively with one another. The images on the cover of this book show how an understanding of basic English skills is relevant in everyday life. People read books for enjoyment and to gather information. Newspapers tell about current events. Telephones allow people to speak and listen to one another. Dictionaries give definitions, correct spelling, and pronunciation of words. Computers can be used to write personal letters and reports for school. How do you use English skills in your everyday life?

ISBN 0-130-23313-7
Printed in the United States of America

6 7 8 9 10 11 12   05 04 03

1-800-321-3106
www.pearsonlearning.com

Contents

Chapter 8   Verb Phrases   162

Chapter 9   Verbs and Sentence Patterns   184

A Note to the Student

The purpose of this book is to help you develop the English skills you need to succeed in today's world. You will learn about different kinds of sentences, and how to capitalize and punctuate them. You will learn about nouns, pronouns, verbs, adjectives, and adverbs. You will also learn about the parts of a paragraph. Some of this information may not seem very useful right now. However, a solid understanding of basic English will help you to communicate well throughout your life—at school, at home, and on the job.

For example, suppose you want to figure out how to use adverbs in written instructions. You may want to know what English skills you need to work as a flight attendant or a sports commentator. *Basic English* can help you find the answers to your questions. In every chapter, there are special features that show you how basic English relates to your life. The **English in Your Life** and **Communicating on the Job** features take basic English out of the classroom and into the real world.

You probably hear a lot about writing skills in school. Do you wonder what this has to do with you? Whether you are taking a test or applying for a job, you need to write clearly and effectively. *Basic English* has many activities that allow you to practice writing in real-world situations. You will also find **Writing Lessons** to help you succeed at this skill.

What about the reference tools that you see in books and in the library? The **Using References** features take the mystery out of reference materials. You will learn how to use a table of contents, an index, a dictionary, and an Internet search engine. These materials will help you find information you need for school and for everyday life.

Throughout the book you will find notes in the margins of the pages. These handy **margin notes** are there to remind you of something you already know.

You will also find several study aids in the book. At the beginning of every chapter, you will find **Learning Objectives**. They will help you focus on the important points in the chapter. You will also find **Words to Know**, a look ahead at the vocabulary you may find challenging. The colorful photos, charts, and drawings in the book bring English concepts to life. **Test Tips** and **Writing Tips** in the Chapter Review will help you prepare for—and succeed on—tests.

Everyone who put this book together worked hard to make it useful, interesting, and enjoyable. The rest is up to you. We wish you well in your studies. Our success is in your accomplishment.

Chapter 1 Sentences

Chapter 2 Punctuation

Machines like these print thousands of newspapers every day. News writers group words into sentences to communicate meaning.

Newspapers contain articles on many different topics. In the local news section, writers report on events in the community.

Read the news article and answer the questions.

1. Which group of words does not express a complete thought? *The First*

2. Which group of words asks a question? *Third*

3. How does the writer show excitement? *the next*

Too Hot to Handle!

The temperature reached 100 degrees over the weekend. It is expected to hit 105 degrees tomorrow. How can people keep cool? Doctors suggest staying inside and drinking plenty of water. It is going to be a long, hot summer!

1

We use sentences to communicate with each other. What do you think is being communicated in this picture?

Chapter 1 ▶ Sentences

Words to Know

sentence	a group of words that expresses a complete thought
subject	the part of a sentence that tells *who* or *what* the sentence is about
predicate	the part of a sentence that tells what the subject *does* or *is*
fragment	a group of words that does not express a complete thought
declarative sentence	tells what someone or something is or does
interrogative sentence	asks a question
imperative sentence	gives a command or makes a request
exclamatory sentence	shows strong feeling
paragraph	three or more sentences that are placed together and relate to the same idea

Sentence Bank Project

Create a sentence bank. Look through newspapers for different kinds of sentences. Cut out sentences that end with periods, question marks, and exclamation points. Group the sentences by kind, and tape them on a sheet of paper.

Learning Objectives

- Define a sentence.
- Identify, capitalize, and punctuate the four kinds of sentences.
- Identify subjects and predicates in declarative, interrogative, and imperative sentences.
- Write complete sentences.
- Apply knowledge of sentences to a letter of complaint and an encyclopedia entry.

A **sentence** is a group of words that expresses a complete thought. Every sentence begins with a capital letter and ends with a punctuation mark.

▶ **EXAMPLE 1**

These are sentences.

The sun shines brightly.

Who rang the doorbell?

Every sentence has two main parts: a **subject** and a **predicate**. The subject tells *who* or *what* the sentence is about. The predicate tells what the subject *does* or *is*.

▶ **EXAMPLE 2**

Subject	Predicate
The sun	shines brightly.
Who	rang the doorbell?

A group of words that does not express a complete thought is called a **fragment**.

▶ **EXAMPLE 3**

These are fragments. They are not sentences.

The sun. (This group of words does not tell what the sun is or does.)

Rang the doorbell? (This group of words does not tell who rang the doorbell.)

Practice A

Look at each group of words. Write *sentence* for each sentence. Write *fragment* for each fragment. The first one is done for you.

1. The man suddenly disappeared.

   sentence

2. Remembered my name.
   Fragment

3. Rachel leaped over the hurdle easily.

   sentence

4. The winner is Sheila.

   sentence

5. A large, noisy crowd.

   sentence

Practice B

Rewrite each fragment as a sentence. The first one is done for you.

6. The large chorus.

   The large chorus sings beautifully.

7. Mario's job at the movie theater.

   Mario's job is at the movie theater

8. Heard a strange noise.

   I was asleep and heard a strange noise

9. The final race.

   Requal finsh the final race.

10. Starts at 7:00 A.M.

    The TV show starts at 7:00 A.M

Practice C

Identify the underlined section as the subject or predicate. The first one is done for you.

11. <u>The airplane</u> landed safely.

    subject

12. Tyrone <u>walked into the store</u>.

    predicate

13. <u>The police officer</u> hurried to the accident.

    subject

14. <u>The pond</u> is frozen solid.

    subject

15. My car <u>makes a strange noise</u>.

    predicate

Remember
A sentence is a group of words that expresses a complete thought.

There are four kinds of sentences.

A **declarative sentence** tells what someone or something is or does. It ends with a period.

An **interrogative sentence** asks a question. It ends with a question mark.

An **imperative sentence** gives a command or makes a request. It usually ends with a period. It may end with an exclamation point.

An **exclamatory sentence** shows strong feeling. It ends with an exclamation point.

▶ **EXAMPLE**

Type	Example
Declarative	Our team won the game.
Interrogative	Who won the game?
Imperative	Please buy tickets for the next game.
Imperative	Get the tickets now!
Exclamatory	That was the best game of the season!

Practice

Label each sentence. Write *declarative, interrogative, imperative,* or *exclamatory.* The first one is done for you.

1. Who plays shortstop on that baseball team?

   interrogative

2. He bought a new CD player.

   declarative

3. Just sign the check over to me.

   imperative

4. What kind of computer is that?

   interrogative

5. The water is too hot! *exclamatory*

6. How many days will you be gone? *interrogative*

7. What a silly suggestion that was! *imperative*

8. Iowa got its name from a Native American word meaning "sleepy ones." *Declarative*

9. Please count them again. *imperative*

10. Do you think you could carry a million one-dollar bills? *interrogative*

11. What a great place this is! *exclamatory*

12. Babe Ruth was a famous baseball player. *declarative*

13. Did you receive the message that I left? *interrogative*

14. I have seen this movie five times. *imperative*

15. Watch out for that falling tree! *exclamatory*

Everyday English

A recall notice tells people that something is wrong with a product. Read this recall notice. Then follow the directions below.

1. Write the three declarative sentences.

2. Write the interrogative sentence.

3. Write the imperative sentence.

4. **CHALLENGE** Explain how you can tell if a sentence is imperative.

Recall Notice

Did you buy Top Performance athletic shoes?

If so, please check the number stamped inside. Any shoes stamped 14927 should be returned. The rubber soles were not glued properly. The store you bought the shoes from will refund your money.

1·3 Capital Letters and End Punctuation in Sentences

Every sentence begins with a capital letter.

▶ **EXAMPLE 1**

The man was a stranger.

Have you seen him before?

Every sentence ends with a punctuation mark. Declarative sentences end with a period. Interrogative sentences end with a question mark. Imperative sentences end with a period or an exclamation point. Exclamatory sentences end with an exclamation point.

▶ **EXAMPLE 2**

Type	Example	Punctuation Mark
Declarative	The man just arrived in town.	period
Interrogative	Did he ride the bus?	question mark
Imperative	Tell me about him.	period
Imperative	Tell me about him at once!	exclamation point
Exclamatory	How mysterious he seems!	exclamation point

Practice A

Rewrite each sentence. Use correct end punctuation. The first one is done for you.

1. What a surprise this is

   What a surprise this is!

2. What is your favorite musical group

3. My aunt lives in North Dakota

4. Listen to the birds sing

5. Watch out for that car

6. Who typed this report ?

7. These fossils were discovered last year,

8. Is this your sandwich ?

9. Send this e-mail to Ms. Thompson !

10. Someone help me !

Practice B

Rewrite each sentence. Use capital letters and end punctuation correctly. The first one is done for you.

11. for years, Cory had wanted a car

    For years, Cory had wanted a car.

12. how could he earn the money he needed

    How could he earn the money he needed?

13. he found a job at the supermarket

    He found a job at the supermarket.

14. it took a long time to save enough money

    It took a long time to save enough money.

15. at last, he had enough

    At last he had enough!

16. where should he go to buy a car

    Where should he go to buy a car?

17. he saw a red convertible at Square Deal Cars

    He saw a red convertible at Square Deal Cars.

18. the car was a dream

    The car was a dream.

19. did he have enough money

    Did he have enough money?

20. to his surprise, the car was very cheap

    To his surprise the car was very cheap.

21. there was one problem

    There was one problem.

(Practice B continued.)

22. the engine would not start

The engine would not start.

23. what did he do

What did he do?

24. tell me

Tell me!

25. he decided to fix the car

He decided to fix the car.

Practice C

Each of the sentences in the paragraph below is missing the end punctuation. Rewrite the paragraph. Use the correct end punctuation in each sentence.

There is a strange noise coming from somewhere in this room, What could it be Look under the bed, It is not coming from under the bed, There it is again Where is it coming from It gets louder by the closet, Open the closet door Be careful It is definitely here in the closet But what is it Oh, I know It is my electronic football game, I must have forgotten to turn it off last night, Whew, that was scary

Everyday English

Arturo works at a local health club. The owner wants to advertise a new water aerobics class. He asked Arturo to make the sign. When Arturo finished typing, he noticed that his sign had no capital letters. All of the end punctuation was also missing.

Rewrite the ad with capital letters and end punctuation.

do you want to get fit fast

well, here is your chance

join our new water aerobics class

classes are held from

6:00 P.M. to 7:00 P.M. every day

(limited spaces are available)

sign up at the front desk

it will be a splash

Subjects and Predicates in Declarative Sentences

1·4

In most declarative sentences, the subject comes before the predicate. The subject tells who or what the sentence is about.

► **EXAMPLE 1**

Look at the subjects in blue type.

People came to see the caves.

Three new **guides** showed the visitors around.

The predicate comes after the subject in most declarative sentences. It usually begins with an action word. The predicate tells what the subject does or is.

► **EXAMPLE 2**

Look at the predicates in blue type.

The group **entered the cave slowly.**

Everyone **looked around.**

In some declarative sentences, the predicate comes before the subject.

► **EXAMPLE 3**

In the sentences below, the predicate is in blue type. Notice where the predicate appears in each sentence.

The girl ran **down the street.**

Down the street ran the girl.

Practice A

Write each sentence. Draw one line under the subject. Draw two lines under the predicate. The first one is done for you.

1. Roger writes to me often.

Roger writes to me often.

2. They went to every football game last year.

3. A messenger will deliver the package tomorrow.

4. From these seeds will spring new plants.

5. Across the lawn rolled an old tennis ball.

6. Donna and he make scented candles.

7. Lobsters have five pairs of legs.

8. Under the couch was Rebecca's missing book.

9. Banks and other businesses will close for the holiday.

10. Nobody wanted to spoil the surprise.

11. Near the chair sat a yawning cat.

12. Julie found her lost necklace.

13. My family and I visited my grandmother.

Practice B

Write each sentence. Add a predicate of your own. The first
one is done for you.

14. Those rusty scissors _____.

    Those rusty scissors should be thrown away.

15. The most experienced detectives in the department *is dead*

16. Muddy footprints *is all over the floor*

17. Most football coaches *is skin*

18. Almost everyone in the whole town *know me*

Practice C

Write each sentence. Add a subject of your own. The first one is done for you.

19. _____ loves to work on cars.

My brother loves to work on cars.

20. _____ swept through the town.

21. _My mother_ appeared from nowhere.

22. _My sister_ was found on the beach.

23. _The bird_ sits outside my window every afternoon.

24. Lying at the bottom of my backpack was _my pen_.

Practice D

Combine the subjects and predicates in the boxes to write ten different declarative sentences.

Subject	Predicate
Kim and Andy	walked on the grass.
We	were looking for food.
Some heavy things	ring loudly and clearly.
The bells	sat under the pine tree.
Bears	fell from the shelf.
The sky	went into overtime.
Some students	cheered for the home team.
The snow and sleet	turned a strange shade of green.
The game	ran through the hall.
Everyone	made the roads dangerous.

1-5 ▷ Subjects and Predicates in Interrogative Sentences

Remember
An interrogative sentence
asks a question and ends
with a question mark.

Every interrogative sentence has a subject and
a predicate.

In some interrogative sentences, the subject comes
before the predicate.

▶ **EXAMPLE 1**

Look at the subjects in blue type.

Who arrived first?

Which package was the largest?

In many interrogative sentences, part of the predicate
comes before the subject.

▶ **EXAMPLE 2**

Look at the predicate in blue type.

Did the butler lie about it?

To find the subject, change the sentence into a
declarative sentence. Then find the subject and
predicate of the new sentence.

▶ **EXAMPLE 3**

In the sentences below, the predicate is in blue type.
Notice where the predicate appears in each sentence.

Did the butler lie about it?

The butler did lie about it.

Practice A

Write the subject of each interrogative sentence. The
first one is done for you.

1. Which poem was the winning entry?

   Which poem

2. What will happen on Sunday?

3. Who will bring a radio?

    who

4. What is on the front page of the newspaper?

5. Which notebook is yours?

    which notebook

6. Who answered the phone?

    who answered

7. Whose gloves are missing?

    whose gloves

8. Which one was the bargain?

    which one

9. Who stars in this movie?

    who stars

10. Whose pen is this?

    whose pen

Practice B

Rewrite each interrogative sentence as a declarative sentence. Draw one line under the subject. Draw two lines under the predicate. The first one is done for you.

11. Do snakes shed their skins?

    Snakes do shed their skins.

12. Did you find the correct answer?

13. Did Lu Yin arrive yesterday?

14. Does the doctor recommend medication?

15. Does that winding path lead to the cabin?

16. Can you hold this book?

17. Did she leave after lunch?

18. Can Jamie help you?

(Practice B continues on next page.) ⇨

19. Will it rain tomorrow?

20. Did Susan and Megan go home?

21. Can you tell me the correct answer?

22. Would you like to see my new office?

23. Will lunch be ready soon?

Practice C

Write each sentence. Add a subject of your own. The first one is done for you.

24. _____ volunteered to help?

Who volunteered to help?

25. Does ___Kim___ have an answer to my question?

26. Can ___you___ fix your car?

27. ___Ice Cream___ is your favorite?

28. Was ___the shop___ crowded today?

Everyday English

Michelle left this message on her friend Jenny's answering machine.

Write the message. Draw one line under each subject. Draw two lines under each predicate.

Jenny, where are you? Why weren't you at the meeting today? Didn't Brian tell you about the new meeting time? Can you please call me when you get home?

Remember
Imperative sentences end with a period or an exclamation point.

 EXAMPLE

An imperative sentence gives a command or makes a request. In most imperative sentences, only the predicate is written or spoken. The subject of the sentence is understood. That subject is always *you.*

Turn off the light.

You turn off the light.

Sing your favorite song for me.

You sing your favorite song for me.

Practice

Write the subject of each sentence. Some of the sentences are imperative sentences. If the subject is understood to be *you*, write *you*. The first one is done for you.

1. Go to Main Street and turn right.

   you

2. Hit the ball to me.

3. Anything is possible.

4. Look at this memo before I send it.

5. Barbara and José will organize the car wash.

6. Never speak to me that way again!

7. Did Tony get a new job?

8. Why won't Mr. Miller be there?

9. Tell me which movie you liked best.

Complete sentences have a subject and a predicate. They also begin with a capital letter and end with a punctuation mark. You can use the READ, PLAN, WRITE, and CHECK steps to write complete sentences.

EXAMPLE

Write a sentence about a recent event in your community. Tell who or what was involved. Also tell what happened. Use capital letters and punctuation marks correctly.

READ   **Do you understand the assignment?**

Write the assignment. Underline the key words.

> Write a <u>sentence</u> about a <u>recent event</u> in <u>your community</u>. Tell <u>who or what was involved</u>. Also tell <u>what happened</u>. Use <u>capital letters</u> and <u>punctuation marks</u> correctly.

PLAN   **Gather your ideas and organize them.**

Use a chart like this one to organize your ideas.

Who or what was involved?	What happened?
the river	flooded Oak Park

WRITE   **Put your ideas into a sentence.**

Create a sentence using the words in your chart. The words in the first column of your chart will be the subject. The words in the second column will be the predicate.

The river flooded Oak Park.
  subject   predicate

CHECK   How can you improve your writing?

Read your sentence to see if it answered the assignment. Add or change some information to make it clearer.

The Red River flooded Oak Park last week.

This sentence gives more information. The words in blue type name the specific river and tell when the flood happened.

Practice

Complete the writing assignments below. Answer the questions below to CHECK your sentences.

1. Write a sentence about someone in the news. Tell who this person is and why this person is in the news.

   CHECK
   Does your sentence answer the assignment?
   What can you add or change to make your sentence clearer?

2. Write another sentence about the person in the first assignment. Explain why this person interests you.

   CHECK
   Does your sentence answer the assignment?
   What can you add or change to make your sentence clearer?

Putting It All Together

A **paragraph** is a group of sentences that are placed together and relate to the same idea. Most paragraphs have at least three sentences.

Write a paragraph about someone who has been mentioned in the news recently. You may use the sentences you have written above. Add more sentences that explain why this person interests you.

ENGLISH IN YOUR LIFE
Writing a Letter of Complaint

Jamal Jones ordered a computer game from a catalog. When he received the disk in the mail, it was damaged. Jamal decided to write a letter of complaint to the catalog company. He asked for a new disk. In his letter he was polite, yet firm.

Read Jamal's letter carefully. Then follow the directions below.

17 Windham Place
Charlotte, NC 59121

January 8, 1999

Gateland Computer Games, Inc.
1500 Industry Road
Seattle, WA 20889

Dear Customer Service Representative:

I received the computer game called **Earth Invader** from your company. The game did not work. The disk must be damaged. I am very disappointed in your product!

Please replace this faulty disk with one that works. I appreciate your cooperation.

Sincerely,

Jamal Jones

Jamal Jones

Writing and Listening
What have you bought that was damaged or didn't work? Write a letter of complaint about this product. Be sure that each sentence has a subject and a predicate. Work with a partner. Read your letters aloud and suggest improvements.

1. Draw a two-column chart. Label one column *Subject* and the other column *Predicate*. List the subject and predicate of each sentence in the correct column.

2. **CRITICAL THINKING** Why is it important to use proper capitalization and end punctuation in a business letter?

USING REFERENCES
Encyclopedia

Encyclopedias give information about thousands of topics. These topics include places, famous people, and important events. An encyclopedia article about a topic is called an entry.

Most encyclopedias are printed as a set of books. Each book is called a volume. Each volume has one or more letters on its side. To find a topic, choose the correct volume. Then search alphabetically for your topic.

Some encyclopedias are electronic. You can use them on a computer. To find a specific entry, type your topic in the search window.

Read this entry from an encyclopedia. Then follow the directions below.

This student uses an encyclopedia.

> **polar bear** Polar bears live near the North Pole. They are larger than other kinds of bears. Some weigh more than 1,800 pounds (800 kg). Polar bears spend much of their time in the water. They eat seals, walruses, and small whales. They also eat berries and seaweed. For more information, see *Arctic Circle* and *seals*.

1. Write a declarative sentence of your own about a fact in the article. Draw one line under the subject and two lines under the predicate.

2. **CHALLENGE** Write two interrogative sentences that could be answered by looking in an encyclopedia.

declarative
exclamatory
fragment
imperative
interrogative
paragraph
predicate
sentence
subject

Vocabulary Review

Complete each sentence with a word from the box.

1. A _____ tells what the subject does or is.
2. To explain something, you use a _____ sentence.
3. To ask a question, you use an _____ sentence.
4. A _____ is a group of sentences about the same topic.
5. To show strong feeling, you use an _____ sentence.
6. A _____ tells what the sentence is about.
7. A _____ is not a complete sentence.
8. To make a request, you use an _____ sentence.
9. A _____ expresses a complete thought.

Chapter Quiz

LESSON 1·1

Defining Sentences
Rewrite each fragment as a sentence.

1. Knows the truth.
2. Which one?
3. The last one on the page.

LESSON 1·2

Test Tip
Punctuation often gives a clue to the type of sentence.

Identifying the Four Kinds of Sentences
Label each sentence. Write *declarative, interrogative, imperative,* or *exclamatory*.

4. Please listen carefully.
5. Did you hear what he said?
6. I wish he would speak louder.
7. What a noisy place this is!
8. Don't talk to me!
9. This is a nice picture frame.

Using Correct Capitalization and End Punctuation
Rewrite each sentence. Use capital letters and end punctuation correctly.

10. something is on fire

11. what can you see

12. everything is all right now

Identifying Subjects and Predicates in Declarative, Interrogative, and Imperative Sentences
Write each sentence. Draw one line under the subject. Draw two lines under the predicate. If the subject *you* is understood, write *you* beside the sentence.

13. My brother's friend is very tall.

14. Will he be coming home today?

15. Look out for that car!

16. Wasn't that a great movie?

Writing Tip
Use a chart in the PLAN step to organize your ideas. CHECK that your paragraph answers the assignment.

Writing Complete Sentences
17. Write a paragraph about a person you admire. Tell who the person is. Give two reasons why you admire the person. Use complete sentences with correct capitalization and end punctuation.

Group Activity

Work with a group to write instructions for emergencies at school. Explain what to do and where to go in case of a fire or another unexpected event. Use complete sentences with correct capitalization and end punctuation. Then have each group member read one step. As a group, suggest ways to improve each step.

What would happen in this picture if there were no stop lights? Punctuation in writing acts like stop lights and street signs. It tells you where to stop or pause. What would happen if there was no punctuation in writing?

Chapter 2 ▶ Punctuation

Words to Know

comma	**(,)**	shows a short pause between words or groups of words
interjection		a word or a group of words that expresses emotion and is followed by an exclamation point or a comma
quotation marks	**(" ")**	show the beginning and end of someone's exact words
colon	**(:)**	introduces a series of items
semicolon	**(;)**	joins two closely-related sentences
hyphen	**(-)**	used between parts of compound numbers, fractions, and some compound words

Flashcard Project

After each lesson, write a sentence on an index card that shows what you learned. Write the sentence on the front with no punctuation. Rewrite it on the back with the correct punctuation. Use your cards to practice punctuating sentences with a partner. Then use the cards to write a summary about what you learned in the chapter.

Learning Objectives

- Use commas to avoid confusion and set off words in a sentence.
- Use commas in a series, in dates, and in place names.
- Use commas and exclamation points with interjections.
- Punctuate and capitalize direct quotations.
- Use colons, semicolons, and hyphens correctly.
- Write sentences with correct punctuation.
- Apply knowledge of punctuation to an advertisement and famous quotations.

Using Commas to Avoid Confusion in a Sentence

When you speak, you often need to pause in the middle of a sentence. By doing this, you show that there is a break in your thought.

The same thing happens in writing. Punctuation marks tell you where to pause or stop. These marks are used to make writing easier to understand.

▶ **EXAMPLE 1**

Incorrect: I do not know why he is acting this way did he hear some good news no wonder he is so excited he won the contest

Correct: I do not know why he is acting this way. Did he hear some good news? No wonder he is so excited. He won the contest!

Use a **comma** in a sentence to indicate a short pause between words. This makes your writing clearer.

▶ **EXAMPLE 2**

Incorrect: In the afternoon traffic filled the streets.

Correct: In the afternoon, traffic filled the streets.

Incorrect: After returning my uncle had dinner.

Correct: After returning, my uncle had dinner.

Practice

Write each sentence. Use a comma where it is needed to make the sentence easier to understand. The first one is done for you.

1. Under a pile of newspapers a mouse was hiding.

    Under a pile of newspapers, a mouse was hiding.

2. After he made his speech Juan did not say another word.

3. On the old desk Conner noticed a book.

4. After the storm was over the lights came on.

5. Whenever Katia went to the movies Paul went with her.

6. With my skates and water bottle I went to the park.

7. I must return the videos he thought.

8. If you tell me when the show starts I will be there on time.

9. At the back of the room he found his backpack.

10. After I read the memo I filed it away.

11. For an afternoon snack Julia ate an apple.

12. When you talk to Jeff tell him I saw his brother.

13. If it is sunny today I will go for a walk in the park.

14. All around the world telephones failed to work.

15. Over the misty clouds the moon shone brightly.

16. For two entire months Alec exercised every day.

17. On a hot summer's evening you often can hear the sound of crickets.

18. At the park people feed the birds.

19. In less than a year I will have saved enough money to buy a stereo.

20. While I do homework I sometimes listen to the radio.

Using Commas to Set Off Words in a Sentence

2·2

Remember
A comma in writing is like a pause in speaking.

Sometimes, a sentence begins with an introductory word or group of words. Use a comma to separate the introductory word or words from the rest of the sentence.

▶ **EXAMPLE 1**

Yes, Jeff is going to New York.

Walking home, I found a one-dollar bill.

Sometimes, a word or group of words interrupts the flow of thought in a sentence. Use commas to set off such a word or words from the rest of the sentence.

▶ **EXAMPLE 2**

Pablo is, I hope, going to help us.

His name, most likely, will never be forgotten.

Sometimes, a person is addressed, or spoken to, by name in a sentence. The name can be at the beginning, at the end, or in the middle of the sentence. Use commas to separate the person's name from the rest of the sentence.

▶ **EXAMPLE 3**

Nick, can you help us? (at the beginning)

Can you help us, Nick? (at the end)

I will be happy, Sara, to help you. (in the middle)

Practice A

Write each sentence. Use commas where they are needed to set off a word or group of words from the rest of the sentence. The first one is done for you.

1. Mary's idea is I think the best one of all.

   Mary's idea is, I think, the best one of all.

2. Excuse me I have a question.

3. This is a problem that of course we can solve together.

4. Matthew I suppose is very popular with his teammates.

5. As usual Jim arrived at the office first.

6. Please can you stop at the store for me?

7. The doctor I think can help us.

8. The answer it seems is simple.

9. This call I hope is for me.

10. No Judy will not read her report today.

11. As always we are waiting for Maria.

12. Hello is anyone home?

13. Yes I am in the living room.

Practice B

Write each sentence. Use commas where they are needed to set off a person's name. The first one is done for you.

14. What movie do you want to see Chen?

What movie do you want to see, Chen?

15. Tim I want to see that new comedy.

16. Wouldn't it be fun Vince to go with them?

17. They haven't asked us to go yet Sara.

18. Vince and Sara do you want to go to the movies with Chen and me?

(Practice B continues on next page.) ⇨

19. What time are you going to work Lynn?

20. José you know that I leave at 6:30.

21. Do you think Belinda that I can get a ride?

22. Sure Lynn I'll be happy to drive you.

Practice C

Write the following paragraph. Add nine commas where they are needed.

I want to thank everyone for working so hard. Susan you have done a great job of finding new customers. Without you our sales would not be so high. Miguel I am so pleased with your new ad designs. I can't forget you Andrea for all your computer training. Yes we would have been in trouble without you. I owe special thanks to you Parker. Working late every night you solved any problems we had. By working as a team we have reached our goal.

Everyday English

Keith is a movie reviewer. He works for a local newspaper. He wrote this week's review, but he left out the commas.

Rewrite Keith's review. Add commas in the correct places.

Go Straight to *Blue Street* ★★★★

Movie fans you do not want to miss *Blue Street*! Although it lasted almost three hours I was never bored. When the movie was over the whole audience cheered. Looking back I think the best parts were the chase scenes.

Using Commas in a Series

A series in writing is formed by three or more of the same kinds of items in a row. Each item can be a single word or a group of words. A comma is used between each item in a series.

EXAMPLE

Gina saw Terry, Kiki, Mitch, and Pam.

Each student had to answer three questions, draw a map, and write an essay.

Jeremy wants to go to Florida, Mexico, or California on vacation.

Practice A

Write each sentence. Use commas to separate the items in a series. The first one is done for you.

1. Carl Jed and Louis agreed to work harder.

   Carl, Jed, and Louis agreed to work harder.

2. Running swimming and skiing are his favorite sports.

3. Has anyone seen Cheryl Patricia or Kathy?

4. Jim drove through Texas New Mexico and Arizona.

5. From his window, he saw flowers grass and trees.

6. Emily likes onions olives and mushrooms on her pizza.

7. **CHALLENGE** Ken and Jill want to paint the house green and tan green and white or blue and white.

Practice B

Use each series below in a sentence of your own. Use commas where they are needed. The first one is done for you.

8. robins sparrows and blackbirds

In the forest, he could hear the sounds of robins, sparrows, and blackbirds.

9. trucks cars and buses

10. blue red and yellow

11. January February and March

12. put his key in the lock opened the door and went inside

13. looked at his watch threw on his coat and ran downstairs

14. New York Boston or Philadelphia

15. morning afternoon and evening

16. camera film batteries

17. came home ate dinner and read a book.

18. Marta Richard and Manny

19. pennies nickels dimes and quarters

20. fell out of my hand rolled across the ground and landed in the mud

2·4 ▶ Using Commas in Dates and in Place Names

Using Commas in Dates

Use a comma to separate the day of the month from the year in a date. If the date is at the beginning or in the middle of a sentence, put another comma after the year. Do not use a comma in a date that has only the name of the month and the year.

▶ **EXAMPLE**

October 2, 1920, was the day of the last baseball triple-header.

Many baseball fans were tired at the end of the day on October 2, 1920.

Those fans will always remember October 1920.

Practice

Write each sentence. Use commas in the dates where they are needed. The first one is done for you.

1. The first drive-in movie opened on June 6 1933.

   The first drive-in movie opened on June 6, 1933.

2. The first U.S. newspaper ad was published on May 1 1704.

3. On May 24 1844 Samuel Morse sent the first message using Morse code.

4. Direct-dial long-distance calls began in November 1951.

5. On February 10 1933 the first singing telegram was sent.

Using Commas in Place Names

Use a comma between the name of a city or town and the name of a state or country.

EXAMPLE 1

The world's oldest zoo is in Vienna, Austria.

It rains often in Portland, Oregon.

Sometimes, the two place names come at the beginning or in the middle of a sentence. Place another comma after the name of the state or country.

EXAMPLE 2

In Vienna, Austria, you will find the world's oldest zoo.

Portland, Oregon, receives much rain.

Practice

Write each sentence. Use commas in the place names where they are needed. The first one is done for you.

1. A large carnival opened in Chicago Illinois.

   A large carnival opened in Chicago, Illinois.

2. New Orleans Louisiana is famous for its music and cooking.

3. The first gas station opened in Bordeaux France.

4. Thomas Edison invented the light bulb in Menlo Park New Jersey.

5. A female boxer defeated a male opponent in Mexico City Mexico.

6. Basketball was invented in Springfield Massachusetts.

7. A famous soapbox derby is held in Akron Ohio.

8. The Gateway Arch is located in St. Louis Missouri.

9. Brooklyn New York once had a baseball team.

10. In Moscow Russia the circus has cows that play football.

11. Have you ever visited the state fair in Columbus Ohio?

12. Did you see the ski race in Park City Utah?

13. We visited a nature center in Sitka Alaska.

14. In Philadelphia Pennsylvania we visited the Liberty Bell.

15. The highest bridge in the country is in Royal Gorge Colorado.

16. Abraham Lincoln was born in Hodgenville Kentucky.

Everyday English

Shayna wants a job at a day-care center. She wrote a cover letter to go with her résumé. Shayna needs to check her letter for mistakes before she sends it. Part of her letter is shown here.

1. Rewrite Shayna's letter. Add commas where they are needed.

2. Add a date to the top of the letter. Use commas where they are needed.

I believe I would do a good job at your day-care center. I have experience patience and a love for kids. I also know first aid and lots of children's songs.

I worked at Sunny Day Care in Toledo Ohio from September 12 1999 until March 14 2000. I have also baby-sat for neighbors friends and relatives for many years.

2·5 ► Using Commas or Exclamation Points with Interjections

An **interjection** is a word or group of words that expresses emotion. Always separate the interjection from the rest of the sentence with a punctuation mark.

Use an exclamation point after an interjection that shows strong emotion. Capitalize the first word of the sentence after the exclamation point.

► **EXAMPLE 1**

Yuck! This food tastes bad.

Really! That surprises me.

Use a comma after an interjection that does not show strong emotion. Do not capitalize the first word of the sentence after the comma.

► **EXAMPLE 2**

Oh, he is not really sure.

Well, you will need to find out.

Practice A

Write each sentence. Use a comma or an exclamation point after each interjection. The first one is done for you.

1. Wow That is a terrific idea.

   Wow! That is a terrific idea.

2. Ouch This paper cut really hurts.

3. Yuck Sally just put peanut butter on her eggs.

4. Hey have you met my cousin?

5. Gosh I don't think we are in Kansas anymore.

6. Wow That is incredible!

7. Well tell us about your exercise program, Coach Lewis.

8. Ah I love the taste of fresh bread first thing in the morning.

9. Great You passed the test.

10. Hurrah I am finished.

11. Sorry I did not see you there.

12. Yeah Our team scored another goal.

13. Sure I can meet you at 5:30.

14. Help Can anybody hear me?

15. Oh, no My computer just crashed.

Practice B

Use an interjection from the box to complete each sentence.
Remember to use the correct punctuation marks.

16. _____ I wouldn't say that.

17. _____ guess who's coming to dinner.

18. _____ I guess you can borrow my notes.

19. _____ My tooth hurts.

20. _____ That was a great game!

21. _____ The water is so refreshing.

22. _____ Our team won the championship.

Hey	Ugh
Well	Oh
Wow	Great
Ouch	Ah

2·6 ▶ Using Punctuation and Capitalization with Direct Quotations

Punctuating Direct Quotations

A quotation can be either indirect or direct. An indirect quotation tells what someone said without using the speaker's exact words.

▶ **EXAMPLE 1**

Watson said that he is not leaving.

A direct quotation tells the exact words a person said. Use **quotation marks** at the beginning and end of each part of a direct quotation. Use commas to separate the quotation from the words that tell who is speaking.

▶ **EXAMPLE 2**

"Holmes," cried Watson, "that's amazing!"

A direct quotation sometimes comes at the end of a sentence. A period is placed inside the quotation marks.

▶ **EXAMPLE 3**

Watson said, "I saw her."

Place exclamation points and question marks that belong to the quotation inside the quotation marks. Place exclamation points and question marks that do not belong to the quotation outside the quotation marks.

▶ **EXAMPLE 4**

Watson exclaimed, "She was on the train!" (inside)

Did Holmes say, "That is important"? (outside)

Sometimes, the direct quotation comes before the name of the speaker. If the quotation is a statement or command, use a comma at the end of it. If it is a question, use a question mark. If it is an exclamation, use an exclamation point.

▶ **EXAMPLE 5**

"The train did not arrive until eleven o'clock," said Holmes.

"Do you see the importance of that?" asked Holmes.

"The body was discovered at ten o'clock!" exclaimed Watson.

Practice A

Write each sentence correctly. Use quotation marks where they are needed. The first one is done for you.

1. Will Rogers said, I never met a man I didn't like.

   Will Rogers said, "I never met a man I didn't like."

2. There are no gains without pains, said Benjamin Franklin.

3. Ken said to meet him in front of the school at three o'clock.

4. Jeff told me he will work my shift on Saturday.

5. The game's not over, Yogi Berra said, till it's over.

Practice B

Write each sentence. Use quotation marks, commas, and the correct end punctuation where they are needed. The first one is done for you.

6. What should I do next asked Bradley.

   "What should I do next?" asked Bradley.

7. Which road goes to Taunton asked the stranger.

8. Jane told me that Bradford Boulevard goes that way.

9. A quicker way said Megan is to take West Street to Route 11.

10. West Street is closed due to roadwork insisted Mike.

11. Jane said that you should take Curtis Drive.

12. Did the stranger say I will ask at the gas station

Capitalizing Direct Quotations

Begin the first word in a direct quotation with a capital letter.

► EXAMPLE 1

Marian asked, "Where did the cat hide now?"

Remember
A sentence is a group of words that expresses a complete thought.

Sometimes, the words that tell who is speaking divide a direct quotation into two parts. If the second part of the quotation is part of the sentence, it should not begin with a capital letter. If the second part of the quotation is a new sentence, it should begin with a capital letter.

► EXAMPLE 2

"Where," asked Marian, "did the cat hide now?" (part of the sentence)

"I know where the cat is," said Fran. "Look over there." (new sentence)

Practice

Write each sentence correctly. Use capital letters where they are needed. The first one is done for you.

1. Mark asked, "do you enjoy French food?"

   Mark asked, "Do you enjoy French food?"

2. Ping Lin said, "the restaurant across the street is good."

3. "should we study," asked Luther, "at the library?"

4. "here comes the train," said Jane.

5. "we'll just make it aboard," said Luz, "if we run."

6. "look over there!" Tasha cried. "a tree fell down."

7. "the last time I was in Ohio," Kevin said, "it rained all week."

8. Justin said, "we had better leave now or we will be late."

9. "did you talk to Marie?" asked Mindy. "she did not call me yet."

10. "Clean up your room," said Mr. Patel. "we are having guests"

11. "I will," Kim said, "as soon as I finish my homework."

12. "Fine," said Mr. Patel, "but they are arriving in one hour."

13. Did she say, "we will go shopping later"?

14. **CHALLENGE** Write the following sentence with correct punctuation and capitalization.

    Mr. Atkins is not here today said Cindi he will be back tomorrow.

Everyday English

Steven interviewed an author for a magazine article he was writing. He used quotations from the author in his article. Part of his article is shown below.

> Ms. Markel said I don't have a favorite book. Then she thought a moment. oh she added maybe I do like one best. I asked her which one that was. it changes she said with a laugh. it's always the last one I wrote.

1. Add the missing commas, quotation marks, and capital letters.

2. **CHALLENGE** Change the first sentence to an indirect quotation.

USING REFERENCES
Book of Quotations

Books of quotations contain sayings by well-known people. Some books include quotations on many topics. Other books focus on one subject, such as sports, politics, or business.

Many books of quotations are organized by topic. The topics are arranged alphabetically. Other books may be arranged in time order or alphabetically by author.

Books of quotations can be useful when writing a speech or a report. They can support an opinion or introduce an idea. When you use a quotation from a book in your writing, be sure to use quotation marks. Also name the person who said it.

Read the quotations about success from a book of quotations. Then follow the directions below.

Success

"The talent of success is nothing more than doing what you can do well, and doing well whatever you do."
– Henry Wadsworth Longfellow

"Whenever a man does the best he can, then that is all he can do . . ."
– Harry S Truman

"There is only one success—to spend your life in your own way."
– Christopher Morley

---

1. List some reasons to use a quotation in a report or in a speech.

2. **CHALLENGE** Explain what success means to you. Choose your favorite quotation above. Use the quotation to support your explanation. Punctuate the quotation correctly.

Using Colons, Semicolons, and Hyphens

Using Colons

Use a **colon** to introduce a series of items. Use a colon between the hour and the minutes to write expressions of time. Use a colon after the greeting in a business letter.

▶ **EXAMPLE**

The photographer brought the following items: cameras, rolls of film, and a tripod. (to introduce a series)

6:15 P.M. (between the hour and minutes)

Dear Mr. Long: (after a business letter greeting)

Practice

Write each sentence. Use a colon where it is needed. The first one is done for you.

1. Yesterday, the sun rose at 730 A.M.

   Yesterday, the sun rose at 7:30 A.M.

2. The movie doesn't start until 915 P.M.

3. After snowing for two days, the storm finally ended at 200 P.M.

4. Tim and Roger enjoy the following sports baseball, basketball, and football.

5. They left the house at 1100 A.M.

6. The newspaper is delivered every day at 630 A.M.

7. Larry will visit the following cities Boston, Philadelphia, Baltimore, and Washington, D.C.

Using Semicolons

You have learned to use a comma to show a pause in a sentence. You also have learned that a period can separate two sentences.

► EXAMPLE 1

Arnold's hands were cold, so he put on his gloves. (pause)

Arnold's hands were cold. He put on his gloves. (separate sentence)

To show a break in thought that is stronger than a comma but not as strong as a period, use a **semicolon**. A semicolon joins two closely related sentences into one sentence. The first word after the semicolon is *not* capitalized.

► EXAMPLE 2

Arnold's hands were cold; he put on his gloves.

Do not use words such as *and, or, but,* or *so* when you use semicolons.

► EXAMPLE 3

The stereo did not work, so we bought a new one. (comma with the word *so*)

The stereo did not work; we bought a new one. (semicolon)

Practice A

Join each pair of sentences using a semicolon. The first one is done for you.

1. Yusef threw out the bread. It was stale.

   Yusef threw out the bread; it was stale.

2. Jack dropped the eggs. Three of them broke.

3. Cheryl came into the kitchen. She slipped on the floor.

4. The three friends laughed. They joked about the mess.

Practice B

Rewrite each sentence using a semicolon. Remember to take out any unnecessary words. The first one is done for you.

5. Randy got into his car, and he headed toward Lisa's house.

Randy got into his car; he headed toward Lisa's house.

6. Randy and Lisa had some free time, and they wanted to go to a movie.

7. They turned to the movie section in the newspaper, and they looked through the listings.

8. They could go to see an adventure movie, or they could go to see a comedy.

9. Randy likes adventure movies, so he suggested the one playing at the Town Theater.

10. Lisa likes adventure movies, and she also enjoys comedies.

11. A new movie had just been released, and it was a comedy.

12. Both movies started soon, and the comedy might be sold out.

13. Time was running out, so they had to choose quickly.

14. They decided not to go to the movies, and they went out to eat instead.

15. **CHALLENGE** Write a sentence about what you did last weekend. Use a semicolon.

Using Hyphens

A **hyphen** is used between parts of certain words. Use a hyphen in compound numbers from twenty-one through ninety-nine. Use a hyphen in a fraction when the fraction describes another word. Use a hyphen in some compound words.

▶ **EXAMPLE**

Compound Number	Fraction	Compound Word
twenty-two	one-fifth	great-aunt
fifty-three	two-sevenths	commander-in-chief
eighty-seven	one-half	father-in-law

Practice

In each sentence below, find the numbers and fractions that should have hyphens. Rewrite the numbers and fractions correctly. The first one is done for you.

1. The eye of a giant squid can be one and one fourth feet wide.

   one-fourth

2. Steak is seventy four percent water.

3. The baby weighed seven and one half pounds.

4. A boy created a house of cards sixty eight stories tall.

5. This baseball bat weighs two and one quarter pounds.

6. A hockey puck weighs about one third pound.

7. A person's brain weighs three and one tenth pounds.

8. An ostrich egg can weigh thirty one pounds.

COMMUNICATING ON THE JOB
Video Store Employee

Roberta Vega just got a job in a new video store. She will greet customers and use the cash register. She also will help people find the videos they want.

The store is getting ready for its grand opening. The store owner asked Roberta to create a flyer to attract customers.

Read Roberta's flyer at the bottom of the page. Then answer the following questions.

1. Which sentence is missing commas? Write the sentence correctly.

Roberta scans the bar code on a video.

2. Which sentence is missing a colon? Write the sentence correctly.

3. Which word in the last sentence should be capitalized?

4. **CRITICAL THINKING** Why is it important to use commas and capital letters correctly in advertisements?

Do you want the newest and most popular videos?

Vince's Videos
is the place to get them!

We have new releases comedies dramas and much more.

The store is open from 1000 A.M. to 11:30 P.M.

The owner, Vince Martelli, says, "drop in and check us out!"

Writing and Reading

With a partner, create a flyer for your favorite store. Include a reason why customers should shop there. Also include the hours the store is open. Be sure to use punctuation and capital letters correctly. Then read your flyer to the class.

Writing: Using Punctuation Correctly in Sentences

Punctuation marks make your writing easier to understand. You can use the READ, PLAN, WRITE, and CHECK steps to write sentences with correct punctuation.

EXAMPLE

What do you like most about your personality? Write a sentence describing your best qualities. List the qualities as a series in your sentence. Use commas to separate each item.

READ   **Do you understand the assignment?**

Answer this question: What are you supposed to write about?

I am supposed to write about what I like most about my personality.

PLAN   **Gather your ideas and organize them.**

Use a sunburst diagram to plan what to write. Write *My Best Qualities* in the center circle. Then list one quality on each ray.

WRITE   **Put your ideas into a sentence.**

Use your ideas in the sunburst diagram to form a sentence. List your qualities in a series.

Quality 1   Quality 2   Quality 3
I am outgoing, funny, and honest.

CHECK   How can you improve your writing?

Does your sentence answer the assignment?
Did you use commas to separate each quality?
Improve your sentence to make it clearer.

What I like most about my personality is that I am outgoing, funny, and honest.

The words in blue type were added. They answer the part of the assignment that asks what you like most about your personality.

Practice

Complete the writing assignments below. Answer the questions to CHECK your sentences.

1. Write a sentence that lists three of your favorite songs, movies, or books. Use commas to separate each item.

    CHECK
    Does your sentence answer the assignment? Did you use commas correctly? How can you make your sentence clearer?

2. Write a sentence that lists three of your hobbies or interests. Use commas to separate each item.

    CHECK
    Does your sentence answer the assignment? Did you use commas correctly? How can you make your sentence clearer?

Putting It All Together

Write an autobiographical sketch of yourself. Describe your best qualities. Also tell about some of your favorite things, hobbies, and interests. You may want to use the two sentences you have written above. Add other sentences that give more information about you.

colon
comma
hyphen
interjection
quotation marks
semicolon

Vocabulary Review

Complete each sentence with a term from the box.

1. A ____ is used between parts of compound numbers.

2. A ____ indicates a short pause between words.

3. An ____ expresses emotion.

4. A ____ joins two closely related sentences.

5. A ____ is used to introduce a series of items.

6. ____ show the beginning and end of someone's exact words.

Chapter Quiz

LESSONS 2·1 to 2·4

Using Commas in Sentences

Write each sentence. Use commas where they are needed in each sentence.

1. Right after we sat down the movie started.

2. Jon what do you think we should do?

3. Ken Jana Frank and Latoya came in together.

4. Cleveland Ohio is where she was born.

5. April 9 1865 marked the end of the Civil War.

LESSON 2·5

Punctuating Interjections

Write each sentence. Use a comma or an exclamation point after each interjection.

6. Hey That was my foot!

7. Wow Your project looks great!

8. Oh I thought you knew that.

9. Well I think I'll go home now.

Punctuating Direct Quotations

Use quotation marks and commas in each sentence.

10. Well Claire said we are almost finished.

11. It is nearly time to turn in our project added Jack.

12. I think said Trevor that we have done our best.

13. I agree Juan said I hope the teacher thinks so, too.

Test Tip
Use colons to introduce lists. Use semicolons between closely related sentences. Use hyphens in fractions.

Using Colons, Semicolons, and Hyphens

Use a colon, a semicolon, or a hyphen in each sentence.

14. I lost my wallet I will need a new one.

15. Here is what you need a can of motor oil, a container, and goggles.

16. He ran three and one half miles.

17. Susan ate a large salad for lunch she decided not to have a snack before dinner.

Writing Tip
Use a Sunburst diagram to PLAN your ideas. CHECK that you used correct punctuation in your paragraph.

Writing: Using Punctuation Correctly in Sentences

18. Write a paragraph about your birthday. Tell when and where you were born. Then list three favorite presents you have received. Make sure you use commas correctly in your paragraph.

Group Activity

Your school is planning a homecoming celebration. Work with a group to create a poster telling about the celebration. The poster should include the date, time, and place of the celebration. It also should tell what activities will be happening. Be sure to use correct punctuation and capitalization. Exchange posters with another group. Suggest ways to improve the other group's poster.

Unit 1 **Review**

Read the passage below to answer questions 1–5. Decide which type of error, if any, appears in each underlined section. Mark the letter for your answer.

(1) <u>Oh no My computer</u> just crashed. I was just finishing my report, which is due (2) <u>tomorrow. did</u> I save it before the (3) <u>computer crashed. Let</u> me see. Well, it is all there. I just need to (4) <u>spell check, print, and save</u> one more time. (5) <u>What a relief that is?</u>

1. A. Spelling Error
   B. Capitalization error
   C. Punctuation error
   D. No error

2. A. Spelling Error
   B. Capitalization error
   C. Punctuation error
   D. No error

3. A. Spelling Error
   B. Capitalization error
   C. Punctuation error
   D. No error

4. A. Spelling Error
   B. Capitalization error
   C. Punctuation error
   D. No error

5. A. Spelling Error
   B. Capitalization error
   C. Punctuation error
   D. No error

Read the passage below to answer questions 6 and 7. Choose the best way to write the passage. Mark the letter for your answer.

(6) <u>"Ted don't forget about the meeting next Friday,"</u> I said. (7) <u>"It is in Akron Ohio." I reminded him."</u>

6. A. "Ted, don't forget about the meeting next Friday," I said.
   B. "Ted, don't forget about the meeting next Friday" I said.
   C. "Ted, don't forget about the meeting next Friday." I said.
   D. No error

7. A. "It is in Akron, Ohio." I reminded him."
   B. "It is in Akron, Ohio" I reminded him.
   C. "It is in Akron, Ohio," I reminded him.
   D. No error

Critical Thinking

Your state wants to raise the age for getting a driver's license. Explain why you agree or disagree.

WRITING Write a paragraph about why the age for a driver's license should or should not be raised. Use correct capitalization and punctuation.

Unit 2 ▸ Nouns

Chapter 3 Common and Proper Nouns
Chapter 4 Noun Forms

A movie shoot is made up of many people, places, and things. The words used to name people, places, and things are called nouns.

Screenwriters use storyboards to sketch out ideas. The storyboard below shows scenes of an action movie. Look at the storyboard, and read the sentences. Then answer the questions.

A plane lands safely on a deserted island.

All aboard hope to be rescued soon.

A clue to an island mystery is found.

1. Where does Scene 1 take place?

2. What people appear in Scene 2?

3. What objects appear in Scene 3?

A common noun names any person, place, thing, event, or idea. List three common nouns that you see in this photograph.

Chapter 3

Common and Proper Nouns

Words to Know

noun	a word that names a person, place, thing, event, or idea
compound noun	a group of words that names a person, place, thing, event, or idea
common noun	a word that names any person, place, thing, event, or idea
proper noun	a word that names a particular person, place, thing, event, or idea
abbreviation	a shortened form of a word

Journal Project

Think about some of your favorite things. For example, what is your favorite food? Your favorite movie? Your favorite piece of clothing? Your favorite music group? Your favorite sport? All of the things you mentioned are nouns. List them in your journal. Then write several sentences using some of the nouns in your list.

Learning Objectives

- Identify nouns.
- Identify compound nouns.
- Identify common and proper nouns.
- Capitalize proper nouns.
- Capitalize abbreviations.
- Write sentences using nouns.
- Apply knowledge of nouns to a job application and library catalogs.

All people and things have names. Most people and things have more than one name. You have more than one name. You have the name you were given at birth. You are a <u>student</u>. You are a <u>son</u> or a <u>daughter</u>. You are a young <u>woman</u> or a young <u>man</u>.

Each of the underlined words could be a name for you. Each word is a **noun**. Nouns are naming words. A noun may name a person, place, or thing. A noun may name an event. A noun may name an idea. An idea may be a feeling or a quality.

▶ **EXAMPLE**

Person	Place	Thing	Event	Idea
man	street	chair	party	loyalty
child	Texas	paper	rally	courage
Jill	school	horse	concert	happiness

Practice A

Draw five columns on a separate sheet of paper. Use these headings: *Person, Place, Thing, Event, Idea*. List each noun in the box below under the correct heading. The first one is done for you.

student	rock	sadness	store	prize
graduation	teacher	equality	parade	house

Person	Place	Thing	Event	Idea
student				

CHALLENGE Add one noun of your own under each heading.

Practice B

Write the nouns in each sentence. There may be more than one noun in a sentence. The first sentence is done for you.

1. A porcupine can float in water.

   porcupine   water

2. Frogs pull in their eyeballs to close their eyes.

3. Penguins are not fish, but they can swim.

4. Lions show love and loyalty to their young.

5. Doves are actually fierce birds.

6. These divers found no treasure.

7. The furniture in her apartment belongs to her sister.

8. It was hard to hide my excitement about the game.

9. Where are the toothbrushes and soap?

10. They are in the suitcase on the bench.

Practice C

Write each sentence. Add nouns of your own. The first sentence is done for you.

11. Nora wants to buy the green _____.

   Nora wants to buy the green dress.

12. She has saved enough _____ from her _____.

13. He took one look at the _____ and laughed.

14. Laurie broke the _____ last _____.

(Practice C continues on next page.) ⇨

15. Tim won a _____ at the _____.

16. Keisha went to the _____ to buy _____.

17. Derrell had to find _____ to write his _____.

18. Shannen listens to the _____ on her way home from _____.

19. Jesse felt much _____ toward his friends.

20. The _____ won the state _____.

Practice D

Write the 15 nouns in the paragraph below. For example, the nouns in the first sentence are *shock* and *morning*.

What a shock I had this morning! I arrived at school just before the bell rang. I rushed to my locker to get my notebook. I expected to see a messy pile of shoes, sweatshirts, and books. Instead, most of my belongings were neatly piled on the floor. My clothes were hung on the hooks. Who had straightened out my locker?

Everyday English

Newspaper headlines have nouns in them. Look at the newspapers on the right. Then follow the directions below.

1. List the five nouns in the headlines.

2. Next to each noun, write if it is a person, place, thing, event, or idea.

Today's Sports
Pitcher Blows Game
in 9th Inning

Local News
Game Seven Determines
Championship

Compound Nouns

A group of words may name a person, place, thing, event, or idea. These groups of words are called **compound nouns**. Some compound nouns have hyphens between the words. Some are written as one word. Some are written as two words.

Compound nouns make sense as a group. For example, the noun *ice cream* means something different from the separate nouns *ice* and *cream*.

Read these groups of words. Each one is a compound noun.

▶ **EXAMPLE**

high school	Fort Mason	Mount Baldy	framework
Stone Avenue	classroom	sister-in-law	commander-in-chief

Practice

Write the nouns in each sentence. Then underline the compound nouns. The first sentence is done for you.

1. The White House is the home of the President.

   <u>White House</u>   home   President

2. St. Louis is in the state of Missouri.

3. The teacher hung posters in the classroom.

4. The junior high school is next to the high school.

5. The maid of honor was late for the wedding.

6. Kim finished her homework before she went to work.

7. Many people eat frozen yogurt instead of ice cream.

A **common noun** is the name of any person, place, thing, event, or idea.

A **proper noun** is the name of a particular person, place, thing, event, or idea. Every important word in a proper noun is capitalized.

▶ **EXAMPLE**

Remember
An idea can be a feeling, such as courage, or a quality, such as happiness.

	Common Noun	Proper Noun
Person	man	John Tyler
Place	state	Nevada
Thing	day	Monday
Event	holiday	Halloween
Idea	religion	Buddhism

Practice A

Write the nouns in each sentence. If the noun is a common noun, write *C* after it. If it is a proper noun, write *P*. The first sentence is done for you.

1. Raul does not have to work at the bank on Saturday.

    Raul P, bank C, Saturday P

2. Alex traveled to India to see his family.

3. The Clarks enjoyed the fireworks on New Year's Eve.

4. Cameron will study English, algebra, and biology next year.

5. Joe told Ann that Spanish was his favorite subject.

6. Mr. Vasquez is the best teacher at Central High School.

Practice B

Write each sentence correctly. Capitalize the proper nouns.
The first sentence is done for you.

7. My sister helen wanted to be a teacher.

My sister Helen wanted to be a teacher.

8. The hotel biltmore was filled with americans.

9. His friend paul speaks spanish.

10. John walked through central park to get to his job on
fifth avenue.

11. My sister is on the basketball team at westwood
high school.

12. Last january, debra visited new mexico.

Everyday English

Iris and Carl wanted to buy a color television. They put a
Want Ad in the local paper. Look at the advertisement they
wrote, and answer the questions below.

1. Which two proper nouns are not
capitalized correctly?

2. Capitalize them correctly.

3. List all the nouns in the ad.

4. CHALLENGE Classify the nouns in this ad
as people, places, or things?

WANTED
Residents in bloomfield need a 19-inch color television. Wilco or Power are brands they prefer. Call Iris or carl at 563-5569.

ENGLISH IN YOUR LIFE
Completing a Job Application

Jason Brock wanted a job at a movie theater. To apply for the job, he had to fill out a job application. The application asked many questions about his education and work experience.

Here is part of the application that Jason filled out. This section asked Jason to list his past jobs.

Read Jason's application. Then answer the questions below.

Employment Record

Please list all employment from the last five years.
Attach extra pages, if needed.

Company: *Super Save Groceries*
Address: *115 Elm Street, Landview, Ohio 99909*
Manager/Supervisor: *Amy Anderson*
Position Held: *cashier*
Dates Employed: *April 1999 to July 1999*
Telephone Number: *999-555-0907*
Reason for Leaving: *The store went out of business.*

1. What proper nouns did Jason use when he filled out the application?

2. What common nouns did Jason use?

3. Rewrite Jason's last answer using a proper noun.

4. **CRITICAL THINKING** Why do you need to use proper nouns when filling out a job application?

Speaking and Listening
Work with a partner to practice answering job interview questions. One person asks the questions. The other person answers them. Then switch roles. Listen carefully for nouns you use in your answers.

Capitalizing Names of Places

The names of places are proper nouns. Capitalize the important words in the names of places. Short words, such as *of* and *and* are usually not important words.

▸ **EXAMPLE**

	Proper Noun	
Street or route	Oak Street	Route 6
City	Miami	Kansas City
State	Maine	North Dakota
Building	Alamo	Empire State Building
Natural feature	Mount Shasta	Gulf of Mexico
Organization	Toledo Tigers	American Legion

Practice

Write each sentence correctly. Capitalize the proper nouns. The first sentence is done for you.

1. The history club visited washington, d.c.

   The history club visited Washington, D.C.

2. They saw the washington monument.

3. They had to wait at the white house.

4. They went on a tour of capitol hill.

5. Everyone enjoyed the picnic in rock creek park.

6. They went for a boat ride on the potomac river.

7. They stopped at colonial restaurant for a quick snack on the way home.

Capitalizing Abbreviations

Some proper nouns can be shortened. A shortened form of a word is called an **abbreviation**. Capitalize the first letter of the abbreviation of proper nouns. Put a period at the end of most abbreviations.

▶ **EXAMPLE 1**

Hill Street	Hill St.
Doctor Wu	Dr. Wu
Mister Ross	Mr. Ross

Capitalize both letters in abbreviations of states in the United States. Do not put a period at the end of these abbreviations.

▶ **EXAMPLE 2**

Texas	TX
New Jersey	NJ
Illinois	IL

Practice

Write each address correctly. Use capital letters and periods where necessary. Underline the abbreviations.

1. ms francie jones
32 denver pl
los angeles, ca 90067

2. dr linda jackson
575 spruce blvd
sitka, ak 22292

3. mr carl rath
49 vista dr
fleming, ky 41816

4. miss robin stein
1516 cleveland rd
dayton, oh 63631

Capitalizing Parts of the Country

Names of parts of the United States are proper nouns. Capitalize the names of parts of the country.

▶ EXAMPLE 1

In the summer, it is hot in the Southeast.

Names of directions are common nouns. Do not capitalize names of directions.

▶ EXAMPLE 2

We will drive north to the White Mountains.

Sometimes, it can be hard to decide if a noun is common or proper. Ask yourself if the word means a region. If so, it is a part of the country and should be capitalized as a proper noun.

Practice

Write each sentence correctly. Capitalize only the proper nouns. The first sentence is done for you.

1. We want to go from the northeast to the southeast.

    We want to go from the Northeast to the Southeast.

2. We plan to drive south until we get to atlanta.

3. My uncle visited the southwest.

4. Is the city of miami in the southeast?

5. The rocky mountains are west of the mississippi river.

6. Cape cod national seashore is in the northeast.

Capitalizing Titles

Books, movies, magazines, and television programs have titles. Titles are proper nouns. Capitalize each important word in a title. Always capitalize the first and last words in a title.

▶ **EXAMPLE**

Great Expectations
(book title)

The Man from Mars
(movie title)

Hollywood Stars
(magazine title)

The Four of Us
(television program)

Practice

Write each title correctly. Capitalize all important words. Capitalize the first and last words. The first one is done for you.

1. ted and sue get married
   Ted and Sue Get Married

2. a tale of two cities

3. the afternoon show

4. teen talk

Everyday English

Maps contain proper nouns. Use the map on the right to answer the following questions. Remember to capitalize proper nouns correctly in your answers.

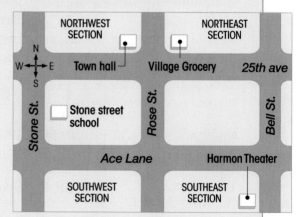

1. Which places on the map are capitalized incorrectly?

2. Which abbreviation on the map is incorrect?

3. **CHALLENGE** Write directions from Stone Street School to Village Grocery.

USING REFERENCES
Library Catalogs

Every library contains a catalog of all of its books. The card catalog is divided into three categories: TITLE, AUTHOR, and SUBJECT.

Most libraries also have a computer card catalog. It contains the same information as the card catalog.

Look at the screen of a computer card catalog below. The "search term" box is where you type in an author's name, a book title, or your subject. You click the "search everything" button if you want all the information possible about a subject.

This student uses the card catalog.

You can use proper nouns to name titles and authors. You can use either common or proper nouns to name subjects.

Enter search term. Then select search type.			
search term:	music		
search type:	SEARCH EVERYTHING / AUTHOR / TITLE / PERIODICAL TITLE		

Answer the questions below using the information on the computer screen.

1. What is the search term on the computer screen? Is it a common or proper noun?

2. If you want to find the names of books by Maya Angelou, what search type do you use?

3. **CHALLENGE** If you want to find a sports article from *The New York Times*, how do you begin your search?

Writing: Using Nouns in Sentences

Many sentences contain common and proper nouns. You can use the READ, PLAN, WRITE, and CHECK steps to write sentences using these nouns.

EXAMPLE

Write a sentence about an important person in your life. Tell why this person is important to you. Use at least one proper noun and one common noun.

READ   **Do you understand the assignment?**

Write the assignment in your own words.

> *Write a sentence that names someone important to me, and explain why the person is important. Use proper and common nouns.*

PLAN   **Gather your ideas and organize them.**

Use an idea web to plan what to write. Put the name of the person in the square that says Topic. Put the reasons why the person is important to you in the Detail circles.

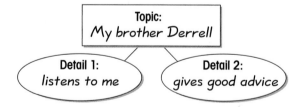

WRITE   **Put your ideas into a sentence.**

Write the information from the idea web in the form of a sentence.

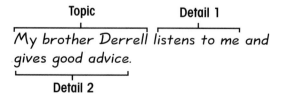

CHECK   How can you improve your writing?

Check that the sentence answers the assignment.
Add or change information to make it clearer.
Make sure you used nouns corectly.

> *My brother Derrell* is an important person
> to me because *he listens to me and gives*
> *good advice.*

The words in blue type were added. They restate the part of
the assignment that says to tell why the person is important
to you.

Practice

Complete the writing assignments below. Answer the
questions in the PLAN step to help you complete your
idea web.

1. Write a sentence about a special place. Explain why you
    like to go there. Use at least one proper noun and one
    common noun.

    PLAN
    What special place can you put in the idea web?
    What reasons can you give as details?

2. Write a sentence about something that you own. Tell
    why this object is important to you. Use at least one
    proper noun and one common noun.

    PLAN
    What object can you put in the idea web?
    What reasons can you give as details?

Putting It All Together

Write a paragraph about special places and things. You may
want to use the two sentences you have written above. Add
other sentences that tell more about special places and things.

abbreviation
common noun
compound noun
noun
proper noun

Vocabulary Review

Complete each sentence with the correct term from the box.

1. A _____ is a naming word.

2. A _____ can be the special name of a particular person.

3. An _____ is a shortened form of a word.

4. A _____ is a group of words that names a person, place, thing, event, or idea.

5. A _____ can be the general name of a thing.

Chapter Quiz

LESSON 3·1

Identifying Nouns

Write the nouns in each sentence. There may be more than one noun in a sentence.

1. Where is the party tonight?

2. It is at the restaurant on the corner.

3. What outfit is Anne going to wear?

4. Bob heard that a live band is going to play.

5. My hope is that it plays my favorite song.

LESSON 3·2

Identifying Compound Nouns

Write the compound noun in each sentence. There may be more than one compound noun in a sentence.

6. After the game, we all went out for frozen yogurt.

7. We visited the Washington Monument on a field trip.

8. The Golden Gate Bridge is in San Francisco.

LESSON 3·3

Identifying Common and Proper Nouns

Write the nouns in each sentence. If the noun is a common noun, write *C* after it. If it is a proper noun, write *P*.

9. The oldest subway is in London.

10. The World Trade Center is the tallest building in New York City.

11. The first car was sold long ago on April Fool's Day.

LESSON 3·4

Test Tip
Capitalize the important words in a title.

Capitalizing Proper Nouns

Capitalize the proper nouns in each sentence.

12. In which part of the united states is oregon?

13. Oregon is north of california, and the pacific ocean forms its western border.

14. The principal of northview high school is mrs. wilson.

15. Amy tan is the author of the book, *the joy luck club*.

LESSON 3·5

Writing Tip
Use an idea web to PLAN what to write. CHECK that your paragraph answers the assignment.

Writing: Using Nouns in Sentences

16. Write a paragraph about your school. Answer the following questions: What is the school's name? Where is it located? What does it look like? Use at least one proper noun and one common noun.

Group Activity

Work with a group to write directions from your classroom to another place in your school. Decide where your directions will lead. Use common and proper nouns correctly. Exchange papers with another group. Check the other group's directions for errors. Suggest ways to improve them.

What do you see in this photograph? List as many different items as you can. Which items are shown only once? These are singular nouns. Which items are shown more than once? These are plural nouns.

Words to Know

singular noun	a noun that names one person, place, thing, event, or idea
plural noun	a noun that names more than one person, place, thing, event, or idea
collective noun	a noun that names a group of people, things, or animals that acts as a unit
possessive noun	a noun that shows ownership or relationship
apostrophe (')	a punctuation mark used with possessive nouns to show ownership or relationship
concrete noun	a noun that names something that can be seen, heard, touched, smelled, or tasted
abstract noun	a noun that names an idea, quality, or feeling

Nouns Chart Project

Draw a four-column chart. Label the columns *Singular, Singular Possessive, Plural, Plural Possessive.* In the first column, list as many singular nouns as you can. Then write the other forms of each noun as you work through the chapter. When you have finished, write a paragraph using several nouns from each column in your chart.

Learning Objectives

- Identify singular and plural nouns.
- Identify collective nouns.
- Spell plural nouns correctly.
- Form possessive nouns.
- Identify concrete and abstract nouns.
- Write sentences using noun forms.
- Apply knowledge of noun forms to a police report and a computer spelling checker.

Singular, Plural, and Collective Nouns

Identifying Singular and Plural Nouns

A **singular noun** names one person, place, thing, event, or idea.

A **plural noun** names more than one person, place, thing, event, or idea. Many plural nouns end in *-s*.

▶ **EXAMPLE**

Singular Noun	Plural Noun
book	books
house	houses
letter	letters
Josh Smith	Smiths

Practice A

Draw two columns on a sheet of paper. Use these headings: *Singular Noun, Plural Noun.* List each noun in the box below under the correct heading. The first one is done for you.

pencil	birthday	writers	garden
letter	record	legs	stores
singers	concerts	faces	song

SINGULAR NOUN	PLURAL NOUN
pencil	

CHALLENGE Add two nouns of your own to each column.

Practice B

Write the nouns in each sentence. If a noun is singular, write *S* after it. If a noun is plural, write *P* after it. The first one is done for you.

1. Let's make plans for our trip next year.

    plans P, trip S, year S

2. The story is about a spaceship and a frightened boy.

3. The campers enjoy the peace and quiet of the mountains.

4. Sean set up our tents near a stream.

5. The manager asked for ideas from the employees.

6. The Jacksons went to the fair with my dad.

7. The hills are covered with flowers for months.

8. Several floats and marching bands were in the parade.

Everyday English

Look at the nutrition facts label. It provides information about spaghetti sauce. Some nouns on the label are underlined.

1. Which of the underlined nouns are plural nouns?

2. Write the following sentence. Add a plural noun.
There are about six _____ in this jar.

3. **CHALLENGE** Write two nouns on the label that are not underlined. Tell if each noun is singular or plural.

Spaghetti Sauce
Nutrition <u>Facts</u>
Serving Size 1/2 cup (120 ml)
<u>Servings</u> Per Container About 6
Amount per serving
Calories   140
Calories from Fat   40
% Daily Value
Total <u>Fat</u> 4.5 g   7%
Saturated Fat 1.5 g   8%
Cholesterol 0 mg   0%
Sodium 610 mg   25%
Total Carbohydrates 23 g 8%
Dietery Fiber 2 g   8%
Sugars 15 g
<u>Protein</u> 2 g

Identifying Collective Nouns

A **collective noun** names a group of people, things, or animals that act as a unit.

Collective Nouns				
audience	committee	flock	herd	panel
class	family	group	team	crowd

Practice

Write the collective noun in each sentence. The first one is done for you.

1. The audience applauded loudly after the concert.

   audience

2. The committee will meet tomorrow afternoon.

3. Our class will go on a field trip to the museum.

4. Our team won first place at the swim meet.

5. The teacher asked each group to make a presentation.

6. A flock of sheep was grazing in the field.

7. The skaters performed for a panel of judges.

8. The Wu family eats dinner together every night.

9. The crowd waits for the concert to start.

10. A committee of experts solved the problem.

Spelling Plural Nouns Correctly

Nouns That End with *x, s, z, ch,* or *sh*

The plural form of many nouns is made by adding -*s* to the end of the word. However, nouns that end with *x, s, z, ch,* or *sh* are treated differently. The plural form of these nouns is formed by adding -*es* to the end of the word.

▶ **EXAMPLE**

Singular Noun	Plural Noun
box	boxes
guess	guesses
buzz	buzzes
lunch	lunches
flash	flashes

Practice A

Write the plural form of each singular noun. The first one is done for you.

1. tax *taxes*   **2.** address

3. wish   **4.** watch

5. wax   **6.** beach

7. sandwich   **8.** waltz

9. business   **10.** patch

11. leash   **12.** dress

Practice B

Rewrite each sentence. Change the noun in parentheses to its plural form. The first one is done for you.

13. We baked three (batch) of cookies.

   We baked three batches of cookies.

14. There are several (church) in my neighborhood.

15. Many houses in the country have large (porch).

16. All of the (coach) will attend the dinner.

17. I need some (match) to light the birthday candles.

18. These (branch) on your tree need to be trimmed.

19. Your baseball landed in those (bush).

20. Our team had only two (loss) this season.

21. Can you help me carry those (box) upstairs?

22. Gina packed two (lunch) for her brother and sister.

23. The secretary sent three (fax).

24. The (quiz) were based on last night's homework.

25. Jason ate two (bunch) of grapes.

26. The mother gave her baby many (kiss).

27. We made sure to ask for hall (pass).

28. Maria made two great (catch) in the game.

Nouns That End with *y*

Some singular nouns end with a vowel and a *y*. Make the plural form of these nouns by adding -*s*. Some nouns end with a consonant and a *y*. Make the plural form of these nouns by changing the *y* to *i* and adding -*es*.

▶ EXAMPLE

Singular Noun	Plural Noun	
day	days	
turkey	turkeys	Add -*s*
valley	valleys	
joy	joys	
pony	ponies	
candy	candies	Change *y* to *i* and add -*es*
duty	duties	
diary	diaries	

Practice

Rewrite each sentence. Change the noun in parentheses to its plural form. The first one is done for you.

1. Where did you put my (key)?

   Where did you put my keys?

2. The best races will be the (relay).

3. The fly landed on the (strawberry).

4. The (stairway) led down to the bay.

5. Read your (summary) of the stories.

6. The student wrote the (essay) over the weekend.

7. Please put the (trophy) on the bookcase.

8. The (pony) stayed in the barn.

Nouns That End with *f* or *fe*

Some singular nouns end with *f*, *ff*, or *fe*. Make the plural form of some of these nouns by adding *-s*. Make the plural of others by changing the *f* to *v* and adding *-es*.

▶ **EXAMPLE**

Singular Noun	Plural Noun
chef	chefs
cliff	cliffs
safe	safes
leaf	leaves
half	halves
life	lives

Add *-s*

Change *f* to *v* and add *-es*

Practice

Rewrite each sentence. Change the noun in parentheses to its plural form. The first one is done for you.

1. The boat came too close to the (reef).

   The boat came too close to the reefs.

2. Please cut the (loaf) of fresh bread.

3. The detective found both (half) of the letter.

4. The (cliff) overlook the ocean.

5. The hero saved the (life) of many people.

6. The autumn (leaf) were beautiful this year.

7. The men introduced their (wife).

8. The women wore white (scarf) around their necks.

Nouns That End with *o*

Some nouns end with a vowel and an *o*. Make the plural form of these nouns by adding -*s*.

Some nouns end with a consonant and an *o*. Make the plural form of these nouns by adding -*es*. Some nouns that end with a consonant and *o* refer to music. Make these nouns plural by adding -*s*.

▶ **EXAMPLE**

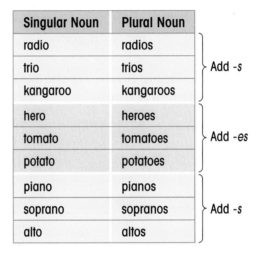

Singular Noun	Plural Noun
radio	radios
trio	trios
kangaroo	kangaroos
hero	heroes
tomato	tomatoes
potato	potatoes
piano	pianos
soprano	sopranos
alto	altos

Add -*s*

Add -*es*

Add -*s*

Practice

Rewrite each sentence. Change the noun in parentheses to its plural form. The first one is done for you.

1. This music hall has two (piano).

   This music hall has two pianos.

2. Several (radio) were playing loudly.

3. Tom and Eduardo are (hero).

4. Chen sang two (solo) at the concert.

5. Isaac saw two (tornado) in the sky.

Irregular Nouns

Some plural nouns do not end with -s. These nouns become plural by changing other letters in the word.

Singular Noun	Plural Noun
man	men
foot	feet
mouse	mice
tooth	teeth

Some nouns are the same in the singular and plural forms.

Singular Noun	Plural Noun
fish	fish
deer	deer
sheep	sheep
series	series

Practice

Rewrite each sentence. Change the noun in parentheses to its plural form. The first one is done for you.

1. Tomorrow, I shall have my (tooth) cleaned.

   Tomorrow, I shall have my teeth cleaned.

2. There are three (series) of questions on the test.

3. We saw five (fish) near the pier.

4. Several (woman) joined the committee.

5. **CHALLENGE** The (child) saw several (goose) on the pond.

Possessive Nouns

A **possessive noun** shows ownership or relationship. It contains an **apostrophe**. An apostrophe is a punctuation mark used to show that something belongs to or is related to a person or thing.

EXAMPLE 1

This is Robert's car. (The car belongs to Robert.)

Devin is Tasha's cousin. (Devin is related to Tasha.)

Add an apostrophe and an -*s* to most singular nouns to form the possessive.

EXAMPLE 2

Singular Noun
the cat's tail
his aunt's ring

Remember
A plural noun names more than one person, place, thing, event, or idea.

Add just an apostrophe to most plural nouns that end with *s* to form the possessive. Add an apostrophe and an -*s* to plural nouns that do not end with *s* to form the possessive.

EXAMPLE 3

Noun Ending in *s*	Plural Noun Not Ending in *s*
my friends' parents	the men's locker room
the Smiths' house	those children's coats

Practice A

Write the possessive noun in each sentence. The first one is done for you.

1. We have tickets for tomorrow night's play.

   night's

2. These stories' heroes are interesting.

3. What is the Andersons' phone number?

4. The players read the season's schedule.

5. That store's sign was damaged by the storm.

6. The teacher graded all of the students' reports.

7. All my aunts and uncles will be at my cousin's house.

8. Why don't you ask Ted's sister to the party?

Practice B

Rewrite each sentence. Change the noun in parentheses to its possessive form. The first one is done for you.

9. Tomorrow is (Father) Day.

Tomorrow is Father's Day.

10. This (lesson) subject is possessive nouns.

11. Keep the (boxes) contents a secret.

12. Mrs. Rudolph answered the (women) questions.

13. The two (nations) leaders met in Paris.

14. The (candidates) ideas seemed very different.

15. He will replace his (watch) broken strap.

Practice C

Read the following paragraph. Write the four possessive nouns.

Yesterday, I found an old trunk in the attic. When I opened it, I found my grandfather's Medal of Honor. Underneath it was my grandmother's wedding dress. I also found my dad's first report card. Each of these items told a story about my family's history.

Practice D

Write each sentence. Add a possessive noun of your own. The first one is done for you.

16. The _____ water supply is getting low.

   The town's water supply is getting low.

17. What is your _____ name?

18. The _____ dessert was fruit.

19. Randy met the _____ father.

20. The _____ crops are blackberries and potatoes.

21. The _____ notebook was in her locker.

22. There were many items on the _____ menu.

Practice E

Make two columns on a sheet of paper. Use these headings: *Possessive Noun, Plural Noun*. List each noun in the box under the correct heading. The first one is done for you.

POSSESSIVE NOUN	PLURAL NOUN
newspaper's	

newspaper's	towns
uncles	phones
schools'	women's
doctors	city's
painters'	heads

CHALLENGE Add two nouns of your own to each column.

USING REFERENCES
Computer Spelling Checker

Most computer programs have a spelling checker. This tool allows you to check your work for spelling errors.

For each misspelled word, the program gives a list of correct spellings. Find the correct word. Then replace the misspelled word with the correct one.

The spelling checker does not know some proper nouns. If you know the word is spelled correctly, tell the spelling checker to ignore that word. If you do not know the correct spelling, check the dictionary.

The spelling checker may not find all mistakes. For example, you might use an incorrect word but spell it correctly. Because of this, always check your work carefully.

Look at the computer spelling checker. Then answer the questions below.

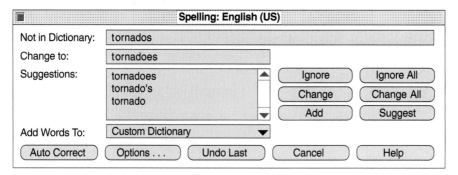

1. What is the correct spelling of the plural noun?

2. Which of the suggestions is a possessive noun?

3. **CHALLENGE** What can you do if the spelling checker does not suggest the correct word?

4·4 ► Concrete and Abstract Nouns

A **concrete noun** names something you can see, hear, touch, smell, or taste. Concrete nouns include people, places, and things.

An **abstract noun** names an idea, quality, or feeling.

► **EXAMPLE**

Concrete Noun	Abstract Noun
elephant	strength
flower	beauty
flag	patriotism

Practice A

Write the abstract noun from each group. The first one is done for you.

1. chicken   apple   hunger
   hunger

2. bicycle   car   transportation

3. happiness   laughter   joke

4. kitten   weakness   baby

5. smoke   danger   flames

6. justice   lawyer   jury

7. medal   trophy   pride

8. career   desk   computer

Practice B

Write the nouns in each sentence. If the noun is concrete, write *C* after it. If the noun is abstract, write *A* after it. The first one is done for you.

9. My stomach was growling with hunger.

   stomach C, hunger A

10. Bill received a medal for his courage.

11. The soldiers fought for peace.

12. Christina has a good idea for our book.

13. The cheering fans expressed their pleasure with the concert.

14. In her happiness, Martha jumped for joy.

15. **CHALLENGE** Write a sentence of your own using an abstract noun.

Everyday English

Billboards show advertisements for companies. Some billboards use both concrete and abstract nouns. Look at this billboard. Then answer the following questions.

Stereo Warehouse
4144 Main Street
Visit our store to find the best deals in town.
Quality and value are our top priorities.

1. What concrete nouns are used on the billboard?

2. What abstract nouns are used on the billboard?

3. **CHALLENGE** Choose one sentence to rewrite. Change one abstract noun to a concrete noun.

COMMUNICATING ON THE JOB
Police Officer

Shara Doli is a police officer. As part of her job, she writes police reports. These reports can be about a theft, an attack, a car accident, or another problem.

When Officer Doli writes a report, she must give clear and correct information. She has to describe things clearly, yet she must be brief.

Officer Doli wrote the following report.

Read the police report, and follow the directions below.

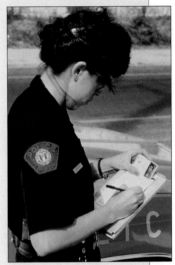

Officer Doli writes a police report.

> On January 28, at 5:15 P.M., a woman saw a man running from her car. He was carrying several items. She said that the man's hair was brown. He was wearing black pants and boots. The woman's purse, keys, and watch were missing from her car.

1. Write each singular noun in the report. Next to it, write the plural form of the noun.

2. Write the possessive nouns in the report.

3. **CRITICAL THINKING** Why do you think many theft reports include concrete nouns?

Writing and Speaking
Write two questions Officer Doli might ask the witness. Then role-play with a partner. One person is the police officer and asks the questions. The other person is the witness and answers them. Make sure nouns are used correctly.

Writing: Using Noun Forms in Sentences

Many sentences use different forms of nouns. You can use the READ, PLAN, WRITE and CHECK steps to write sentences using different noun forms.

▶ **EXAMPLE**

Your school is creating a time capsule. Write a sentence about three items you would put in it. Explain why you chose these items. Use one singular noun, one plural noun, and one possessive noun.

READ   **Do you understand the assignment?**

Write the main idea of the assignment.

Write a sentence about three items you would put in a time capsule. Explain your choices.

PLAN   **Gather your ideas and organize them.**

Use a tree map to organize your ideas. Write *Items for Time Capsule* in the top square. List your three items in the bottom circles.

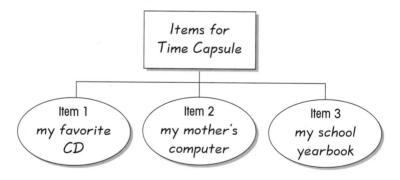

WRITE   **Put your ideas into a sentence.**

Include the three items in the tree map in your sentence.

I would put my favorite CD, my mother's computer, and my school yearbook in the time capsule.

CHECK   How can you improve your writing?

Make sure your sentence answers the assignment.
Check that you used nouns correctly.

*I would put my favorite CD, my mother's computer,
and my school yearbook in the time capsule* because
these items reflect present-day life.

The words in blue type were added to complete the
assignment. They include a plural noun and explain
why the items were chosen.

Practice

Complete the writing assignments below. READ each
assignment and answer the questions that follow.

1. You are stranded on a deserted island. Write a sentence
   that lists three items you would want to have with you.
   Use concrete nouns.

   READ
   What will you write about?
   What noun forms will you use in your sentence?

2. Write a sentence that explains why you chose one of the
   items above. Use an abstract noun.

   READ
   What will you write about?
   What noun form will you use in your sentence?

Putting It All Together

Write a paragraph about being stranded on a deserted island. Tell
what three items you would take with you, and explain why. You
may want to use the two sentences that you have written above.
Add other sentences to explain your choice of items.

abstract

apostrophe

collective

concrete

plural

possessive

singular

Vocabulary Review

Complete each sentence with a word from the box.

1. . A_____ noun shows ownership or relationship.

2. A _____ noun names one person, place, thing, event, or idea.

3. A noun that names something you can hear, see, touch, taste, or smell is a _____ noun.

4. A noun that names an idea, quality, or feeling is an _____ noun.

5. A _____ noun names more than one person, place, thing, event, or idea.

6. A punctuation mark used with a possessive noun to show ownership or relationship is an _____.

7. A _____ noun names a group of people, things, or animals that acts as a unit.

Chapter Quiz

LESSON 4·1

Identifying Singular, Plural, and Collective Nouns
Write the nouns in each sentence. If a noun is singular, write *S* after it. If it is plural, write *P*. If it is a collective noun, write *C*.

1. Tony has two rolls of film.

2. The employee wore a uniform.

3. That shirt comes in four sizes.

4. The group of teenagers went to the concert.

5. The audience danced to the music.

Spelling Plural Nouns Correctly
Change the noun in parentheses to its plural form.

  6. Sarah ate two (sandwich) for lunch.

  7. Michael placed the books on the (shelf).

  8. Mother served (potato) with dinner.

Forming Possessive Nouns
Change the noun in parentheses to its possessive form.

  9. The baseball (players) tips were interesting.

  10. After five (days) work, the women took a day off.

  11. (Denise) sister looks just like her.

Test Tip
A concrete noun can be seen, heard, tasted, smelled, or felt; an abstract noun cannot.

Identifying Concrete and Abstract Nouns
Write the nouns in each sentence. If the noun is concrete, write *C* after it. If it is abstract, write *A*.

  12. The big wave pounded against the ship.

  13. Check the quality of your report.

  14. The patriots fought for liberty and freedom.

Writing Tip
READ the assignment carefully to decide what you should write about. Use a tree map to PLAN your ideas.

Writing: Using Noun Forms in Sentences
  15. Write a paragraph that tells what you would wish for if you could wish for any three things. Explain each choice. Use at least one abstract noun.

Group Activity

Work with your group to write a description of things in your classroom. Tell who owns these items. Include singular, plural, and possessive nouns. Then exchange papers with another group. Suggest ways to improve the other group's description.

Unit 2 **Review**

Read the passage below to answer questions 1–5. Choose the word or group of words that belongs in each space. Mark the letter for your answer.

___(1)___ who visit ___(2)___ may feel as if they are moving slowly. Compared to ___(3)___, they probably are. Some of the fastest ___(4)___ in the ___(5)___ live there.

1. A. Tourist's
   B. Tourists
   C. tourist's
   D. tourists

2. A. new York
   B. new york
   C. New York
   D. New york

3. A. New Yorkers
   B. New Yorker's
   C. New Yorkers'
   D. New Yorker

4. A. walker
   B. Walkers
   C. walker's
   D. walkers

5. A. united States
   B. United States
   C. United states
   D. united states

Read the passage below to answer questions 6–8. Decide which type of error, if any, appears in each underlined section. Mark the letter for your answer.

A woman and her son stand in line at (6) <u>yale grocery store</u>. She decides she has (7) <u>the right number of cereal boxes but not enough tomatos</u>. The cashier recognizes her and says hello. (8) <u>The womans son smiles at the cashier</u>.

6. A. Spelling error
   B. Capitalization error
   C. Punctuation error
   D. No error

7. A. Spelling error
   B. Capitalization error
   C. Punctuation error
   D. No error

8. A. Spelling error
   B. Capitalization
   C. Punctuation error
   D. No error

Critical Thinking
Your school is setting up a drug prevention program. Provide three ideas that you think the program should promote.
WRITING Write a letter to your principal. Explain the ideas that you think the program should promote. Use noun forms correctly.

Unit 3 ▷ Pronouns

Chapter 5   **Pronouns and Antecedents**

Chapter 6   **Pronouns That Ask and Point**

You have learned that nouns are used to name people, places, things, events, and ideas. Pronouns are used to take the place of nouns. All the people and things in this photograph of the United Nations can be named by pronouns.

The United Nations has headquarters in New York City. Representatives from many nations go there to give speeches about world issues.

Read the speech, and answer the questions.

1. What noun does the pronoun *you* refer to?

2. What noun does the pronoun *it* take the place of?

3. What word does the speaker use to refer to himself?

Good evening, ambassadors. You are here tonight to join me in a celebration. We are celebrating the success of last year's effort to help end hunger. It was successful because all our nations worked together.

This is a photograph of Mount Everest. *List some nouns that you see in the photograph. Pronouns take the place of nouns. Use the pronouns <u>he</u>, <u>she</u>, <u>it</u>, and <u>they</u> to replace the nouns that you listed.*

Chapter 5

Pronouns and Antecedents

Words to Know

pronoun	a word that takes the place of one or more nouns
personal pronoun	a pronoun that identifies the speaker, the person spoken to, or the person or thing spoken about
antecedent	the noun or nouns that the pronoun refers to or stands for
reflexive pronoun	a pronoun that refers to a noun or pronoun already named
possessive pronoun	a pronoun that shows ownership or relationship
indefinite pronoun	a pronoun that does not replace a particular noun; the antecedent often is not known

Graphic Organizer Project

Create a spider map for pronouns. Draw a circle. Write the word *Pronouns* in the center. Then draw four lines that radiate from the circle. Write one of the following on each line: *Personal*, *Reflexive*, *Possessive*, and *Indefinite*. From each line, draw five lines. As you read the chapter, write pronouns for each category on your organizer. Then write a sentence for each pronoun.

Learning Objectives

- Identify personal pronouns and their antecedents.
- Use reflexive pronouns.
- Use possessive pronouns.
- Use indefinite pronouns.
- Write sentences using pronouns and antecedants.
- Apply knowledge of pronouns and antecedents to a thank-you note and a biography.

5·1 ▶ Personal Pronouns and Antecedents

Identifying Personal Pronouns

A **pronoun** is a word that takes the place of one or more nouns. Pronouns can take the place of common and proper nouns.

One type of pronoun is a **personal pronoun**. A personal pronoun identifies the speaker, the person spoken to, or the person or thing spoken about.

	Personal Pronoun
The speaker	I, me, we, us
The person spoken to	you
The person or thing spoken about	he, him, she, her, it, they, them

▶ **EXAMPLE**

Bill and Kim watched the game.

We watched the game. (The speaker)

The three girls left.

You left. (The person spoken to)

Tyler hit the ball.

He hit the ball. (The person spoken about)

Practice A

Write the two personal pronouns in each sentence. The first one is done for you.

1. We often go camping with him.

   We, him

2. She sent me a postcard from New York.

3. When did you receive it?

4. I will bake a cake for you.

5. Give them to us later, please.

6. They will help us tomorrow.

7. Did you tell her the news?

8. Where did you put them?

9. We wanted it to be a surprise.

10. I should go to dinner with them.

Practice B

Rewrite each sentence. Replace the word or words in parentheses with the correct personal pronoun. The first one is done for you.

11. (Gina) wrapped (the gift) in blue paper.

She wrapped it in blue paper.

12. (Mr. Krantz) will fix (the sprinkler).

13. (Rick and Sal) delivered (the packages).

14. Borrow (the tape) from (Elizabeth).

15. (All the team members) are counting on (John).

16. (Bruce) is studying (that book) carefully.

17. (Davis) checks (the schedule) every day.

18. Only (Lou) can unlock (the safe).

19. (The question) puzzled (Judy).

20. (Pam and Jessie) told (Will) about (the party).

Identifying Antecedents

An **antecedent** is a word or group of words that a pronoun refers to or stands for.

▶ **EXAMPLE**

Meg is fond of jigsaw puzzles. She bought a new puzzle today.

antecedent: Meg   pronoun: she

Mary invited Brad and Pablo, but they can't come.

antecedent: Brad and Pablo   pronoun: they

The cat likes people to pet him.

antecedent: The cat   pronoun: him

Practice

Write the personal pronoun and antecedent in each sentence. The first one is done for you.

1. Alex and Tracy asked Sharon to go with them.

   them, Alex and Tracy

2. That book is interesting because it tells a true story.

3. Mrs. Rogers, will you be home tomorrow?

4. Ed was here, but he had to leave.

5. Bob called to Jan, but she did not hear.

6. Cal spoke to Li and Juan when they arrived.

7. Jorge explained why he was not at the game.

8. Morgan mailed the letters after she copied them.

9. Diane invited Kevin, but he did not reply.

10. The room was warm because it was so crowded.

Pronoun-Antecedent Agreement

A pronoun must agree with its antecedent. The antecedent and pronoun must be the same in number. If the antecedent is singular, the pronoun must be singular. If the antecedent is plural, the pronoun must be plural.

Singular Pronoun	Plural Pronoun
I, me, you, he, him, she, her, it	we, us, you, they, them

EXAMPLE 1

Robin will wash the floor and wax it. (singular)

Grace and Jake know they will be late. (plural)

The antecedent and pronoun must be the same in person. If the antecedent is masculine, the pronoun must be masculine. If the antecedent is feminine, the pronoun must be feminine.

Masculine Pronoun	Feminine Pronoun
he, him	she, her

EXAMPLE 2

Mr. Perez goes fishing whenever he can. (masculine)

Sandra will help if she is not working. (feminine)

Practice

Write each sentence. Add a personal pronoun of your own. Remember that a pronoun must agree with its antecedent. The first one is done for you.

1. Rosa invited Min to visit _____ next week.

   Rosa invited Min to visit her next week.

2. Lauren, did _____ put the dog outside?

3. Open the door for Raul when _____ rings the bell.

(Practice continues on next page.) ⇨

4. Andy said hello when we saw _____ yesterday.

5. I wanted Paul to play the piano, but _____ played the drums instead.

6. Ruby asked Linda to drive _____ to the airport.

7. Carmen and Shelby explained what _____ were doing.

8. Tyrone and I got lost as _____ explored the woods.

9. When you finished your library book, where did you put _____?

10. David and I loved the gifts you bought for _____.

11. The deer were grazing on our lawn, but Tom did not stop _____.

12. **CHALLENGE** Write a sentence of your own. Use at least one personal pronoun and an antecedent.

Everyday English

Jamie has planned a surprise party for her brother. Read the invitation she sent, and answer the following questions.

1. What is the antecedent for *it* in the *What* part of the invitation?

2. What is the antecedent for *me* under the *Given By* part of the invitation?

3. What personal pronoun could Jamie have used instead of *Juan* at the end of the last sentence?

4. **CHALLENGE** Who is the antecedent for *you* in the first line of the invitation?

YOU ARE INVITED!

What: It is a surprise birthday party for Juan!
When: 8:00 P.M. on May 3
Where: Bruno's Italian Restaurant
Given By: Jamie

Call Jamie at 555-123-4567 by April 25.
Call me for directions too!
Remember, Juan does not know about the party. Don't tell Juan!

A **reflexive pronoun** refers back to a noun or pronoun already named. Reflexive pronouns end in *-self* or *-selves*.

Singular Reflexive Pronoun	Plural Reflexive Pronoun
myself	ourselves
yourself	yourselves
herself, himself, itself	themselves

A reflexive pronoun is used in one of two ways in a sentence. It adds new information, or it gives extra importance to the word it refers to.

▶ **EXAMPLE**

Robert washed the dishes himself. (new information)

Robert himself washed the dishes. (extra importance)

We went to the town council meeting ourselves. (new information)

We ourselves went to the town council meeting. (extra importance)

Practice A

Write the reflexive pronoun in each sentence. The first one is done for you.

1. Rosalie knitted that sweater herself.

   herself

2. Carlos said that he needed to be by himself.

3. Did you make the decorations yourselves?

4. They seldom do anything for themselves.

5. She herself drove the truck.

6. Reuben completed the job himself.

(Practice A continues on next page.) ⟳

7. We cleaned up the park ourselves.

8. I painted the house myself.

9. I cannot believe you built that deck yourself!

10. Did Jack leave by himself?

11. The snack itself was enough for a meal.

12. Perry himself needed to talk to her.

13. Are you doing all the work yourself?

Practice B

Write each sentence. Add a reflexive pronoun of your own.
The first one is done for you.

14. Ken and Angelo prepared the meal _____.

Ken and Angelo prepared the meal themselves.

15. Bonnie wanted the bicycle for _____.

16. The problem may take care of _____.

17. We have decided to paint the house _____.

18. All of you can do that for _____.

19. Marcus _____ decided not to run for office.

20. I need to tell him the news _____.

21. The students _____ are planning the entire show.

22. **CHALLENGE** Write a sentence of your own. Use a
reflexive pronoun.

5·3 Possessive Pronouns

A **possessive pronoun** shows ownership or relationship. Some possessive pronouns come before nouns. The possessive pronouns in the box below must be used before a noun.

Singular Possessive Pronoun	Plural Possessive Pronoun
my	our
your	your
his, her, its	their

EXAMPLE 1

This is Jill's book.

This is her book.

The Smiths' dog is very playful.

Their dog is very playful.

Remember
A possessive noun shows ownership or relationship.

Some possessive pronouns are used in place of possessive nouns. The possessive pronouns in the box can take the place of a possessive noun.

Singular Possessive Pronoun	Plural Possessive Pronoun
mine	ours
yours	yours
his, hers, its	theirs

EXAMPLE 2

This book is Jill's.

This book is hers.

The playful dog is the Smiths'.

The playful dog is theirs.

Practice A

Write the possessive pronoun in each sentence. The first one is done for you.

1. Here are our cousins from Detroit.

    our

2. I just washed my hair.

3. Their guitars came from Spain.

4. Mine has a red sticker on it.

5. How old is her brother?

6. The artist forgot to sign her name.

7. Do you like my new car?

8. I tried to duplicate theirs.

9. That tree lost all of its leaves.

10. I told him that your house is for sale.

Practice B

Write the correct form of the pronoun in parentheses in each sentence. The first one is done for you.

11. Which office is (your, yours)?

    yours

12. They say the prize should be (theirs, their).

13. Tell us which seats are (our, ours).

14. She says (him, his) records were burned in the fire.

15. How many of (my, mine) cookies are left?

16. The Marlows will lend us one of (their, theirs).

Practice C

Write each sentence. Add a possessive pronoun of your own.
The first one is done for you.

17. The Gundersons remodeled _____ house last year.

The Gundersons remodeled their house last year.

18. Hannah is training _____ dog.

19. Matt and I will bring _____ tomorrow.

20. Daniel stayed home because of _____ cold.

21. Did you notice which one is _____?

Everyday English

Sam's dog, Chief, cut his paw. Sam took Chief to a veterinarian. An assistant wrote down instructions on how to care for Chief. However, the assistant made an error when using a pronoun. Read the instructions. Then answer the questions.

1. What is the possessive pronoun in the first sentence?

2. Rewrite the second sentence. Replace the possessive noun with a possessive pronoun.

3. CHALLENGE Why is the pronoun *him* not correct in the third sentence? What pronoun is correct?

KIT 'N' KAPOODLE Animal Clinic
500 MacArthur St.
Wayne, NJ 07400
555-234-5678

Give your dog one pill daily for five days. If he will not swallow it himself, hide it in the dog's food. Keep him paw dry. Put a clean bandage on it every day.

5·4 Indefinite Pronouns

A pronoun that takes the place of an unnamed noun is called an **indefinite pronoun**. The antecedent of an indefinite pronoun often is not known.

Singular Indefinite Pronoun		Plural Indefinite Pronoun	Indefinite Pronoun That May Be Singular or Plural
another	neither	both	all
anybody	nobody	few	any
anyone	no one	many	most
anything	nothing	others	none
each	one	several	some
either	other		such
everybody	somebody		
everyone	someone		
everything	something		

▶ **EXAMPLE**

Everyone heard the noise. (singular)

Both were in the next room. (plural)

All is well. (used as singular)

All of them are here. (used as plural)

Practice A

Write the indefinite pronouns in each sentence. The first one is done for you.

1. Does anybody know anything about computers?

   anybody, anything

2. Both of them were invited, but neither came.

3. Some were easy, but most were difficult.

4. All will be judged carefully before any is chosen.

5. Many went to the museum, but few saw everything.

6. Does anyone want another?

7. Nobody had time to do either.

8. Although I tried on several, none fit.

9. This is something Charlene wants everyone to hear.

10. Neither said anything about the surprise party.

11. Several went, but few stayed.

12. If each brings some, there will be too many.

13. Everyone waited for someone to say something.

14. I need one or the other to finish most of this project.

15. The restaurant had something for everybody.

Practice B

Write the paragraph. Add indefinite pronouns of your own.

>   Is _____ interested in hearing about my trip? Does
> _____ want to see my pictures? They are _____
> here in this album. _____ are great shots. _____
> have said that _____ look like postcards. A _____
> turned out blurry. _____ was on the camera lens.
> I wiped the lens to remove _____ that was on it.
> When this didn't work, I tried to find _____ to help me.

CHALLENGE Write a sentence of your own at the end of the
paragraph. Use an indefinite pronoun.

5·5 Writing: Using Pronouns and Antecedents in Sentences

Pronouns help writers avoid repeating the same words over and over. You can use the READ, PLAN, WRITE, and CHECK steps to write sentences using pronouns.

▶ **EXAMPLE**

Write a sentence about someone whom you admire. Tell who it is, and give three reasons why you admire this person. Be sure to include at least one personal pronoun.

READ **Do you understand the assignment?**
Write the assignment in your own words.

Write a sentence about someone I admire, and tell why I admire the person. Use a personal pronoun.

PLAN **Gather your ideas and organize them.**
Use a tree map to organize your ideas. Write the name of the person in the top square. Write three reasons why you admire this person in the bottom circles.

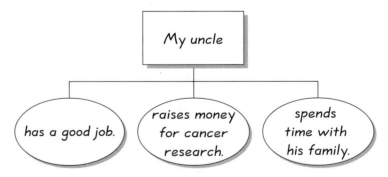

WRITE **Put your ideas into a sentence.**
Create a sentence using the ideas in your diagram.

I admire my uncle because he has a good job and helps to raise money for cancer research.

CHECK   How can you improve your writing?

Make sure your sentence answers the assignment.
Add or change information to make it clearer. Make
sure the pronouns agree with their antecedents.

*I admire my uncle because he has a good job,
spends time with his family, and helps
to raise money for cancer research.*

The words in blue type were added. They help to
complete the assignment, which asks you to give
three reasons why you admire the person.

Practice

Complete the writing assignments below. Answer the
question in the READ step to check your understanding of
the assignment.

1. Write a sentence about your favorite actor. Tell who he
or she is and why this person is your favorite. Use at
least one reflexive pronoun.

READ
What are you supposed to write about?

2. Write a sentence about a movie or television show this
actor starred in. Tell why you think he or she did a good
job. Use at least one possessive pronoun.

READ
What are you supposed to write about?

Putting It All Together

Write a paragraph about your favorite actor. You may use
the two sentences you have written above. Add other
sentences to complete your paragraph.

Jordan Perez and Reggie Ormand are best friends. They both are hockey fans. Jordan's father bought them two tickets for last Saturday night's hockey game.

Here is the thank-you note Reggie sent to Jordan's father after the game.

Read Reggie's note carefully. Then follow the directions below.

«««««««« **Thank You** »»»»»»»»

Dear Mr. Perez,

Thank you very much for the hockey ticket for last Saturday's game. Jordan and I had an awesome time. We cheered so loudly we lost our voices in the third period. Nobody enjoyed the game more than I did!

Thanks again!

Sincerely,
Reggie

1. Write the antecedent for the pronoun *you* in the first sentence.

2. Write the possessive pronoun in the thank-you note.

3. **CRITICAL THINKING** Why is it important to use pronouns correctly in a thank-you note?

Writing and Speaking

Write a thank-you note to someone who has done something special for you. Be sure to use pronouns to avoid repetition. Exchange notes with a partner. Read your partner's note aloud to make sure it is clear.

USING REFERENCES
Biographical Reference Book

If you need to know more about an important person, you can look in a biographical reference book. This reference book has biographies, or life stories, of well-known people. The information in a biographical reference book is arranged alphabetically by last name.

Read the article about César Chávez from a biographical reference book. Then answer the questions below.

This student uses a biographical reference book for his report.

Chávez, César Estrada

César Chávez (SHAH vehz) was born in 1927 on a farm in Arizona. He was ten when his parents had to sell their farm to pay their bills. They became migrant workers. As Chávez grew up, he wanted to help migrant workers have better lives. In 1962, he helped grape pickers in California get better working conditions. In 1966, he started the National Farm Workers Association. Until his death in 1993, Chávez devoted himself to improving the lives of others.

---

1. What is the antecedent for the pronoun in the third sentence?

2. What two different possessive pronouns can you find?

3. What is the reflexive pronoun in the article?

4. What is the indefinite pronoun in the article?

5. **CHALLENGE** Write a sentence of your own that tells your opinion of César Chávez. Use at least two pronouns.

antecedent
indefinite
personal
possessive
pronoun
reflexive

Vocabulary Review

Complete each sentence with a word from the box.

1. The antecedent of an ____ pronoun may be unknown.

2. An ____ is a noun that a pronoun refers to.

3. A ____ takes the place of a noun.

4. A ____ pronoun refers to a noun or pronoun named earlier.

5. To show ownership, use a ____ pronoun.

6. A ____ pronoun identifies the speaker, the person spoken to, or the person or thing spoken about.

Chapter Quiz

LESSON 5·1

Test Tip
The following are personal pronouns: *I, he, she, it, me, him, her, we, you, us, they, them.*

Identifying Personal Pronouns and Their Antecedents

Write the personal pronoun and antecedent in each sentence.

1. Rachel said that she was not going to the game.

2. Chris practiced ball after he did his homework.

3. Coach, who do you want to guard Jamie?

LESSON 5·2

Using Reflexive Pronouns

Write each sentence. Add a reflexive pronoun of your own.

4. I like to walk home by ____.

5. They let ____ in the back door.

6. Did you do the whole project ____?

Using Possessive Pronouns

Write the correct pronoun in each sentence.

7. (My, Mine) homework is almost finished.

8. Jan said that (her, hers) is broken.

9. Is that car (their, theirs)?

10. The dog wagged (it, its) tail.

Using Indefinite Pronouns

Write each sentence. Add an indefinite pronoun of your own.

11. Is ____ out there?

12. I ate ____ of the strawberries.

13. ____ warmed up before the game.

14. ____ in the room laughed.

Writing Tip
Make sure to READ the assignment carefully. Write down the important words. Use a tree map to PLAN your writing.

Writing: Using Pronouns and Antecedents in Sentences

15. Write a paragraph about your home. Tell where you live, who else lives there, and what you like to do when you are home. Include at least two pronouns. Be sure that they agree with their antecedents.

Group Activity

Work with a group to write an introduction about your school for the school's yearbook. Tell what makes the school and student body special, what the school has to offer students, and what the school is proud of. Be sure to use complete sentences with pronouns and antecedents. Then exchange paragraphs with another group. Suggest ways to improve the other group's work.

The words _this_, _that_, _these_, and _those_ are pronouns that are used to point things out. Use one of these pronouns to describe something in this photograph of a car show.

Pronouns That Ask and Point

Chapter 6

Words to Know

interrogative pronoun	a pronoun that is used to ask a question
demonstrative pronoun	a pronoun that points out one or more nouns
relative pronoun	a pronoun that connects a noun or pronoun with a group of words that tells more about it

Trivia Game Project

Use the following topics to create questions for a trivia game: music, movies, sports, television, and people in history. Write one question about each topic on one side of an index card. Write the answer on the other side. Be sure to use at least one interrogative pronoun in each question. Use a demonstrative or relative pronoun in each answer. Use the index cards to create a game board.

Learning Objectives

- Identify and use interrogative pronouns.
- Identify and use demonstrative pronouns.
- Identify and use relative pronouns.
- Write sentences using pronouns.
- Apply knowledge of pronouns to written instructions and Internet search engines.

6·1 Interrogative Pronouns

An **interrogative pronoun** is used to ask a question. The words in the box are interrogative pronouns.

Interrogative Pronouns				
who	whom	whose	what	which

Who and *whom* refer to a person or people. *Who* refers to the subject of a sentence. *Whom* refers to someone other than the subject.

Whose is used to ask about ownership or relationship. *What* refers to people, places, things, events, and ideas. *Which* is used when there is a choice between two or more people, places, things, events, or ideas.

Interrogative pronouns can be used in all four types of sentences.

▶ **EXAMPLE**

Tell me who is going to be there. (imperative sentence)

To whom did you send the letter? (interrogative sentence)

Whose is that? (interrogative sentence)

I don't know what to do! (exclamatory sentence)

I am not sure which of these shirts is on sale. (declarative sentence)

Practice A

Write the interrogative pronoun in each sentence. The first one is done for you.

1. Whose jacket is it?

   Whose

2. With whom did you go to dinner?

3. I don't know which to choose!

4. Who came to the office?

5. Whose dog was lost?

6. Who won the Heisman Trophy last year?

7. Tell me what caused the argument.

8. For whom is this package?

9. Marla knows which of the three racers won.

10. What is the meaning of this sign?

Practice B

Write the correct interrogative pronoun in parentheses in each sentence. The first one is done for you.

11. (Which, Who) of the students asked for directions?

    Which

12. (Who, Whose) homework is this?

13. I do not know (who, whom) is at the door.

14. (What, Which) is the process for making a cake?

15. (What, Which) of the pipes were repaired?

16. (Who, Whom) admired his athletic ability?

17. For (who, whom) are you waiting?

18. No one knows (which, what) caused the fire.

19. Next to (who, whom) do you want to sit?

20. I cannot remember (who, whom) borrowed my notes.

21. Write a report about (who, whom) you admire most.

22 Do you know (whose, whom) is the red car?

23. (Which, What) is his name?

24. Tell me (what, which) of the three is important.

25. I can't imagine (what, which) is taking so long!

Practice C

Write each sentence. Use the correct interrogative pronoun. The first one is done for you.

26. By _____ was that song recorded?

By whom was that song recorded?

27. _____ handwriting is on the envelope?

28. Tell me _____ was at the party.

29. That is _____ is so amazing about this invention!

30. _____ of the members signed this petition?

31. In your letter, include for _____ you worked.

32. To _____ was the letter addressed?

33. _____ of your assignments will you do first?

34. _____ will you say when you meet the mayor?

35. _____ of these colors do you like the best?

36. **CHALLENGE** Write two sentences of your own using interrogative pronouns.

Demonstrative Pronouns

A **demonstrative pronoun** points out one or more nouns. The words in the box are demonstrative pronouns.

Demonstrative Pronoun	
Singular	**Plural**
this	these
that	those

Remember
A singular noun names one person, place, thing, event, or idea. A plural noun names more than one.

Use *this* and *that* when referring to singular nouns or pronouns. Use *these* and *those* when referring to plural nouns or pronouns.

Use *this* and *these* when referring to nouns or pronouns that are close by. Use *that* and *those* when referring to nouns or pronouns that are farther away.

▶ **EXAMPLE**

Then he handed me this. (singular, close by)

That is my favorite pen. (singular, farther away)

These are your assignments. (plural, close by)

Please give me those. (plural, farther away)

Practice A

Write the demonstrative pronoun in each sentence. The first one is done for you.

1. This is a serious problem.

 This

2. Are those the messages you sent?

3. That only happened once.

4. I think these once belonged to him.

Write each sentence. Add a demonstrative pronoun of your own.
For some sentences, there is more than one correct answer. The
first one is done for you.

5. Who would do _____?

    Who would do that?

6. _____ is Robert's favorite part.

7. Which of _____ did Sheila buy?

8. _____ are the rules.

9. By whom was _____ written?

10. Complete _____ today.

11. _____ are all for sale.

12. **CHALLENGE** Write two sentences of your own
using demonstrative pronouns.

Everyday English

Lesha wants to order her favorite
magazine. She will need to fill out
a subscription card. Read the card,
and follow the directions below.

1. Which words are demonstrative
pronouns?

2. Rewrite the fourth sentence. Use a
demonstrative pronoun to
replace the subject *It*.

3. **CHALLENGE** Add a sentence of your own to the
subscription card. Use a demonstrative pronoun.

**THIS IS YOUR BIG CHANCE to
subscribe to MUSIC MONTHLY!**

This is the best music magazine you'll find. Our
low rate is only 99¢ an issue. It is more than 66%
OFF the cover price.

  ☐ OK! Send me **MUSIC MONTHLY** for 99¢ an issue.
  ☐ 1 year (12 issues) ☐ 6 months (6 issues)

NAME (Please Print)
_____

ADDRESS
_____

CITY STATE ZIP
_____ ☐ Payment enclosed ☐ Bill me later

USING REFERENCES
Internet Search Engines

A search engine on a computer is used to find information on the Internet. It lists thousands of Internet sources.

To use a search engine, log onto the Internet. The home page of your Internet Service Provider contains a search box. In this box, type in a key word. A key word describes the topic of your search. Then click on the search button. Your search results will appear.

Read the search engine results, and answer the questions below.

These students use the Internet.

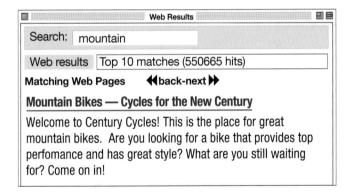

Web Results

Search: mountain

Web results | Top 10 matches (550665 hits)

Matching Web Pages ◀◀back-next▶▶

Mountain Bikes — Cycles for the New Century

Welcome to Century Cycles! This is the place for great mountain bikes. Are you looking for a bike that provides top perfomance and has great style? What are you still waiting for? Come on in!

1. Which sentence contains a demonstrative pronoun?

2. Which sentence contains an interrogative pronoun?

3. **CHALLENGE** What question could you type in the search box for more information on mountain bikes? Use an interrogative pronoun.

6·3 ▶ Relative Pronouns

A **relative pronoun** connects a noun or pronoun with a group of words that tells more about it. The words in the box are relative pronouns.

Relative Pronouns				
who	whom	whose	that	which

A relative pronoun refers to a noun or pronoun in the sentence. This antecedant usually comes right before the relative pronoun.

Who and *whom* refer to a person or people. Use *who* when referring to a subject. Use *whom* when referring to someone else. *Whose* shows ownership or relationship.

▶ **EXAMPLE 1**

The woman who is speaking is my aunt.

pronoun: who   antecedent: woman

The man to whom I spoke is my uncle.

pronoun: whom   antecedent: man

The boy whose dog is lost offered a reward for its return.

pronoun: whose   antecedent: boy

That and *which* refer to places or things. Use *that* when adding necessary information about a noun or pronoun. Use *which* when adding information that is not needed to make the meaning of the sentence clear.

▶ **EXAMPLE 2**

The pie that Nora baked is delicious.

pronoun: that   antecedent: pie

The book, which has a red cover, is on the shelf.

pronoun: which   antecedent: book

Practice A

Write the relative pronoun and its antecedent in each sentence.
The first one is done for you.

1. She could find no one who spoke English.

  who, no one

2. Ted has a voice that carries far.

3. She was a woman whose ideas were ahead of her time.

4. The couple whom they interviewed saw the accident.

5. The man who spoke first was very funny.

6. We need someone whom we can trust.

7. Have you seen the man who moved next door?

8. The hammer, which you were looking for, is right here.

Practice B

Write each sentence. Use the correct relative pronoun. The first
one is done for you.

9. The dog _____ I want is a boxer.

  The dog that I want is a boxer.

10. The woman _____ came to the door did not live there.

11. The records, _____ are old and scratched, belong to him.

12. The girl _____ kitten got lost was very sad.

13. The story _____ he told was unbelievable.

14. **CHALLENGE** Write a sentence of your own using a
relative pronoun.

Practice C

Write each underlined pronoun. If the pronoun is interrogative, write *I*. If the pronoun is demonstrative, write *D*. If it is a relative pronoun, write *R*. The first one is done for you.

15. The dress <u>that</u> she wore had yellow stripes.

that, R

16. <u>This</u> is my house.

17. <u>Who</u> is on the phone?

18. Tell me <u>what</u> the meaning of this is.

19. She is the actress <u>whom</u> we saw in the play.

20. Please hand me <u>those</u>.

21. The person <u>who</u> bought this gift is thoughtful.

22. The pizza, <u>which</u> Paul bought, was not eaten.

Everyday English

Sports Town athletic store is looking for a manager. The store owner placed this ad in the newspaper. However, she used one pronoun incorrectly. Read the ad. Then answer the following questions.

1. What are the two relative pronouns?

2. Which relative pronoun is used incorrectly? Tell why it is incorrect.

3. **CHALLENGE** Add a sentence to the ad. Use a relative pronoun.

Looking for a job that has great benefits?

We are seeking a store manager whom has 3 to 5 years of experience

Send your résumé to:
Sports Town
P.O. Box 156
Irving, TX 75063

Include hours available and salary requirements.

Lee Young is working on a house construction crew for the summer. Today is his first day on the job. The construction supervisor could not be on the work site with Lee. He left Lee the following written instructions for the day.

Read the supervisor's instructions, and answer the questions below.

> Today, you will work with Hank. He will show you how to frame a house. Only use the boards that are stacked by the shed. Do not use the boards that are inside the shed. The boards are for the deck. We will build it last. If you have questions about what to do, ask Hank.

1. Use a relative pronoun to combine the first two sentences.

2. Rewrite the fifth sentence. Replace the subject with a demonstrative pronoun.

3. Add a sentence to the end of the instructions. Use an interrogative pronoun.

4. **CRITICAL THINKING** Why is it important to use pronouns correctly in instructions?

Speaking and Listening
Work with a partner to give instructions on how to cover a book. One student gives the instructions and demonstrates. The other student listens carefully and then follows the instructions. Switch roles. Be sure to use pronouns correctly.

6·4 ▶ Writing: Using Pronouns That Ask and Point in Sentences

Interrogative, demonstrative, and relative pronouns help ask questions and point things out. You can use the READ, PLAN, WRITE, and CHECK steps to write sentences using these types of pronouns.

▶ **EXAMPLE**

You have a job interview tomorrow. Write a sentence about what you plan to wear. Explain why you chose these clothes. Use a relative pronoun.

READ **Do you understand the assignment?**
Write the assignment in your own words.

> *Write a sentence about what I am going to wear to my job interview and why I made this choice. Use a relative pronoun.*

PLAN **Gather your ideas and organize them.**
Use a sunburst diagram to organize your ideas. Write *Interview Clothes* in the center circle. On each ray, write what you plan to wear.

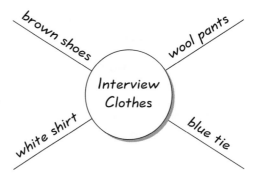

WRITE **Put your ideas into a sentence.**
Include the items in your diagram in your sentence.

> *For my job interview, I will wear the white shirt, blue tie, wool pants, and brown shoes that I bought last week.*

CHECK   **How can you improve your writing?**

Make sure your sentence answers the assignment. Add information that tells why you chose that clothing. Be sure you used pronouns correctly.

> *For my job interview, I will wear the white shirt, blue tie, wool pants, and brown shoes that I bought last week* because they look neat and clean.

The words in blue type were added to explain why this clothing was chosen.

Practice

Complete the writing assignments below. Use a sunburst diagram to help when you answer the questions under PLAN.

1. Write two basic questions that an employer might ask in an interview. Use interrogative pronouns.

   PLAN
   What determines if an applicant is right for the job?
   What information does an employer need to know?

2. Write a sentence that explains why it is important to be prepared for an interview. Use a relative pronoun.

   PLAN
   What will you gain from being prepared?
   Why is it a good idea to practice interviewing?

Putting It All Together

Write a paragraph that explains why job interviews are important. You may include the sentences you have written above. Add other sentences that explain your ideas.

| demonstrative |
| interrogative |
| relative |

Vocabulary Review

Complete each sentence with a word from the box.

1. A ____ pronoun connects a noun or pronoun with a group of words that tells more about it.

2. A ____ pronoun points out people, places, things, events, and ideas.

3. An ____ pronoun asks a question.

Chapter Quiz

LESSON 6·1

Using Pronouns That Ask

Write each sentence. Use the correct interrrogative pronoun.

1. ____ called on the phone this morning?

2. ____ do you think that word means?

3. I wonder ____ won the game.

4. ____ of the three sweaters will you choose?

5. For ____ is the last slice of cake?

6. Tell me ____ to do with this.

LESSON 6·2

Using Demonstrative Pronouns

Write each sentence. Add a demonstrative pronoun of your own.

7. ____ is the greatest book I have ever read.

8. ____ are the ones I made myself.

9. You told me ____ yesterday.

10. I cannot carry two of ____ at one time.

11. ____ are the shoes I like.

12. Do you believe ____?

Test Tip
That, which, who, whom, and *whose* are relative pronouns.

Using Relative Pronouns
Write each sentence. Use the correct relative pronoun.

13. Jane is wearing a jacket ____ matches her jeans.

14. I live in Georgeville, ____ is 10 miles from here.

15. He is the one ____ bike I borrowed.

16. The person to ____ I introduced you is my aunt.

Identifying Interrogative, Demonstrative, and Relative Pronouns
Write each underlined pronoun. If the pronoun is interrogative, write *I*. If the pronoun is demonstrative, write *D*. If it is a relative pronoun, write *R*.

17. <u>Which</u> way is the school?

18. I think <u>that</u> is the right way.

19. <u>This</u> is the street <u>that</u> I usually take.

Writing Tip
Use a sunburst diagram to PLAN what to write. CHECK that you used pronouns correctly.

Writing: Using Pronouns in Sentences
20. You are going to interview the mayor of your city. Write three questions to ask the mayor. For example, you may want to ask about public parks or recycling efforts. Use interrogative pronouns.

Group Activity

Work with a group to create a questionnaire. Choose one of the following topics: music, sports, movies, or hobbies. Have each group member write one question, such as *Who is your favorite athlete?* Be sure to use different interrogative pronouns. Then exchange questionnaires with another group. Answer the questionnaire with your group members.

Unit 3 **Review**

Read the passage below to answer questions 1–5. Choose the word that belongs in each space. Mark the letter for your answer.

Julie had promised to walk __(1)__ neighbor's dog after school on Tuesday. Julie forgot __(2)__ she had basketball practice that day. __(3)__ would do it for her? She could not think of __(4)__ to ask. Her brothers were too busy with __(5)__ own basketball practice.

1. A. her's
   B. its
   C. his
   D. her

2. A. that
   B. which
   C. whom
   D. who

3. A. Who
   B. Whom
   C. Whose
   D. What

4. A. something
   B. everyone
   C. anyone
   D. everybody

5. A. his
   B. himself
   C. theirs
   D. their

Read the passage below to answer questions 6 and 7. Choose the best way to write the passage. Mark the letter for your answer.

Todd lost a book that I borrowed from the library. (6) She says we should split the cost of the book. (7) I think he should pay for the book myself. I told him that yesterday, and I have not seen him since.

6. A. They says we should split the cost of the book.
   B. He says we should split the cost of the book.
   C. We says we should split the cost of the book.
   D. No error

7. A. I think he should pay for the book himself.
   B. I think he should pay for the book hisself.
   C. I think he should pay for the book itself.
   D. No error

Critical Thinking

Your class needs to raise money for a class trip. What three questions do you think must be answered to plan a successful fundraiser? **WRITING** Write a paragraph explaining your fundraising plan. Include the answers to your three questions. Use pronouns correctly.

Unit 4 ▶ Verbs

Behind the scenes of a television newscast, a producer decides how to combine words and action to tell a story. Words that are used to express action are called verbs.

Written scripts and live action video come together to make a newscast. Look at the television screen and the news script. Then answer the questions.

1. What action is shown in the picture?

2. What words in the news script express the action?

> **Newscaster:**
> Heavy rain flooded Highway 9 yesterday.
>
> The flood delayed travelers for hours.

Look at this photograph. What action do you see? You need to use verbs to answer this question. Verbs are words that express action.

Words to Know

verb	a word that expresses action or a state of being
action verb	a word that expresses physical or mental action
linking verb	a word that expresses what is or what seems to be
tense	the time of the action or being expressed by a verb
present tense	a verb form that shows action or being at the present time
past tense	a verb form that shows action or being in the past
irregular verb	a word that does not form its past by adding -d or -ed

Verb Table Project

Did you know that everything you do now or have done in the past can be named by verbs? On a sheet of paper, list favorite memories from your past. Also list five things you enjoy doing now. Then create a table. Label the first column *Past Tense Verbs* and the second column *Present Tense Verbs*. Write all the action words from your lists in the correct columns of the table. Do you notice a pattern? Keep adding to your lists and table as you work through this chapter.

Learning Objectives

- Identify verbs.
- Identify action verbs.
- Identify linking verbs.
- Recognize present tense verb forms.
- Determine subject-verb agreement.
- Use past tense verb forms.
- Use irregular past tense verb forms.
- Write sentences using verbs.
- Apply knowledge of verb forms to a résumé and a dictionary entry.

A **verb** expresses an action or a state of being. A verb sometimes expresses an action that cannot be seen or heard.

Every sentence must have a verb. A sentence may have more than one verb.

Michelle hit the ball into the stands. (action)

She is a new member of the team. (state of being)

She thought about the home run. (action that cannot be seen or heard)

Michelle raced around the bases and slid into home base.
(more than one verb)

Practice A

Write the verb or verbs in each sentence. The first one is done for you.

1. Rick takes the bus to school.

   takes

2. The lion roared loudly.

3. Ms. Brown went to the phone and dialed a number.

4. Nadia and I are first cousins.

5. Snow fell late last night.

6. Julio misses his brother.

7. Those pears look delicious!

8. Sam is a wonderful cook.

9. Both drivers stopped suddenly.

10. They read the chapter carefully and answered the questions.

11. Miguel felt tired after the game.

12. Jimmy read three books last week!

13. Ashley sometimes turns on the radio and dances.

14. Sara decided on a blue shirt with long sleeves.

15. Mr. Rubén thought about the problem.

16. Lu looks unhappy this morning.

17. The dish slipped from Glen's hands and crashed to the floor.

18. Tim exercises every day.

19. Everyone on the team wished for a home run.

20. Alejandra woke up, jumped out of bed, and made breakfast.

Practice B

Write each sentence. Add one or more verbs of your own.
The first one is done for you.

21. Roberto _____ baseball caps for his collection.

    Roberto buys baseball caps for his collection.

22. I _____ a dollar for the parking meter.

23. Craig _____ upset after his team lost the game.

24. Alison _____ dinner and _____ to work.

25. The group often _____ at the library.

(Practice B continues on next page.) ⇨

26. I _____ he will go with us on the trip.

27. Megan _____ questions before beginning a project.

28. The perfume _____ like a rose garden.

29. Julie _____ her science homework.

30. She _____ a great artist.

31. I _____ all of the words to that song.

32. Luther and Mary _____ brownies every weekend.

33. She _____ a glass of juice and _____ it to her sister.

34. Joe _____ the window and _____ the door.

35. I _____ to my locker and _____ the books I needed in my backpack.

Everyday English

Jason is reading the instructions for his new popcorn maker. Read the instructions and follow the directions below.

1. List the seven verbs in the instructions.

2. Write these instructions. Add a verb of your own.

    a. _____ the popcorn popping.

    b. _____ melted butter on the popcorn.

    c. _____ your snack.

Jumbo Air Popper

Instructions for Use

1. Remove the top.
2. Pour the kernels into the popper.
3. Replace the top.
4. Place a large bowl underneath the dispenser.
5. Plug the cord into the wall.
6. Unplug the cord when the popping stops.

Top

Popcorn dispenser

Bowl

Plug

Action Verbs

An **action verb** expresses physical or mental action. A mental action cannot be seen or heard.

▶ **EXAMPLE**

The pitcher throws the ball hard. (physical action)

The batter swings with power. (physical action)

He thinks it is an unbelievable story. (mental action)

Everyone believes the story. (mental action)

Practice A

Write the action verb in each sentence. The first one is done for you.

1. We swim in the lake each summer.

   swim

2. Sheila never judges other people.

3. Marvin drives to his office in the city each day.

4. The plane landed safely during the snowstorm.

5. Lu eats a balanced diet.

6. The council considered the plan with care.

7. Those birds fly south in the winter.

8. They wrote their term papers on the computer.

9. Tara always jogs on the beach at sunset.

10. The weather bureau predicts rain for tomorrow.

Practice B

Write each sentence. Use an action verb from the box.
The first one is done for you.

11. Vito _____ a new stereo.

Vito purchased a new stereo.

12. We _____ a big surprise for Lauren.

13. Lupe _____ into the room.

14. Melissa _____ a new car.

15. I _____ until midnight.

16. Caitlin _____ across the ice.

17. They _____ the sand sculpture.

18. Tony _____ an interesting speech.

worked	slid
delivered	picked
ordered	played
planned	wanted
skipped	purchased
rushed	liked

Practice C

Write the action verb in each sentence. Then replace it with another
action verb that makes sense. The first one is done for you.

19. Enrique drives his car.

drives, paints

20. Tammy eats breakfast each morning.

21. The government passed a new law.

22. The teens laughed with their friends.

23. The girls threw the basketball.

24. The company believes it has a good product.

A **linking verb** expresses what is or what seems to be. It links the subject of a sentence with a word that describes it.

▶ **EXAMPLE 1**

Jerry is our friend.

(*Our friend* describes the subject *Jerry*.)

He always looks happy.

(*Happy* describes how the subject *he* looks.)

The verb *to be* is the most common linking verb. The forms of the verb *to be* are *am, is, are, was,* and *were.* The chart below contains some other common linking verbs.

▶ **EXAMPLE 2**

Common Linking Verbs Each of these verbs can be used as a linking verb.			
act	feel	remain	sound
appear	grow	seem	stay
become	look	smell	taste

Many linking verbs also can be action verbs. It depends on how they are used in a sentence. If the subject is performing the action, the verb is an action verb. If not, the verb is a linking verb.

▶ **EXAMPLE 3**

Linking: Their father appeared angry. (not performing action)

Action: The singer appeared in a play. (performing action)

Linking: I looked sad. (not performing action)

Action: I looked at the page. (performing action)

Linking: The runner grew tired. (not performing action)

Action: The man grew a beard. (performing action)

Practice A

Write the linking verb in each sentence. The first one is done for you.

1. Emily is a fine singer.

    is

2. They remained quiet throughout the whole play.

3. The potatoes taste salty.

4. Suddenly, Marta grew quiet.

5. Sondra and Neil are hard workers.

6. Little by little, the sky became cloudy.

7. That sounds wise to me.

8. Ray was captain of the team.

Practice B

Write each sentence. Use a form of *to be* or another linking verb. Refer to the box on page 141. The first one is done for you.

9. They sometimes _____ funny.

    They sometimes look funny.

10. The telephone call _____ for Dennis.

11. I never _____ bored.

12. The party guests _____ happy.

13. You _____ my best friend.

14. These flowers _____ sweet.

15. The patients _____ ill.

16. **CHALLENGE** Write the verb in each sentence. Write *A* next to the action verb. Write *L* next to the linking verb.

The salsa tastes spicy.
The chef tastes all the food himself.

Practice C

Read the following paragraph. Write the seven linking verbs.

Rain forests cover less than six percent of the earth. Some of the largest rain forests are in South America and Africa. The rain forest is hot, humid, and rainy. The climate is perfect for plants to grow. About 70 percent of all the plants in the forest are trees. Over the years, many trees were cut for lumber. People grew concerned about the effect on the environment. They became aware of the problems to the world's climate. People are working to save the forests, but they still remain in danger.

Everyday English

Kyle and his friends are choosing a video at the video store. They read the video jacket to find out more about the movie.

1. Write the linking verb in the movie title.

2. List the seven linking verbs in the movie summary.

3. **CHALLENGE** Rewrite the video jacket. Replace two linking verbs with action verbs. Underline your action verbs.

Nick Is Out of Control

Bob Garcia is great as troubled teen Nick Jones in *Nick Is Out of Control*. When Nick becomes a rock star almost overnight, his parents grow concerned. Suddenly, their son looks strange. Nick's friends are worried and upset. Something seems wrong — very wrong.

★★★★
"Stunning performances!"

7-4 ▸ Present Tense Verb Forms

Verbs express **tense**, or time. Verbs can express past, present, and future tense.

The **present tense** shows action or being that is happening now. The present tense also can show repeated action.

▶ **EXAMPLE**

The cat hides under the sofa. (action in the present)

The cat is under the sofa. (being in the present)

The cat hides there whenever the dog comes into the room. (repeated action)

Practice

Write the present tense verb in each sentence. The first one is done for you.

1. They often camp in the woods.

   camp

2. The whistle blows at five o'clock.

3. Greg makes the greatest tacos in the world.

4. Those flowers bloom only in the spring.

5. He studies in his room every afternoon.

6. Gina sleeps late on Saturdays.

7. She runs a marathon every fall.

8. John is a talented football player.

Subject-Verb Agreement

Making Subjects and Verbs Agree

When the subject and a verb in a sentence agree, the verb matches its subject in number. Most verbs have both a singular and a plural present tense form. Use singular verbs with singular subjects. The singular subject may be a noun or the pronoun *he*, *she*, or *it*.

▶ **EXAMPLE 1**

Subject	Singular Present Tense Verb Form
The dog	runs.
He (She, It)	runs.

Use plural verbs with plural subjects. The plural subject may be a noun or the pronoun *I*, *you*, *we*, or *they*.

▶ **EXAMPLE 2**

Subject	Plural Present Tense Verb Form
The dogs	run.
I (You, We, They)	run.

Practice

Write each sentence. Use the correct form of the verb in parentheses. The first one is done for you.

1. That band (perform, performs) at every assembly.

   That band performs at every assembly.

2. Each cast member (play, plays) several roles.

3. The Chans (spend, spends) holidays in Seattle.

4. The jury members (argue, argues) over every point.

5. His friends (call, calls) at all hours of the night.

Subject-Verb Agreement with Indefinite Pronouns

You have learned that an indefinite pronoun takes the place of an unnamed noun. Use a singular verb with a singular indefinite pronoun. Use a plural verb with a plural indefinite pronoun.

Some indefinite pronouns may be singular or plural. Use a singular verb when the pronoun refers to a specific person or one person or thing. Use a plural verb when the pronoun refers to more than one person or thing.

Singular Indefinite Pronoun		Plural Indefinite Pronoun	Indefinite Pronoun That May Be Singular or Plural
another	neither	both	all
anybody	nobody	few	any
anyone	no one	many	most
anything	nothing	others	none
each	one	several	some
either	other		such
everybody	somebody		
everyone	someone		
everything	something		

► **EXAMPLE**

Everyone eats lunch at school. (singular pronoun; singular verb)

Several eat lunch at school. (plural pronoun; plural verb)

Most of the class eats lunch at school. (*Most* used as a singular pronoun; singular verb)

Most of the students eat lunch at school. (*Most* used as a plural pronoun; plural verb)

Practice A

Write the correct form of the verb in parentheses. The first one is done for you.

1. Many _____ to come. (want)

   want

2. Each _____ her own opinion. (have)

3. Few _____ with the chairperson. (agree)

4. Nobody _____ ready. (feel)

5. Several _____ glad to leave. (be)

6. Both _____ Spanish well. (speak)

7. Neither _____ broccoli. (like)

8. Either _____ a fine choice. (be)

Practice B

Read each sentence. If the indefinite pronoun is singular, write *S*. If it is plural, write *P*. The first one is done for you.

9. Some of the characters are interesting.

   P

10. None is cheap.

11. Most of the team plays well.

12. All of those painters use bold brush strokes.

13. All of the cereal is gone.

14. Some of the new movies look interesting.

Subject-Verb Agreement with Compound Subjects

A sentence may have two or more subjects. When the subjects are joined by *and*, you usually use a plural verb form.

▶ **EXAMPLE 1**

The paper and the pencil are on the table.

Sometimes, the subjects are joined by *or* or *nor*. In this case, the verb agrees with the last noun or pronoun.

▶ **EXAMPLE 2**

Plural: Either the paper or the pencils are on the table.

Singular: Neither the papers nor the pencil is on the table.

Practice

Write the correct form of the verb in parentheses. The first one is done for you.

1. Keesha and Maria _____ brilliantly. (skate)

    skate

2. Neither my cat nor my dog _____ in the house. (sleep)

3. The blue shoes and the red shoes _____ my feet. (hurt)

4. Either Ellie or her friends _____ every week. (call)

5. Some gloves or a hat _____ a nice gift. (make)

6. The blue or white shirt best _____ those pants. (match)

7. Jake, Leslie, and their parents _____ a Labor Day party every year. (throw)

Subject-Verb Agreement with Titles

Use a singular verb form with the title of a book or movie. Use a singular verb form with the name of an organization or country.

Space Pioneers **is** my favorite movie.

Great Expectations **has** many interesting characters.

The Philippines **is** an island country.

The United Nations **meets** here.

Practice

Write the correct form of the verb in parentheses. The first one is done for you.

1. The Library Association _____ to raise money. (plan)

   plans

2. The United States _____ to sign that agreement. (want)

3. *The Canterbury Tales* _____ a series of short stories by Geoffrey Chaucer. (be)

4. The Bahamas _____ an island country south of Florida. (be)

5. The Red Cross _____ people when disaster strikes. (help)

6. *War and Peace* _____ the longest book I ever read. (be)

7. Honduras _____ bananas to many other countries. (sell)

Subject-Verb Agreement with Amounts

When you think of an amount as a single unit, use a singular verb form. When you think of an amount as separate units, use a plural verb form.

▶ **EXAMPLE**

One third of the town is registered to vote. (One third refers to one section of the town. It is singular.)

One third of the town's residents are registered to vote. (One third refers to many residents. It is plural.)

Practice A

Think of each amount in these sentences as a single unit. Write the correct form of the verb in parentheses. The first one is done for you.

1. Two thirds of the team _____ the flu. (have)

    has

2. Twenty-five dollars _____ too much money for that cap. (be)

3. One half of the fleet _____ tomorrow. (sail)

Practice B

Think of the amounts in these sentences as separate units. Write the correct form of the verb in parentheses. The first one is done for you.

4. One half of the women _____ every day. (help)

    help

5. One third of the trucks _____ out of service. (be)

6. A quarter of the projects _____ completed. (be)

Past Tense Verb Forms

Past tense verb forms show action or being that has already happened. Many past tense verb forms are made by adding -d or -ed to the present tense plural form.

▶ EXAMPLE

Present Tense	Past Tense
Today, they work hard.	Yesterday, they worked hard.
Today, they share their work.	Yesterday, they shared their work.

Practice A

Write the past tense verb form in each sentence. The first one is done for you.

1. The news shocked the world.

   shocked

2. She photographed many important people.

3. We arrived early.

4. Raymond stayed for three hours.

5. She talked about Alberto all the time.

6. I invited him to the meeting.

7. They danced for hours.

8. The show started with a song.

9. Heather noticed the new guest.

10. Martin asked a tricky question.

Practice B

Write the verb in each sentence. Then write if the verb is in the present tense or in the past tense. The first one is done for you.

11. Pioneers crossed the country in covered wagons.

crossed, past tense

12. Lightning flashed during the storm.

13. The storm ended suddenly.

14. We often see lightning in this part of the country.

15. The chorus learned a new song.

16. I feed the dogs after school.

17. Ingrid started the discussion.

18. Jason asked his mother for the car keys.

19. **CHALLENGE** Snakes shed their skin as they grow.

Practice C

Write each sentence. Add a past tense verb form of your own. The first one is done for you.

20. I _____ at each of her jokes.

I laughed at each of her jokes.

21. She _____ a coin to decide who would go first.

22. Ms. Garza _____ to hire a new secretary.

23. We _____ home after the soccer game.

24. My mother _____ my favorite dinner.

ENGLISH IN YOUR LIFE
Writing a Résumé

Philip Franco wants to work as a home health aide. He volunteers at the local nursing home. He decides to write a résumé. A résumé tells about a person's skills and experiences.

Here is part of Philip's résumé. This part includes his skills and experiences as a volunteer.

Read Philip's résumé, and follow the directions below.

Summary

I am a volunteer nurse's aide at the Lincoln Park Nursing Home. I help elderly people with their daily tasks.

Skills and Experience
- Walk residents to cafeteria and courtyard
- Give meals to residents
- Play checkers with residents
- Change bed linens

1. Write the five present tense action verbs.

2. Write the linking verb.

3. Philip no longer volunteers at the nursing home. Change the present tense verbs to past tense verbs.

4. **CRITICAL THINKING** Why is it a good idea to use action verbs in a résumé?

Writing

What job would you like to have some day? Start to build your résumé. Create a two-column chart. Label the first column *Skills*. Label the second column *Experience*. Fill in the chart with the skills and experience you have that relate to this job. Use action verbs. Then write a summary of your skills and experience.

Irregular Past Tense Verb Forms

Not all verbs form the past tense by adding *-d* or *-ed*. Some form the past tense in other ways. These are called **irregular verbs**. Some common irregular verbs are in the box below.

EXAMPLE

Present Tense	Past Tense	Present Tense	Past Tense
begin	began	grow	grew
blow	blew	know	knew
burst	burst	lie	lay
choose	chose	ring	rang
come	came	run	ran
do	did	see	saw
drink	drank	sleep	slept
drive	drove	speak	spoke
eat	ate	steal	stole
fall	fell	swim	swam
fly	flew	take	took
freeze	froze	tear	tore
give	gave	throw	threw
go	went	wear	wore

Practice A

Write the two irregular past tense verbs in each sentence. The first one is done for you.

1. When she began her speech, she wore a flower in her hair.

   began, wore

2. Lo Yi went home and slept.

3. The race began when the bell rang.

4. Snow fell, and the pipes froze.

5. Only Mike knew which one they chose.

6. Melinda stole the ball and threw it in the hoop.

7. I ran to my room and burst into tears.

8. Marie came to my house and ate dinner with my family.

Practice B

Write each sentence. Use an irregular past tense verb from the box on page 154. The first one is done for you.

9. Lee _____ the movie.

    Lee saw the movie.

10. I _____ all the old papers in the trash.

11. The bag was so full that it _____.

12. Jen _____ to my house yesterday.

13. The professor _____ loudly during his speech.

14. Nicole _____ out the candles on her cake.

15. The tired dog _____ down in the grass.

16. You just _____ me a good idea.

17. We _____ about the party as we _____ home.

18. He _____ asleep early and _____ late.

19. I _____ it was Rosa who _____ the doorbell.

20. Diego _____ how fast Sue _____.

Practice C

Rewrite each sentence. Use the past tense form of the verb in parentheses. The first one is done for you.

21. The student (run) around the track.

The student ran around the track.

22. The plane (fly) them directly to Washington.

23. My best jeans (tear) in the wash.

24. I (drive) my date home last night.

25. Marco (see) what Terry (do).

26. We (eat) pizza and (drink) soda.

27. I (know) my sister (wear) my new shirt before I (do).

28. **CHALLENGE** Write a sentence of your own. Use at least two irregular past tense verbs.

Everyday English

Tyler received a birthday gift from his aunt. Read Tyler's thank-you note that he mailed to her. Then answer the questions below.

1. What are the five irregular verbs in the note?

2. **CHALLENGE** Which verb in the note is the same in the present tense and the past tense?

Dear Aunt Sara,

Thanks for the new jacket that you gave me. I really needed it. I wore out my other jacket. Just the other day, a pen burst in the pocket and left ink stains. I also lost two of the buttons. This jacket looks and fits great!

Thanks again.
Tyler

USING REFERENCES
Dictionary

A dictionary gives information about words. The syllables show you the different parts of the word. The pronunciation tells you how to say the word.

The part of speech tells you how the word is used in a sentence. If the word is a verb, the entry lists the present and past tense forms.

A dictionary also helps you understand word meanings. The most common meaning of a word is listed first. Then other meanings are given. Some dictionaries give a sentence after a meaning to show how the word is used.

This woman uses a dictionary.

Look at the entry, and answer the questions below.

> **speak** (spēk) *v.* **speaks** (spēks), **spoke** (spōk), **spo • ken** (spō-kən), **speak • ing** (spē-king). **1. a.** to utter words, talk. *They speak to each other.* **b.** to express oneself before a group. *She will speak at the meeting.* **2.** to make a written statement. *Steinbeck's novels spoke of the common person.*

1. What part of the entry tells you *speak* is a verb?

2. Write the past tense form of the verb *speak*. Then write its pronunciation.

3. Is *speak* a regular or irregular verb? How do you know?

4. Write the sentence that helps you see how to use *speak* to mean *express oneself before a group*.

5. **CHALLENGE** Write a new sentence for each meaning of the word *speak*.

Writing: Using Verbs in Sentences

Complete sentences contain verbs. You can use the READ, PLAN, WRITE, and CHECK steps to help you use verbs correctly in sentences.

EXAMPLE

Think about someone you know who has an interesting job. Write two sentences that explain what this person's job is and why you think it is interesting. Use two linking verbs and two action verbs.

READ   Do you understand the assignment?

Write the assignment in your own words.

> Write two sentences about someone with an interesting job. Tell why the job is interesting. Use two linking verbs and two action verbs.

PLAN   Gather your ideas and organize them.

Use a chart to organize your ideas. Write what the job is in the first column. Write why the job interests you in the second column.

What	Why
personal trainer	meets many different people

WRITE   Put your ideas into sentences.

Write two sentences using the words in your chart.

> My cousin Mark is a personal trainer. His job is interesting because he meets many different people.

Make sure your sentences answer the assignment. Find ways to make the sentences clearer. Check that you used verbs correctly.

> *My cousin Mark is a personal trainer. His job is interesting because he meets many different people* and trains them on the latest exercise equipment.

The words in blue type were added to complete the assignment. A second action verb was used.

Practice

Complete the assignments below. Use a chart like the one on page 158 when you answer the questions under PLAN.

1. Write two sentences about a job you would like to have some day. Explain why that job interests you. Use at least one linking verb and one action verb.

    PLAN
    What job would you like to have?
    What is interesting about this job?

2. Write two sentences about the type of training you need for the job. Explain why this training is necessary. Include at least one linking verb and one action verb

    PLAN
    What school or classes might you need to take?
    Why is schooling or training helpful?

Putting It All Together

Write a paragraph about a career goal you have. How can you achieve this goal? You may wish to include the sentences you have written. Begin your paragraph with a sentence that connects all your ideas.

action verb

irregular verb

linking verb

past tense

present tense

tense

verb

Vocabulary Review
Complete each sentence with a word from the box.

1. An ____ expresses a physical action.

2. A ____ expresses a state of being.

3. An ____ changes its spelling to show past action.

4. The ____ tells when the action takes place.

5. The ____ tells about an action that already happened.

6. The ____ tells about an action that is happening now.

7. Every sentence must have a ____.

Chapter Quiz

LESSONS 7·1 to 7·3

Identifying Action and Linking Verbs
Write the verb in each sentence. Then write if it is an action verb or a linking verb.

1. Jimmy bought a new fishing pole.

2. He fishes at the lake.

3. The group of friends remained quiet.

4. Something tugged on the line.

5. Jimmy and his friends cooked a fish dinner.

LESSON 7·4

Recognizing Present Tense Verb Forms
Write the present tense verbs in each sentence.

6. Cara saves and prints her work.

7. The teacher reads and grades it.

8. Ben puts on his glasses and watches the movie.

Determining Subject-Verb Agreement
Write the correct form of the verb for each sentence.

9. My cats and dog (is, are) great pets.

10. Neither (likes, like) to bargain.

11. Two thirds of the students (goes, go) to the games.

12. The book *Products of Asia* (is, are) at the bookstore.

13. Nobody (wants, want) to go to the meeting.

Test Tip
Irregular past tense verbs change their spelling.

Using Past Tense Verb Forms
Write the past tense form of each verb in parentheses.

14. Jamie _____ his driving test yesterday. (take)

15. He _____ it on the first try. (pass)

16. Jamie _____ his mother home. (drive)

17. She _____ proud of him. (feel)

Writing Tip
Use a chart to PLAN what to write. CHECK that your sentences answer the assignment.

Writing: Using Verbs in Sentences

18. Write a paragraph about an electronic item in your house, such as a phone or a VCR. Answer these questions: What does the item look like? What special features does it have? When was the last time you used it? Include a linking verb and a past tense verb in your paragraph.

Group Activity

Work in a small group to write a course description for your English class. Tell what the class is, what students learn in the class, and what former students have gained from taking the class. Use action verbs in the present and past tense. Exchange descriptions with another group. Suggest ways to improve the other group's description.

What has just happened in this photo? What is happening right now? What will happen in the future? Verb phrases can be used to describe action in the past, present, or future.

Chapter 8 ▶ Verb Phrases

Words to Know

verb phrase	a phrase made up of one or more helping verbs and a main verb
main verb	the verb in a verb phrase that tells what happens or what is
helping verb	the verb in a verb phrase that helps the main verb tell what happens or what is
present participle	a verb form that shows continuing action
past participle	a verb form that shows completed action
future tense	the verb form that shows action in the future
active voice	the verb form that shows the action is done *by* the subject
passive voice	the verb form that shows the action is done *to* the subject

Journal Project

Look at the photograph on page 162. In your journal, write sentences that describe the action in this photo. As you learn more about verb phrases in this chapter, change or add to your sentences. Include at least one example of every verb form you learn about. Then put your sentences into a paragraph that describes the photo.

Learning Objectives

- Use *to be* and *to have* to form present and past participles.
- Identify verb phrases with *to do* and other helping verbs.
- Identify verb phrases that are interrupted by *not*.
- Identify future tense verb phrases.
- Identify active and passive voice.
- Write sentences using verb phrases.
- Apply knowledge of verb phrases to a description of services and an almanac entry.

Verb Phrases with *To Be*

Identifying Verb Phrases

A **verb phrase** is made up of a **main verb** and one or more **helping verbs**. The main verb tells what happens or what is. The helping verb helps the main verb tell what happens or what is.

▶ **EXAMPLE**

Sentence:	Tom is speaking.
Verb phrase:	is speaking
Helping verb:	is
Main verb:	speaking

Practice

Write the verb phrase in each sentence. Draw one line under each main verb. Draw two lines under each helping verb. The first one is done for you.

1. The bread was rising in the oven.

   was rising

2. I am hoping for a call from my friends.

3. All the leaves were changing colors.

4. She was planning a trip to Chicago.

5. Alex and Bev are preparing for the party.

6. The jury is deciding if she is guilty.

7. The President was speaking to the public.

8. The students were listening to the directions.

Using Present Participles

The main verb in a verb phrase often is the **present participle**. The present participle shows continuing action. It is formed by adding *-ing* to the plural form of the verb. Usually, if the plural form ends with *-e,* drop the *e* before adding *-ing*.

The present participle always follows a form of the helping verb *to be*. Verb phrases with *am, is,* or *are* and a present participle show continuing action in the present. Verb phrases with *was* or *were* and a present participle show continuing action in the past.

▶ **EXAMPLE**

Those cowboys ride horses. (present tense verb)

Those cowboys are riding horses. (present participle; continuing action in the present)
The cowboys were riding horses. (present participle; continuing action in the past)

Practice

Rewrite each sentence. Change the verb to a verb phrase. Use a form of the verb *to be* and the present participle. The first one is done for you.

1. They go to the gym.

    They are going to the gym.

2. Your money gains interest daily.

3. The clouds get thicker.

4. They watch a movie on television.

5. It becomes a serious problem.

6. I look for an apartment.

Have, _has_, and _had_ are forms of the verb _to have_. They are often used as helping verbs in verb phrases.

The helping verb _to have_ is followed by a **past participle**. A past participle is a verb form that shows completed action. It is usually formed by adding _-d_, _-ed_, _-n_, or _-en_ to the plural form of the verb. Some past participles are formed from irregular verbs. Notice how each past participle in the box is formed.

► **EXAMPLE**

Plural Verb Form	Past Participle
agree	has agreed
speak	have spoken
sing	had sung

Practice A

Write the verb phrase in each sentence. The first one is done for you.

1. They have asked an important question.

   have asked

2. The rider had fallen off her horse.

3. We have known them for three years.

4. The clerk has added up the figures.

5. Will and Yon Hee have spoken to the manager.

6. I wish I had known about the test.

7. **CHALLENGE** Have you had a flu shot?

Practice B

Rewrite each sentence. Change the verb to a verb phrase. Use a form of the verb *to have* and the past participle. The first one is done for you.

8. We give several suggestions.

    We have given several suggestions.

9. No one wastes time.

10. The brave rescue workers risk their lives.

11. Their baby grew a lot in the past weeks.

12. The audience applauds each diver.

13. Each student writes a paragraph.

14. I choose not to take the job.

15. Pilar tossed the paper into the wastebasket.

Everyday English

Roberto is a firefighter. He has been asked to give a speech at a local school. He will talk about his job and about fire safety. He wrote some notes for his speech. These notes will help him remember what to say.

Look at Roberto's notes.

1. Write the verb phrases that contain a form of the helping verb *to have*.

2. Rewrite the following sentence using a form of *to have*:
I work at the Northside Fire Station.

> • Your teacher has asked me to talk to you about my job and fire safety.
> • I have been a firefighter for nine years. I work at the Northside Fire Station.
> • Have any of you studied fire safety before? I want you to help me prevent fires from starting.

Verb Phrases with *To Do*

A form of *to do* can be used as a helping verb in a verb phrase. The main verb follows *to do*. It is always a plural verb form. *Do* and *does* are present tense forms of the verb *to do*. *Did* is the past tense verb form.

The helping verb *to do* has three main uses. It is used in questions, with the word *not*, and for emphasis.

▶ **EXAMPLE 1**

Do you like baseball? (in a question)

I do not like baseball. (with the word *not*)

I do like baseball. (for emphasis)

Remember
An interrogative sentence asks a question and ends with a question mark.

In interrogative sentences, the subject will come between a helping verb and a main verb. Notice the verb phrases in blue type.

▶ **EXAMPLE 2**

Does Jane like her classes?

Which class does she like best?

Practice A

Write the verb phrase in each sentence. The first one is done for you.

1. We did see it happen.

   did see

2. Did it rain last night?

3. We do agree with them.

4. They do talk a lot!

5. Rachel does enjoy sports.

6. Those oranges do contain a lot of juice.

7. Did Doug tell you that?

8. They really do have interesting ideas.

9. What do you think is the problem?

10. Susanna did vote in the election.

11. The announcer does speak very well.

12. The concert tickets did sell quickly.

Practice B

Change each question to a statement. Use only the words in the question. Underline the verb phrase. The first one is done for you.

13. Do they like pizza?

They <u>do like</u> pizza.

14. Did Alec send the e-mail message?

15. Does Stephen play the guitar?

16. Did Sandra have a good time on her vacation?

17. Does Elliot know how to drive?

18. Did Alan change his phone number?

19. Does he remember the way to your house?

20. Did Leticia meet Carol at the airport?

21. Do these keys belong to you?

22. **CHALLENGE** Write one statement and one question of your own using a form of the helping verb *to do*. Underline the verb phrases in your sentences.

8·4 Other Helping Verbs

Other helping verbs are sometimes used in verb phrases to change the meaning of a sentence.

The helping verbs *can, could, may, might, must, should,* and *would* are followed by a plural verb form.

Read the sentences in the chart. Think about what they mean.

► **EXAMPLE**

Sentence	Helping Verb
He sings.	
He can sing.	can
He could sing.	could
He may sing.	may
He might sing.	might
He must sing.	must
He should sing.	should
He would sing.	would

Practice A

Write the verb phrase in each sentence. The first one is done for you.

1. I could wear my purple socks.

   could wear

2. We should eat a more balanced diet.

3. Singers must breathe properly.

4. It might explode!

5. Opossums can hang by their tails.

Practice B

Rewrite each sentence. Change the verb to a verb phrase. Use one of the helping verbs in the chart on page 170 and the plural form of the verb. The first one is done for you.

6. Insects destroy plants.

Insects can destroy plants.

7. The sailors lower the anchor every evening.

8. I change my mind about what to wear.

9. All the chefs prepare their favorite recipes.

10. You have a good time at the dance.

11. Someone slipped on that wet floor.

12. She forgot to finish her homework.

13. **CHALLENGE** Complete the sentence below. Use a helping verb from the chart on page 170. Supply a main verb of your own.

Marco _____ his car.

Practice C

Read the following paragraph. Write the eight verb phrases that contain a helping verb from the chart on page 170.

I see dark clouds outside the window. It might rain today. I should get my umbrella. But I might miss the bus. Maybe I can make it. I would be very upset if it rained on my new clothes. I must hurry. Where can that umbrella be? Oh no! I just remembered. I left it at work last week! Now it is raining! Could anything else go wrong?

The word *not* changes the meaning of a sentence. The word *not* usually comes between the words in a verb phrase. However, it is not part of the verb phrase. It is a part of speech called an adverb. You will learn more about adverbs in Chapter 11.

▶ **EXAMPLE**

Sentence	Verb Phrase
They have arrived.	have arrived
They have not arrived.	have arrived
Bill is expecting them.	is expecting
Bill is not expecting them.	is expecting

Practice A

Write the verb phrase in each sentence. The first one is done for you.

1. We did not watch that program.

   did watch

2. They did not prepare well enough.

3. Li did not read that book.

4. We are not beginning until ten o'clock.

5. Stephen was not asking for a big favor.

6. The judges have not selected a winner.

7. I could not find my keys.

8. **CHALLENGE** I didn't tell Jerald.

Practice B

Rewrite each sentence by adding *not*. The first one is done for you.

9. Who has practiced her speech?

Who has not practiced her speech?

10. The suspect did confess.

11. Carey was laughing at Pat's joke.

12. The meeting has started on time.

13. I did give up!

14. Which one has broken?

15. The driver did stop at the stop sign.

16. The police officer was watching from her car.

17. Kayla was going to leave early.

Everyday English

All medicines have instructions and warnings printed on their labels. It is important to read these instructions before taking the medicine.

Read the instructions. Follow the directions below.

1. Write the two verb phrases in the instructions.

2. Which verb phrases are interrupted by the word *not*?

3. CHALLENGE Rewrite the last sentence using the word *not*.

Directions: Take 2 tablets every 4 to 6 hours for pain or fever. Do not take more than 8 tablets within 24 hours. Do not use this with any other pain medicine. Take with food or milk. Never give this product to children under 6 years of age.

8·6 Future Tense

The **future tense** shows action or being that will occur in the future. To form the future tense, use a verb phrase with *will* or *shall* and a plural verb form.

Future tense verb phrases may be interrupted by the word *not* or by the subject of an interrogative sentence.

EXAMPLE

Tomorrow, I will go to work.

Next week, I shall meet with the city council.

Kevin will not be late for the rehearsal on Friday.

Will you drive me to the airport?

Practice A

Write the verb phrase in each sentence. The first one is done for you.

1. Gail will buy drawing paper.

   will buy

2. After the game, we shall celebrate our victory.

3. Perhaps Beth will show us her vacation photos.

4. In case of danger, a warning whistle will sound.

5. Gary will stay home this weekend.

6. They will solve the problem together.

7. When will you tell her the good news?

8. Where will you go on vacation next year?

9. That box will not hold all of these books.

Practice B

Write the verb in each sentence. Then write if it is in the past, present, or future tense. The first one is done for you.

10. Someday, I shall learn yoga.

    shall learn, future tense

11. Before the test, Gordon studied hard.

12. You will not be sorry.

13. Last week, the Romanos cleaned out their garage.

14. Barry enjoys all sports.

15. He was on the baseball team last year.

16. We shall meet again.

Everyday English

Each day, weather reports are given on television and radio. They also can be found in daily newspapers. Read this weather report that was given on the radio.

1. Write the four future tense verb phrases.

2. Change the verb phrase in the last sentence to future tense.

3. **CHALLENGE** Why do you think weather reports often contain future tense verbs?

> The temperature right now is 57 degrees. Today's high will reach 76 degrees. Tomorrow will be sunny and 72 degrees. Thursday, a cold front will blow through. Temperatures will drop into the 40s. Then on Friday, it warms up again to 68 degrees.

Kurt Hernandez is a landscaper in Florida. He plants and trims shrubs and trees. He also mows and waters lawns. Kurt reads information about plant care to help him do his job well.

When Kurt finishes a job, he writes a note to the customer. He lets the customer know what services he completed.

Read Kurt's note, and answer the questions below.

These landscapers plant flowers.

> I completed several things today. I have mowed the grass. I also have finished trimming your new shrubs. I had planted new flowers last week. I watered them well today. They are doing fine. I may cut a few tree branches next time. Your lawn is looking great!

1. Which verb phrases contain a form of the verb *to be*?

2. Which verb phrases contain past participles?

3. **CRITICAL THINKING** Why do you think Kurt used so many past participles in his note?

Writing and Reading

Kurt leaves a note the day before he does a job. Rewrite Kurt's note. Change all of the verb phrases to the future tense. Then exchange papers with a partner. Read your partner's note. Check that your partner used verb phrases correctly.

In each of the sentences you have studied so far, the subject does the action. The verb in this kind of sentence is in the **active voice**.

In other sentences, the action is done *to* the subject. These sentences use verbs in the **passive voice**. These sentences always need a verb phrase. To make the passive voice, use a form of *to be* and a past participle.

Remember
A past participle is a verb form that shows completed action.

 EXAMPLE

Active Voice	Passive Voice
The band gave a concert.	A concert was given by the band.
Mr. Lee teaches that class.	That class is taught by Mr. Lee.

Use the active voice in your writing as much as possible. Use the passive voice only when the person or thing doing the action is unknown or unimportant.

Practice A

Read the following sentences. Write the letter of the sentence that has the verb phrase in the passive voice. The first one is done for you.

1. **A.** Leroy brought the pretzels.
   B. The pretzels were brought by Leroy.

   B

2. **A.** Traffic was slowed by heavy rain.
   B. Heavy rain slowed traffic.

3. **A.** William Hudson wrote *Green Mansions*.
   B. *Green Mansions* was written by William Hudson.

Practice B

Rewrite each sentence. Change the verb form to the passive voice. The first one is done for you.

4. No one witnessed the accident.

> *The accident was witnessed by no one.*

5. Snowplows clear the road.

6. Leslie knitted all those sweaters.

7. Many people like that movie star.

8. A postal worker delivered this package.

9. Troy scored the winning touchdown.

10. The mayor cut the red ribbon.

Practice C

Rewrite each sentence. Change the verb form to the active voice. The first one is done for you.

11. The telephone was invented by Alexander Graham Bell.

> *Alexander Graham Bell invented the telephone.*

12. A press conference was held by the President.

13. The meeting was attended by everyone.

14. The car was fixed by a mechanic.

15. The last question was answered by John.

16. The show is viewed by millions of people.

17. The thief was captured by the police.

USING REFERENCES
Almanac

An almanac is a book that contains facts and statistics on many topics. It tells about the weather, countries, businesses, people, and other subjects. It also includes facts about different sports.

Some almanacs include facts from the entire world. Others focus on a specific country or state. Some concentrate only on one particular subject.

Each year, a new almanac with the latest information is published. Almanacs use many verb phrases to tell about past and present events.

Read the almanac entry about the 1998 baseball season. Follow the directions below.

> Fans were watching the 1998 baseball season with great excitement. Mark McGwire and Sammy Sosa were trying to break Roger Maris's home run record. By October, both had passed his record of 61 home runs in a single season. The final homer was hit by McGwire. At the end of the season, he had set a new record with 70 home runs. Sosa did not finish far behind with 66. Who will break this new record?

1. Find the seven verb phrases used in the almanac entry.

2. Which sentence uses a passive verb phrase? Change it to the active voice.

3. CHALLENGE What important event from the past year might be included in an almanac? Write a sentence about this event. Use a verb phrase.

Writing: Using Verb Phrases in Sentences

8·8

Many sentences contain verb phrases. You can use the READ, PLAN, WRITE, and CHECK steps to write sentences with verb phrases.

▶ **EXAMPLE**

Write two sentences that list two things you could do to improve your community. Explain how each action will help your community. Be sure to use verb phrases.

READ **Do you understand the assignment?**

Write the assignment in your own words.

> *Write two sentences about how I can help to improve my community. Explain how my actions will help. Include verb phrases.*

PLAN **Gather your ideas and organize them.**

Use an idea web to plan what you will write. List one thing you can do and might do.

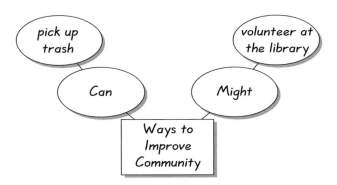

WRITE **Put your ideas into a sentence.**

Write two of the ideas from your web in sentence form.

> *I can pick up trash in my neighborhood. I might volunteer at the local library.*

CHECK   How can you improve your writing?

Make sure that your sentences answer the assignment. Add or change information to make them clearer. Make sure you used verb phrases in your sentences.

To help keep my community clean, **I can pick up trash in my neighborhood. I might volunteer** *to* **help children read** *at the local library.*

The words in blue type were added. They explain how each action will help the community.

Practice

Complete the assignments below. Answer the questions to CHECK your sentences.

1. Write two sentences about how you can help recycle. Be sure to use verb phrases in your sentences.

   CHECK
   Do your sentences answer the assignment?
   How can you make your writing clearer?

2. Write two sentences about how you can help conserve water. Be sure to use verb phrases in your sentences.

   CHECK
   Do your sentences answer the assignment?
   How can you make your writing clearer?

Putting It All Together

Write a paragraph about ways that you can help to save the environment. You may include the sentences that you have written. Add a sentence that introduces your ideas. Check that you used verb phrases correctly in the paragraph.

a.	active voice
b.	future tense verb
c.	helping verb
d.	main verb
e.	passive voice
f.	past participle
g.	present participle
h.	verb phrase

Vocabulary Review

Find the term in the box that matches each definition. Then write the letter for that term.

1. includes a helping verb and a main verb

2. shows action in the future

3. helps the main verb

4. shows completed action

5. shows that the action is done to the subject

6. tells what happens or what exists

7. shows continuing action

8. shows that the action is done by the subject

Chapter Quiz

LESSON 8·1

Using *To Be* to Form Present Participles

Rewrite each sentence. Change the verb to a verb phrase. Use a form of the verb *to be* and the present participle.

1. Ayanna made a video of her friends.

2. I save my money to buy a new watch.

3. The books sat on the shelf.

4. She cooks eggs for breakfast.

LESSON 8·2

Using *To Have* to Form Past Participles

Rewrite each sentence. Change the verb to a verb phrase. Use a form of the verb *to have* and the past participle.

5. Who finished the test?

6. Many people answered the ad.

7. The band plays for hours.

Test Tip
In a question, another word will
come between the helping verb
and the main verb.

Identifying Verb Phrases
Write the verb phrase in each sentence.

8. Did Stacy walk to school?

9. He must speak clearly.

10. We have not found your keys.

11. Can you help me with my project?

12. Will you meet me at 8:00?

13. I shall fix the computer.

14. The boys will order pizza for dinner.

Identifying Active and Passive Voice
**Write each verb phrase. Write an *A* if it is in the
active voice. Write a *P* if it is in the passive voice.**

15. He was playing a guitar.

16. The fire was started by lightning.

17. They were waiting on line at the movie theater.

Writing Tip
Use an idea web to help you
PLAN your paragraph. CHECK
that you used verb phrases in
your sentences.

Writing: Using Verb Phrases in Sentences
18. Write a paragraph about your favorite sandwich.
How do you make the sandwich? What foods
might you eat with it? Who else might like it?
Include verb phrases in your paragraph.

Group Activity
Work with a group to create an advertising flyer for a new
product that could be sold in a school store. Name the product.
Make a sketch of it on the flyer. Tell what the product can do and
why a student should buy it. Check that all your verb phrases
contain a helping verb and a main verb.

This picture of a pottery class shows one way people can be creative. Who is creating something in the picture? Your answer is the subject. What is being created? Your answer is the direct object. Use these answers to write a sentence about the picture.

Chapter 9

Verbs and Sentence Patterns

Words to Know

simple subject	the subject noun or pronoun of a sentence
simple predicate	the main verb or verb phrase of a sentence
direct object	a noun or pronoun that receives the action of a verb
indirect object	a noun or pronoun to whom or for whom an action is done
object complement	a word that follows the direct object and refers to it
predicate nominative	a noun or pronoun that follows a linking verb or verb phrase and renames the simple subject

Sentence Bank Project

On fifteen index cards, write five simple subjects, five simple predicates, and five direct objects. Group the subject cards together. Make two holes at the top of the cards. Use yarn or string to bind them. Repeat this process for the predicate and direct object cards. Use your word sets to form as many sentences as possible. Write your sentences in your sentence bank.

Learning Objectives

- Identify and use simple subjects and simple predicates.
- Identify and use direct objects.
- Identify and use indirect objects.
- Identify and use object complements.
- Identify and use predicate nominatives.
- Write sentences with different sentence patterns.
- Apply knowledge of sentence patterns to a story and an index entry.

Simple Subjects and Simple Predicates

You have already learned that the subject tells who or what the sentence is about. The **simple subject** is the noun or pronoun in the subject. So, the simple subject is the subject noun or pronoun of the sentence.

► **EXAMPLE 1**

The entire graduating class stood up and cheered.

Complete subject: The entire graduating class

Simple subject: class

The predicate tells what the subject does or is. The **simple predicate** is the verb or verb phrase in the predicate. So, the simple predicate is the main verb or verb phrase of a sentence.

► **EXAMPLE 2**

They applauded wildly for five minutes.

Complete predicate: applauded wildly for five minutes

Simple predicate: applauded

Everyone had listened carefully to the speech.

Complete predicate: had listened carefully to the speech

Simple predicate: had listened

Practice A

Write the simple subject and simple predicate in each sentence. The first one is done for you.

1. The happy group prepared a delicious dinner.

   group prepared

2. The alert lifeguard ran quickly toward the water.

3. The brilliant sun rose over the swaying trees.

4. The tiny mouse scurried quickly across the field.

5. The school's colors are blue and white.

6. Several young women walked into the room.

7. They explained the report in detail.

8. The response to the play was outstanding.

9. Each actor bowed deeply.

10. The audience cheered loudly for each actor.

11. Somebody in the room heard the announcement.

12. **CHALLENGE** All of the members had not left the meeting yet.

Practice B

Write each sentence. Add a simple subject of your own. The first one is done for you.

13. The _____ began five minutes ago.

The race began five minutes ago.

14. The _____ ran around the field.

15. _____ was declared the winner.

16. _____ set a new record for the event.

17. The _____ presented the gold medal.

18. A famous _____ sang the national anthem.

19. One _____ carried flowers to the winner.

20. _____ was so nervous that her hands shook.

(Practice B continues on next page.) ⇨

(Practice B continued.)

21. The _____ thanked everyone for the award.

22. The winner's _____ was very proud.

23. _____ was a wonderful day.

24. The _____ will be remembered for years.

Practice C

Write each sentence. Add a simple predicate of your own.
The first one is done for you.

25. My friend Jack _____ me a book.

My friend Jack gave me a book.

26. The tall man _____ loudly.

27. She _____ designer dresses.

28. The storm _____ late in the evening.

29. His supervisor _____ him for his hard work.

30. Everyone _____ the story.

31. All of her friends _____ rock music.

32. Somebody _____ the envelope.

33. We _____ our packages upstairs.

34. They _____ the office at noon.

35. I _____ the dog for a walk.

36. They _____ in the car all day long.

USING REFERENCES
Index

An index is a listing of the main topics in a book. The topics are listed in alphabetical order. An index is found in the back of a book.

Each major topic that is listed in an index is called a main entry. Look at the page numbers listed next to the entry. These numbers tell you where the topic appears. You also may see other entries listed below the main entry. These are subentries. They give more specific information about a topic.

Sometimes, a topic refers to a different main entry for more information. It will say *See* or *See also*, followed by an entry name.

Look at the index below. Then answer the questions below.

Thunderstorm, 265
Tides, 290–293
 See also Oceans;
 Waves
 high tides, 290
 moon and, 291
 sun and, 291
Time zones, 204–205

1. What three subjects are listed as main entries?

2. What three subjects are listed as subentries?

3. CHALLENGE Write three subentries that could be listed under *Oceans*? Use one of them as the simple subject in a sentence.

Direct Objects

Identifying Direct Objects

A **direct object** receives the action of a verb. It is a noun or a pronoun.

Remember
An action verb expresses a physical or mental action. A linking verb tells what is or what seems to be.

A direct object comes after the verb or verb phrase. It always follows an action verb. It never follows a linking verb.

We cooked dinner.

We ate the soup.

A sentence may have more than one direct object.

Marta is bringing cookies and cupcakes.

Pilar bought milk and bread at the store.

Practice A

Write the direct object in each sentence. The first one is done for you.

1. Caroline bought food.

   food

2. He took the photograph.

3. Mr. Kwan drove his car.

4. Nicki put the book on the table.

5. Chris did his homework on the bus.

6. Carmen dropped the glass on the floor.

7. Roberto mowed the lawn.

Practice B

Write the two direct objects in each sentence. The first one is done for you.

8. Did Brittany order soup or salad?

soup, salad

9. Sasha has two dogs and a cat.

10. Ben mailed a letter and a postcard.

11. Will you take a raincoat or an umbrella?

12. Mark visited New York and Boston.

Practice C

Write each sentence. Add a direct object noun of your own. The first one is done for you.

13. Hayato speaks _____.

Hayato speaks Japanese.

14. The store manager ordered more _____.

15. You are helping many _____.

16. Several students wanted this _____.

17. Letisha painted the _____.

18. The refrigerator kept the _____ cold.

19. We ate _____ for dinner.

20. Lucas planted _____ in the front yard.

Pronouns as Direct Objects

A direct object can be a pronoun. The pronoun can be singular or plural. The following pronouns can be used as direct objects.

Direct Object Pronoun	
Singular	**Plural**
me	us
you	you
him, her, it	them
this, that	these, those

◄ EXAMPLE

Nancy asked him. (singular pronoun)

The pilot landed it safely. (singular pronoun)

A loud noise awoke us last night. (plural pronoun)

Kyle saw them. (plural pronoun)

Practice A

Write the direct object in each sentence. The first one is done for you.

1. Gerald helped us yesterday.

    us

2. Mrs. Gravas gave this to my mother.

3. Gwen likes him.

4. Brian found them.

5. Lupe called me at home.

6. Nadine planted these last year.

7. You really surprised her.

Practice B

Write each sentence. Add a direct object pronoun of your own.
The first one is done for you.

8. Pedro could not locate _____.

   Pedro could not locate them.

9. Carl distributed _____ to the audience.

10. Anna took _____ home.

11. Brandon met _____ at the supermarket.

12. Mei Chu enjoyed _____ more than I did.

13. Some of the people saw _____ yesterday.

14. I gave him _____ for his birthday.

15. **CHALLENGE** Write a sentence using a direct object pronoun.
   Draw a line under the direct object pronoun.

Practice C

Read the following paragraph. Write the 12 direct objects.
Remember that a direct object can be a noun or a pronoun.
The first one is done for you.

> Lenka and I are planning a surprise party for Mimi. We
> must do many things before the big day. I will bake the cake.
> I will prepare it right before the party. Lenka is making
> decorations and invitations. I will find a very special present
> for Mimi. She really wants a new camera. She takes many
> pictures. Perhaps we could use the camera at the party. We
> can make a photo album of the event, as well. Then she will
> always remember her special day.

> *party*

Indirect Objects

An **indirect object** tells *to whom* or *for whom* an action is done. It is a noun or a pronoun.

The following pronouns can be used as indirect objects: *me, you, him, her, it, us,* and *them.*

EXAMPLE 1

Gina gave the dog some food.

Gina gave what?	food (direct object)
To whom?	dog (indirect object; noun)

Gina gave him some food.

Gina gave what?	food (direct object)
To whom?	him (indirect object; pronoun)

An indirect object comes after the verb and before the direct object in a sentence. It always follows an action verb. It never follows a linking verb. An indirect object never comes after the word *for* or *to.*

EXAMPLE 2

Gina gave the dog some food.

Indirect object: dog

Gina gave some food to the dog.

NOT an indirect object: to the dog

Practice A

Write each sentence. Draw one line under the direct object. Draw two lines under the indirect object. The first one is done for you.

1. Chee lent Rick his car.

   Chee lent <u>Rick</u> his <u>car</u>.

2. Carmen promised me some cookies.

3. Josh and Gia showed us the dance.

4. Ellen sent Craig a postcard.

5. Tina left her mother this note.

6. Isaac's grandfather told me the story.

7. Mrs. Puccio asked Joe a question.

8. Our team leader taught us the rules.

9. My mother made my sister pancakes for breakfast.

10. Cory bought his brother groceries.

11. The angry man mailed the dog's owner the bill.

12. Mr. Chu gave the landlord a check.

13. Calvin showed us a picture.

14. **CHALLENGE** Write a sentence using a direct object and an indirect object. Draw a line under the direct object. Draw two lines under the indirect object.

Practice B

Write each sentence. Add an indirect object of your own. The first one is done for you.

15. Someone sent _____ a letter.

Someone sent him a letter.

16. Julianna told _____ a joke.

17. That coupon saved _____ some money.

(Practice B continued.)

18. Dr. Kahn showed _____ the report.

19. Mrs. Carson gave _____ the books.

20. My dad made _____ a sandwich.

21. I cooked _____ some soup.

22. Did you save _____ a seat?

23. The judge awarded that _____ the trophy.

24. Carl drew _____ a picture of his new house.

25. Reuben tossed _____ the ball.

26. Did you lend _____ your notes for the science test?

27. She wrote her _____ a letter.

28. The teacher gave the _____ some homework.

Everyday English

Joe's Pizza Palace wants to get more business during the week. Joe put a coupon in the newspaper to attract customers.

Look at the coupon and follow the directions below.

1. Write the three direct objects.

2. Write the indirect object.

3. **CHALLENGE** Rewrite the last sentence using an indirect object.

JOE'S PIZZA PALACE

"We serve our customers food fit for a king."

Call today and save money on a large pizza.
We bring hot pizza to you in 30 minutes or less!

Mon.–Thurs. only   Expires June 30

Rachel Stein fell at the skating rink and hurt her ankle. Her mother took her to the emergency room. Rachel told the doctor what happened at the rink. It was important for her to speak clearly and accurately when she told the story.

Read Rachel's story carefully, and follow the directions below.

> We were at the rink. My friend showed me a trick. I tried it. However, I twisted my ankle and fell on the wooden floor. I could not move my foot. The guard gave me ice to put on my ankle. My mom is a nurse. She wants me to get an X-ray.

1. Write the six direct objects.

2. Write the two indirect objects.

3. **CRITICAL THINKING**   Why is it important to use direct and indirect objects when telling a story?

Speaking and Listening
Think about a memorable event from your childhood. Find a storytelling partner. One person tells his or her story. The other person listens carefully and takes notes. Then switch roles. Tell your partner's story to the rest of the class. As you tell the story, listen for your use of direct and indirect objects.

Object Complements

An **object complement** follows a direct object and refers to it. An object complement renames or tells more about the direct object. An object complement is a noun or an adjective.

EXAMPLE

The club made Henrietta president.

Direct object: Henrietta

Object complement: president

(The noun *president* renames *Henrietta*.)

She proved herself capable.

Direct object: herself

Object complement: capable

(The adjective *capable* tells more about *herself*.)

Practice A

Write each sentence. Draw one line under the direct object. Draw two lines under the object complement. The first one is done for you.

1. They found the house deserted.

    They found the house deserted.

2. That made Jeremy suspicious.

3. They considered the noises strange.

4. The visitors made themselves comfortable.

5. The voters elected her mayor.

6. I found the salesclerk helpful.

7. The long flight made the travelers very tired.

8. They judged you innocent.

9. The car's airbags help keep us safe.

10. The committee made her chairperson for next year.

Practice B

Write each sentence. Add an object complement of your own.
The first one is done for you.

11. I found the music _____.

I found the music beautiful.

12. The teacher made the lesson _____.

13. Some people consider her _____.

14. Abby's stories always make me _____.

15. I certainly would not call him _____.

16. The members just named me _____.

17. I have always found science _____.

18. That e-mail message made Lucy _____.

19. A good comedy always makes me _____.

20. I consider this car _____ for me.

Remember
A linking verb tells what is or what seems to be.

A **predicate nominative** renames, describes, or identifies the simple subject. The predicate nominative is a noun or a pronoun.

The predicate nominative follows a linking verb or verb phrase. It never follows an action verb.

▶ **EXAMPLE 1**

Mario was the first person to arrive.

Simple subject: Mario

Linking verb: was

Predicate nominative: person

(The noun *person* renames *Mario*.)

The following pronouns can be used as predicate nominatives: *I, you, he, she, it, we* and *they*.

▶ **EXAMPLE 2**

That tall man is he.

Simple subject: man

Linking verb: is

Predicate nominative: he

(The pronoun *he* identifies *man*.)

Practice A

Write each sentence. Draw one line under each linking verb. Draw two lines under each predicate nominative. The first one is done for you.

1. The recipient could be you!

The recipient could be you!

2. Those people are voters.

3. They all are applicants.

4. The winner is she.

5. The party was a great success.

Practice B

Write each sentence. Add a predicate nominative of your own. The first one is done for you.

6. We may become _____.

   We may become friends.

7. Johan will be a _____.

8. Ms. Hernandez became a _____.

9. What is that noise? It could be a _____!

10. Sandra Jones is an excellent _____.

Everyday English

Sean told Marc about a new TV show. It plays on Monday nights. Marc looked in the TV listings in the newspaper. He wanted to read about tonight's show. Read the listing. Then follow the directions below.

1. Write the four linking verbs or verb phrases.

2. Write the four predicate nominatives.

3. CHALLENGE What is the predicate nominative in the last sentence? What word does it rename?

8:00 P.M.

(4) City Dwellers Tom Parks is a plumber. Hank Wu is an apartment landlord. Wu hires Parks to fix a broken pipe. Soon afterward, Parks becomes a tenant in the building. Then things begin to go wrong. This could be trouble for these city dwellers.

Writing Sentences with Different Sentence Patterns

Many sentences contain both a direct object and an indirect object. Others have either an object complement or a predicate nominative. You can use the READ, PLAN, WRITE, and CHECK steps to write sentences using these sentence patterns.

▶ **EXAMPLE**

Write two sentences about the last gift you received. In the first sentence, tell what the gift was and who gave it to you. Use a direct object and an indirect object. In the second sentence, tell why you received the gift. Use a predicate nominative.

READ **Do you understand the assignment?**

Rewrite the assignment in your own words.

Write two sentences about the last gift I received. Tell what the gift was, who it was from, and why I received it. Use a direct object, an indirect object, and a predicate nominative.

PLAN **Gather your ideas and organize them.**

Use a chart to organize your ideas.

What is the gift?	*a black leather coat*
Who is it from?	*my grandmother*
Why did I get it?	*for my birthday*

WRITE **Put your ideas into a sentence.**

Create sentences using the words in the chart.

Last month, my grandmother sent me a black leather coat. It was for my birthday.

CHECK How can you improve your writing?

Make sure your sentences answer the assignment. Add missing information.

Last month, my grandmother sent me a black leather coat. It was a present for my birthday.

The predicate nominative in blue type was added to complete the assignment.

Practice

Complete the writing assignments below. Answer the questions under PLAN to create a chart.

1. Write two sentences about the last gift you gave. Tell what the gift was, the person you gave it to, and how the person felt about it. Use a direct object, an indirect object, and an object complement.

   PLAN
   What gift did you give? To whom did you give it?
   How did the person feel about the gift?

2. Write two sentences about the next gift you plan to give. Tell what the gift will be, who you will give it to, and what the occasion will be. Use a direct object, an indirect object, and a predicate nominative.

   PLAN
   What gift will you give? To whom will you give it?
   What is the occasion?

Putting It All Together

Write a paragraph about gifts that you have given and plan to give. You may want to use the sentences you have written above. Add other sentences to connect your ideas.

direct object
indirect object
object complement
predicate nominative
simple predicate
simple subject

Vocabulary Review

Complete each sentence with a term from the box.

1. The subject noun or pronoun of a sentence is called the ____.

2. The main verb or verb phrase of a sentence is called the ____.

3. A noun or pronoun that receives the action of a verb is called a ____.

4. A noun or pronoun that follows a linking verb and renames the simple subject is called a ____.

5. A word that follows the direct object and refers to it is called an ____.

6. A noun or pronoun to whom or for whom an action is done is called an ____.

Chapter Quiz

LESSON 9·1

Identifying Simple Subjects and Simple Predicates
Write the simple subject and simple predicate in each sentence.

1. Many airports give flying lessons.

2. All students need many flying hours.

3. Michelle joined an aircraft group.

4. She hopes to pilot her own plane someday.

LESSONS 9·2 and 9·3

Identifying Direct Objects and Indirect Objects
Write each sentence. Draw one line under the direct object. Draw two lines under the indirect object.

5. Grandmother baked us a pie.

6. I served my brother a piece.

7. He poured me a glass of milk.

Identifying Object Complements

Write the object complement in each sentence.

8. My family named our dog Champ.

9. We consider her part of the family.

10. Champ has proven herself a great watchdog.

Identifying Predicate Nominatives

Write each sentence. Draw one line under each linking verb. Draw two lines under each predicate nominative.

11. Montell is a policeman.

12. He may become a detective.

13. He is a good candidate for the job.

Writing: Using Different Sentence Patterns

14. Write a paragraph about your favorite teacher from last year. Tell who the teacher was, what the teacher taught you, and what you liked about this teacher. Be sure to include the following: a direct object, an indirect object, an object complement, and a predicate nominative.

Group Activity

Work with a group to form a small business. Write a paragraph telling what service or product your company provides. If you choose a service, tell what job each group member does. If you choose a product, explain why the product is special. Be sure to use different sentence patterns in your paragraph. Exchange paragraphs with another group. Suggest ways to improve the other group's work.

Unit 4 **Review**

Read the passage below to answer questions 1–5. Choose the word or words that belong in each space. Mark the letter for your answer.

Last year, Evelyn __(1)__ the first female baseball player on our team. She __(2)__ played only softball before joining the team. She __(3)__ our team win the state championship. She __(4)__ voted the Most Valuable Player. Evelyn __(5)__ remembered for all of her hard work and talent.

1. **A.** became
   B. is becoming
   C. becomes
   D. have become

2. **A.** have
   B. has
   C. had
   D. having

3. **A.** helped
   B. help
   C. helps
   D. helping

4. **A.** is
   B. was
   C. were
   D. are

5. **A.** are
   B. have been
   C. should
   D. will be

Read the passage below to answer questions 6 and 7. Choose the best way to write the passage. Mark the letter for your answer.

When the moon is full for the second time in one month, it is called a blue moon. (6) <u>This condition have occurred once every few years.</u> The expression *once in a blue moon* means "very seldom." (7) <u>Over the years, a blue moon has meaned any rare kind of moon.</u>

6. **A.** This condition occur once every few years.
   B. This condition had occurred once every few years.
   C. This condition occurs once every few years.
   D. No error

7. **A.** Over the years, a blue moon is meaning any rare kind of moon.
   B. Over the years, a blue moon has meant any rare kind of moon.
   C. Over the years, a blue moon have meant any rare kind of moon.
   D. No error

Critical Thinking

Your school is conducting a three-month "Helping Hands" project. List three ways your school can help the less fortunate.

WRITING Write a paragraph that explains how your school can help the less fortunate. Use verbs in the future tense.

Unit 5 ▶ Adjectives and Adverbs

Chapter 10 Adjectives

Chapter 11 Adverbs

Scientists track the journey of whales from the north to the south. These scientists use adjectives and adverbs to describe what they see. Adjectives are words that describe nouns and pronouns. Adverbs are words that describe verbs, adjectives, and other adverbs.

Scientists take notes in an observation log about the whales they see. Read the log, and answer the questions.

1. When and where did this scientist see the whales?

2. What words are used to describe the whales?

3. What word is used to describe how the whales were swimming?

Whale Observation Log

DATE: *April 19*

LOCATION: *Gulf of St. Lawrence*

NOTES: *Two whales were spotted about one and a half miles off the coast. They appeared to be a female whale and a small calf. They were swimming slowly at about 7 miles per hour.*

207

Look carefully at the photograph. Write a sentence that describes the scene. You will probably use adjectives to paint a clear picture in words. Adjectives are words that describe nouns or pronouns.

Chapter 10 ▷ Adjectives

Words to Know

adjective	a word that describes a noun or a pronoun
articles	a special group of adjectives that includes the words *the, a,* and *an*
predicate adjective	an adjective that comes after a linking verb and tells about the subject of the sentence
proper adjective	an adjective that refers to the name of a particular person, place, thing, event, or idea
comparative adjective	an adjective that compares two people, places, things, events, or ideas
superlative adjective	an adjective that compares three or more people, places, things, events, or ideas

Riddle Project

Write riddles about the following objects: camera, car, basketball, stereo, and computer. Add adjectives and other words to these sentences: *I am _____, _____, and _____. What am I?* For example, you might write the following riddle for a school bus: *I am big, yellow, and take kids to school. What am I?* Then trade papers with a partner. Compare the adjectives you each used.

Learning Objectives

- Identify adjectives.
- Use articles, predicate adjectives, and proper adjectives correctly.
- Use adjectives to make comparisons.
- Spell adjectives correctly.
- Use specific adjectives for clarity.
- Write sentences using adjectives.
- Apply knowledge of adjectives to a medical description and a telephone-book advertisement.

An **adjective** is a word that describes a noun or pronoun. Adjectives usually tell what kind, which one, or how many. Many times, an adjective comes before a noun in a sentence.

▶ **EXAMPLE**

She bought yellow flowers. (tells what kind)

Those flowers are in the vase. (tells which ones)

Ten flowers fit into the vase. (tells how many)

Practice A

Write the adjectives in each sentence. Each sentence has more than one. The first one is done for you.

1. Ancient Egyptians slept on hard pillows.

    Ancient, hard

2. Susan bought twelve chocolate cupcakes.

3. That white dog has beautiful blue eyes.

Practice B

Write each sentence. Add adjectives of your own. The first one is done for you.

4. The _____ coat is in the closet.

    The leather coat is in the closet.

5. We went to a _____ sale at a _____ store.

6. Her _____ brother plays _____ baseball.

7. **CHALLENGE** Write two adjectives that tell about color, two that tell about size, and two that tell how many.

The words *the*, *a*, and *an* make up a special group of adjectives called **articles**. An article always comes before the noun it describes.

The is a definite article. It refers to a specific person, place, thing, event, or idea. *A* and *an* are indefinite articles. They refer to any one of a group of things.

▶ **EXAMPLE 1**

The concert sold out quickly. (definite article)

One fan stood in line for eight hours to buy a ticket. (indefinite article)

Use *a* when the word that follows it begins with a consonant. Use *an* when the word that follows it begins with a vowel or sounds as if it begins with a vowel.

▶ **EXAMPLE 2**

The lead singer plays a guitar. (consonant)

He also plays an electric piano. (vowel)

He performed for an hour. (vowel sound)

The article *the* can be used with singular or plural nouns. The articles *a* and *an* are used only with singular nouns.

▶ **EXAMPLE 3**

The divers saw a sting ray and an octopus.

Practice A

Write the articles in each sentence. The first one is done for you.

1. Jackie saw a show about the making of a movie.

   a, the, a

2. The special effects were amazing.

3. A model ship was used for part of the filming.

Practice B

Write each sentence. Fill in the blanks with *a* or *an*. The first one is done for you.

4. José took _____ trip to _____ island.

    José took a trip to an island.

5. He found _____ starfish and _____ oyster shell.

6. José built _____ huge sand castle on the beach.

7. _____ exciting tour of the island lasted _____ hour.

8. _____ computer created the image of _____ iceberg.

9. She made _____ out in that inning.

10. _____ person in the crowd let out _____ cheer.

Everyday English

Derek decided to cook breakfast. He found an easy recipe for French toast. However, the recipe has some mistakes. Look at the recipe, and follow the directions below.

1. One article is used incorrectly in Step 1. Rewrite the sentence with the correct word.

2. An article is missing in Step 2. Rewrite the sentence and add the missing word.

3. **CHALLENGE** Step 5 uses an indefinite article incorrectly. Rewrite the step correctly.

FRENCH TOAST

Step 1: In a bowl, mix a egg and a cup of milk.

Step 2: Soak slice of bread in the egg and milk.

Step 3: Repeat Steps 1 and 2 with another slice of bread.

Step 4: Cook slices of bread for 3-5 minutes on each side.

Step 5: Serve a French toast with powdered sugar or maple syrup.

Adjectives can come after a form of the verb *to be* or another linking verb. These adjectives are called **predicate adjectives**. A predicate adjective tells about the noun or pronoun that is the subject of the sentence.

Remember
A linking verb connects the subject of a sentence with a word that describes it.

▶ **EXAMPLE**

More than one adjective can be used to describe the subject. Some sentences have more than one predicate adjective.

The flower is red. (The adjective *red* tells about the noun *flower*.)

The man grew tired of waiting. (The adjective *tired* tells about the noun *man*.)

The room was bright and cheerful. (The adjectives *bright* and *cheerful* tell about the noun *room*.)

The ocean felt cool and refreshing. (The adjectives *cool* and *refreshing* tell about the noun *ocean*.)

Practice A

Write the adjective in each sentence. Then write the subject it describes. Do not write the articles. The first one is done for you.

1. The street was dark and deserted.

    dark, street; deserted, street

2. The man was alone.

3. He became frightened.

4. The noise was sudden and loud.

5. It seemed startling.

6. The restaurant looked inviting.

Practice B

You are going to meet your cousins for the first time. You make plans to meet them at the airport. They asked, "How will we recognize you?" Write each sentence. Add an adjective that might describe you. The first one is done for you.

7. My eyes are _____ _____.

    My eyes are dark brown.

8. You may notice my hair because it is _____ and _____.

9. I am somewhat _____ and quite _____.

10. I may be wearing _____ jeans or _____ pants.

11. I may have a _____ flower in my hand.

12. My jacket is _____ .

13. I am so _____ to meet you!

14. **CHALLENGE** Write another sentence that describes you. Use a predicate adjective. Draw one line under the subject. Draw two lines under the predicate adjective.

Practice C

Read the following paragraph. Write the seven predicate adjectives.

> Mission control, we have just landed on Mars. The atmosphere appears hot and dry. There is no water. The soil is red and sandy. It seems almost burnt. Small rocks are scattered on the ground. They may be pieces of meteorites. Several small holes are located on the surface. Most are not deep, but they are very long.

10·4 Proper Adjectives

Proper adjectives are formed from proper nouns. A proper adjective refers to the name of a particular person, place, thing, event, or idea.

Proper adjectives begin with capital letters.

Proper Noun	Proper Adjective
America	American
the South	Southern
Rome	Roman

EXAMPLE

Mexican food can be spicy.

The Mayan ruins are interesting.

My friend's family is Russian.

Practice A

Write the proper adjective in each sentence. Then write the noun it describes. The first one is done for you.

1. Italian cooking is very popular in this country.

Italian, cooking

2. Neapolitan pizza is many people's favorite.

3. There is nothing like a California sunset.

4. *Hamlet* is my favorite Shakespearean play.

5. My mother's family is Spanish.

6. We bought a large Persian rug.

7. The Swiss airline was rated number one.

Practice B

Write each sentence. Add a proper adjective of your own.
The first one is done for you.

8. Have you ever tasted _____ olives?

    Have you ever tasted Greek olives?

9. The author of that book is _____.

10. He enjoys _____ music.

11. My cousin just bought a _____ cat.

12. Caroline's great-grandmother was a _____ immigrant.

13. He spent all of his _____ currency.

14. **CHALLENGE** Write a sentence about your cultural background. Use a proper adjective.

Everyday English

The names of some foods contain proper adjectives. Look at this menu from a sandwich shop. It contains an error. Follow the directions below.

1. Write each proper adjective and the noun it describes.

2. One proper adjective is not capitalized. Capitalize it correctly.

3. **CHALLENGE** Add a proper adjective to the last sentence.

Sandwiches

Ham & Cheese Sliced ham, Swiss cheese, lettuce, tomato, and mustard served on rye bread

Meatball Parmigiana Meatballs, spaghetti sauce, and mozzarella cheese served on Italian bread

Pita Pocket Sliced ham, feta cheese, and black olives served in a greek pita

All sandwiches are served with fries or a small Caesar salad.

Comparative Adjectives

Adding -er and -est to Adjectives

Adjectives can be used to compare two or more people, places, things, events, or ideas.

Adjectives that compare two items are called **comparative adjectives**. They often end in *-er*.

Adjectives that compare three or more items are called **superlative adjectives**. They often end in *-est*.

▶ **EXAMPLE**

Did you know that the World Trade Center is taller than the Empire State Building? (comparative)

Did you know that the World Trade Center is the tallest building in New York City? (superlative)

Practice

Write the correct form of the adjective for each sentence. The first one is done for you.

1. Nina's hair is (longer, longest) than Carrie's.

    longer

2. This room is the (bigger, biggest) in the house.

3. This is the (harder, hardest) job he has ever had.

4. My uncle is (older, oldest) than my mother.

5. This road is (steeper, steepest) than the other one.

6. Your room is (cleaner, cleanest) than it was yesterday.

7. She told the (funnier, funniest) story of all!

8. Which of the two questions is (easier, easiest)?

Using *More* and *Most*

Use *more* and *most* with adjectives that have three or more syllables. Use *more* and *most* with some adjectives that have two syllables.

Use *more* when you are comparing two items. Use *most* when you are comparing three or more items.

▶ EXAMPLE

This game was more exciting than the last one.

I was the most eager to learn about the author's life.

Practice

Rewrite each sentence. Use either *more* or *most* with the adjective in parentheses. The first one is done for you.

1. He is the (talented) singer in the chorus.

   He is the most talented singer in the chorus.

2. A crocodile may be (dangerous) than an alligator.

3. What is the (endangered) animal in the world?

4. Daria seems to be (responsible) than Steve.

5. Which of the two watches is (accurate)?

6. He was one of Hollywood's (successful) actors.

7. That test was (difficult) than last week's test.

8. That was the (challenging) game we have played this season.

9. Did you buy the (expensive) sweater?

10. The puppy has (energy) than its mother.

Using *Less* and *Least*

Use *less* when you compare two items. Use *least* when you compare three or more items.

► EXAMPLE

Your parents were less convinced than mine were.

Julie's parents were the least convinced of all.

Practice

Write each sentence. Use *less* or *least*. The first one is done for you.

1. Mandy was _____ tired than her brother.

   Mandy was less tired than her brother.

2. Sam was the _____ frightened of anyone in the room.

3. Flora is _____ certain than I am about passing the test.

4. She is _____ concerned than her sister.

5. Who is the _____ experienced swimmer of the two?

6. He is the _____ confident of all.

7. These shoes are _____ expensive than those.

8. After the rain, our street was the _____ flooded.

9. Richard is the _____ interested in cooking of the group.

10. That team was _____ enthusiastic than ours.

Using Other Comparative Adjectives

The adjectives *good* and *bad* both change form when they are used to compare things. The forms of the adjective *good* are *good, better,* and *best.* Use *better* when comparing two items. Use *best* when comparing three or more items.

The forms of the adjective *bad* are *bad, worse,* and *worst.* Use *worse* when comparing two items. Use *worst* when comparing three or more items.

▶ **EXAMPLE**

This movie is better than that one.

It is the best movie I have seen this year.

This movie is worse than that one.

It is the worst movie I have seen this year.

Practice

Rewrite each sentence. Use the correct form of the adjective in parentheses. The first one is done for you.

1. This book is (good) than that one.

   This book is better than that one.

2. This is the (good) restaurant in the city.

3. His performance was even (bad) than it was last year.

4. Our new apartment is even (good) than our old one.

5. It is the (bad) cold he has ever had.

6. His singing voice is (bad) than mine.

7. Alice made the (good) grade in the class.

8. Which of the two shirts looks (good)?

Phone books list the names, addresses, and phone numbers of people and businesses in a specific area.

Most phone books include a section called the *Yellow Pages*. You can use this section to find information about a specific business. You can also use it to find all the businesses that offer similar services or products.

The *Yellow Pages* are arranged by categories, or types of businesses. The categories are listed in alphabetical order. To find the information you need, look up the appropriate category. Then look at the different business listings under that category. Some businesses place ads in the *Yellow Pages* to attract customers.

Look at the listing from the Yellow Pages, and answer the questions below.

First-Place Autopark
"We have the best deals in town!"

● New and Used Cars ● Service Hotline ● Largest Selection

555-1234

9876 Main St.

Five-Star Motors 222 Elm St. 555-0000
Goodson Auto Center 15 Jones Road 555-5555

---

1. What five adjectives are used in this ad?

2. Which two adjectives in the ad are superlative adjectives?

3. **CHALLENGE** Why might a business use superlative adjectives in an ad?

Some one-syllable adjectives end with a vowel followed by a consonant. Double the final consonant before you add -er or -est to these adjectives.

▶ **EXAMPLE 1**

Adjective	Comparative	Superlative
big	bigger	biggest
sad	sadder	saddest

Some adjectives end with a consonant followed by a *y*. Change the *y* to *i* before adding -er or -est to these adjectives.

▶ **EXAMPLE 2**

Adjective	Comparative	Superlative
dry	drier	driest
silly	sillier	silliest

Practice A

Write the comparative and superlative forms for each adjective. The first one is done for you.

1. busy

busier, busiest

2. curly

3. red

4. shiny

5. fat

6. mad

7. funny

8. foggy

9. crazy

10. sleepy

Practice B

Write each sentence. Use the correct form of the adjective in parentheses. The first one is done for you.

11. John was the (angry) of all.

John was the angriest of all.

12. That joke was (funny) than this one.

13. Yesterday was the (hot) day of the year.

14. This is the (heavy) piece of furniture yet.

15. The roads are (wet) today than they were yesterday.

16. Her kitten has the (silky) fur of all.

Practice C

Write each sentence. Add an adjective of your own. The first one is done for you.

17. Wags is the _____ dog I have ever known.

Wags is the friendliest dog I have ever known.

18. Now that I exercise, I am _____ than I was before.

19. Arguing will just make her _____.

20. **CHALLENGE** Now that the snow clouds have moved out of our area, we should see the end of the _____ winter on record. In fact, we are in for some very sunny days. Today was _____ than yesterday. But tomorrow will be the _____ day this week.

10·7 Specific Adjectives

Some adjectives are more specific than others. *Specific* means "clearly stated." You can make your writing clearer and more interesting by using specific adjectives.

EXAMPLE

Nice flowers were in the new vase by the old table.

Fresh yellow flowers were in a crystal vase on the antique table.

The first sentence does not give a clear picture of the flowers on the table. The second sentence gives a clearer picture. Specific adjectives have been added to this sentence.

Practice A

Read each pair of adjectives. Write the adjective that gives the clearer picture. The first one is done for you.

1. bright, brilliant
   brilliant

2. large, gigantic

3. loud, deafening

4. noisy, thunderous

Practice B

Write each sentence. Add a specific adjective before each noun. The first one is done for you.

5. The man approached the dog.
   The frightened man approached the snarling dog.

6. The computer sat on the desk.

7. Ice cream is my sister's favorite treat.

8. The captain steered the ship toward the island.

COMMUNICATING ON THE JOB
Veterinary Assistant

Ed Allen works as a veterinary assistant in an animal clinic. He helps feed, bathe, and care for sick animals. He also listens to owners describe their pet's symptoms. He writes these descriptions clearly for Dr. Santiago, the veterinarian.

Megan Green brought her dog Fritz to the clinic. Something was wrong with Fritz's paw. Ed wrote the following description for Dr. Santiago.

Read Ed's description, and answer the questions below.

Ed assists Dr. Santiago.

Note to the Doctor _____

Fritz's front paw is red and puffy. Megan noticed it three days ago. Fritz will not walk on it. It is much puffier than it was yesterday. He may have cut it on the rusty fence.

1. What adjectives are used in this description?

2. Which adjective in the description is used to make a comparison?

3. **CRITICAL THINKING** How do adjectives improve written and spoken messages?

Speaking and Listening

You are a veterinary assistant. Work with a partner. One person describes a pet's symptoms. The other person listens carefully and writes them down. Then switch roles. Work together to add specific adjectives to each description.

10·8 ▶ Writing: Using Adjectives in Sentences

Adding adjectives to your writing makes your sentences clearer and more interesting. You can use the READ, PLAN, WRITE, and CHECK steps to write sentences with specific adjectives.

▶ **EXAMPLE**

Write two sentences that compare and contrast this school year with last year. Be sure to use specific adjectives.

READ **Do you understand the assignment?**

Rewrite the assignment in your own words.

Write two sentences that tell what is the same and different about this school year and last year. Use specific adjectives.

PLAN **Gather your ideas and organize them.**

Use a Venn diagram to organize your ideas. Write *Last Year* and *This Year* in the circles. Write similarities in the middle section. Write differences in the separate sections.

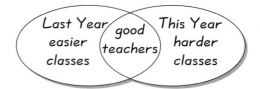

WRITE **Put your ideas into a sentence.**

Use the ideas in your Venn diagram. In the first sentence, compare this year and last year. In the second sentence, contrast the two years.

For the past two years, I have had good teachers. This year my classes are harder than they were last year.

CHECK   How can you improve your writing?

Check that your sentences answer the assignment. Make your ideas clearer by adding specific adjectives to your sentences.

> For the past two years, I have had <u>interesting</u> and <u>fun</u> teachers. This school year my <u>math</u> and <u>science</u> classes are harder than they were last year.

The words in blue type were added. The specific adjectives are underlined.

Practice

Complete the writing assignments below. Use a Venn diagram to help you PLAN your writing.

1. Write two sentences that compare and contrast your personality with your best friend's personality. Use at least one comparative adjective.

   PLAN
   What is the same about your personalities?
   What is different about your personalities?

2. Write two sentences that compare and contrast your interests with your best friend's interests. Use at least one comparative adjective.

   PLAN
   What interests do you and your best friend share?
   What interests do you and your best friend have that are different?

Putting It All Together

Write a paragraph telling how you and your best friend are alike and different. You may wish to use the sentences you have written above. Add other sentences that compare you and your friend.

adjective
article
comparative adjective
predicate adjective
proper adjective
superlative adjective

Vocabulary Review

Complete each sentence with a term from the box.

1. An _____ is a special group of adjectives, including *the, a*, and *an*.

2. An _____ describes a noun or pronoun.

3. A _____ comes after a linking verb and tells about the subject.

4. A _____ is used to compare two nouns or pronouns.

5. A _____ refers to the name of a particular person, place, thing, event, or idea.

6. A _____ is used to compare three or more nouns or pronouns.

Chapter Quiz

LESSONS 10·1 to 10·3

Test Tip
The, an, and *a* are articles.

Identifying Adjectives

Write the adjectives in each sentence. Include the articles. Some sentences have more than one.

1. Trees grow in humid conditions.

2. Some birds have brilliant colors.

3. The fireplace was warm and cozy.

4. Hard hats are often worn at construction sites.

5. Bobby and Rico are very athletic.

6. The elevator is too crowded.

7. That backpack is bigger than mine.

8. Amy lost an umbrella and a hat today.

9. Raúl works as an aide in the hospital.

| **LESSON 10·4** | **Identifying Proper Adjectives** |

Identifying Proper Adjectives

Write the proper adjective in each sentence. Then write the noun it describes.

10. The African gray parrot held the branch with its toes.

11. Let's try that new Chinese restaurant.

12. A tourist crossed the Canadian border.

LESSONS 10·5 and 10·6

Using Comparative Adjectives

Write the correct form of the adjective in parentheses.

13. That was the (scary) story he ever told.

14. Mac is the (good) swimmer on our team.

15. The bald eagle is (fierce) than that tiger.

LESSON 10·7

Using Specific Adjectives

Write each sentence. Add a specific adjective before each noun.

16. The ship was docked near the city.

17. The wind blew the paper into the street.

LESSON 10·8

Writing Tip
Use a Venn diagram to PLAN your paragraph. Then WRITE your ideas in sentence form.

Writing: Using Adjectives in Sentences

18. Write a paragraph that compares and contrasts an airplane and a car. Tell how the two are alike and how they are different. Use adjectives correctly.

Group Activity

Work with a group to create a flyer for a new amusement park. Convince visitors to come to the new park. Write a title and a brief description of each ride. Use adjectives to make your descriptions clear. Then switch flyers with another group. Suggest ways that they can improve their flyers.

Look at this photograph. Use a complete sentence to explain what the people are doing. Now try to give a clearer description of the action. To do this, you will need to use adverbs. Adverbs tell how, where, when, or how many times an action takes place.

Words to Know

adverb	a word that tells more about a verb, verb phrase, adjective, or another adverb
negative	a word or phrase that means "no," such as *not*
contraction	a shortened form of a group of words in which an apostrophe takes the place of the missing letter or letters

Performance Project

Think of two adverbs that can describe each of the following verbs: write, walk, and talk. Write each adverb and verb on a separate index card. Combine your cards with your classmates' cards. One at a time, choose a card, and act out what is on the card for the class. Have the other students guess the adverb and verb that you are acting out. Continue so that each person has a turn. Then choose two of the adverbs and verbs that were acted out. In your journal, write two sentences using these words.

Learning Objectives

- Identify adverbs that tell more about verbs, adjectives, and other adverbs.
- Choose between adjectives and adverbs.
- Use adverbs to make comparisons.
- Avoid double negatives, and use contractions correctly.
- Use specific adverbs.
- Write sentences using specific adverbs.
- Apply knowledge of adverbs to written instructions and a thesaurus entry.

What Is an Adverb?

An **adverb** is a word that tells more about a verb, a verb phrase, an adjective, or another adverb. An adverb tells *how*, *where*, *when*, or *how many times* an action takes place.

► **EXAMPLE**

She hung posters quickly. (tells how)

She hung posters everywhere. (tells where)

She hung posters yesterday. (tells when)

She hung posters twice. (tells how many times)

Practice A

Write the adverb in each sentence. The first one is done for you.

1. The woman spoke quietly.

   quietly

2. Some birds can fly backward.

3. Yo-yos were first used as weapons.

4. Robby wrapped the present slowly.

5. He folded the ends neatly.

6. He tied the bow carefully.

7. His niece hastily ripped open the package.

8. She looked inside.

9. She yelled loudly.

10. I applied for a job today.

11. Allison whispered softly to the children.

12. I tried spinach once.

13. Josh grabbed the rope tightly.

14. I will meet you here at two o'clock.

Practice B

Write the adverb in each sentence. Beside each adverb, write how it is used in the sentence. Write *how, where, when,* or *how many times.* The first one is done for you.

15. They will arrive tomorrow.

tomorrow, when

16. Babe Ruth first became famous as a pitcher.

17. Later, he gained fame as a hitter.

18. Crowds cheered him wildly.

19. Both contestants stepped forward.

20. Murray drummed his fingers impatiently.

21. Kelly called me twice.

22. She did everything differently.

23. She never listened to her friends.

24. I will only tell you this once!

25. **CHALLENGE** Write a sentence of your own using an adverb. Draw one line under the adverb. Next to the sentence, write how the adverb is used in the sentence.

11·2 Adverbs That Tell More About Adjectives

Some adverbs tell more about adjectives. These adverbs tell *to what degree*.

Some examples of adverbs that tell more about adjectives are shown in the box.

Adverbs		
almost	quite	too
especially	rather	truly
extremely	really	unusually
fairly	somewhat	very

Remember
Adjectives describe nouns and pronouns.

That is a very powerful car. (*Very* tells how powerful the car is.)

The car is too expensive for me. (*Too* tells how expensive the car is.)

The engine is rather unsafe. (*Rather* tells how unsafe the engine is.)

Practice A

Write the adverb in each sentence. Beside each adverb, write the adjective it tells more about. The first one is done for you.

1. It was fairly bright in the room.

   fairly, bright

2. We taught her at an especially early age.

3. Cynthia told a very funny story.

4. She was an extremely popular singer.

5. I was quite happy with my grades.

Practice B

Write each sentence. Add an adverb of your own. Use a different adverb in each sentence. The first one is done for you.

6. I thought that movie was _____ scary!

I thought that movie was really scary!

7. The weather was _____ cold.

8. It was _____ good to be true.

9. When buying a car, try not to seem _____ eager.

10. That cashier was _____ unfriendly.

11. The temperature was _____ hot in Florida.

12. CHALLENGE Write a sentence of your own using an adverb that tells more about an adjective.

Everyday English

Charlie received a clothing catalog in the mail. He wants to order a coat from the catalog. Look at the listing, and answer the questions below.

1. What are the five adverbs that tell more about adjectives?

2. What are the five adjectives that the adverbs tell more about?

3. CHALLENGE Which sentence has an adverb that does *not* tell more about an adjective? Write the sentence, and draw a line under the adverb.

100% Wool Topcoat for $129

A TRULY GREAT DEAL!

This Woodlake Collection coat is 100% wool, beautifully tailored, and fully lined. It is especially comfortable over a suit jacket. It's great for those really cold days! The coat should be dry cleaned only.

11-3 Adverbs That Tell More About Other Adverbs

Some adverbs tell more about other adverbs. They tell *to what degree*.

Some examples of adverbs that tell more about other adverbs are shown in the box.

► **EXAMPLE**

Adverbs		
almost	quite	too
especially	rather	truly
extremely	really	unusually
fairly	somewhat	very

The manager spoke fairly briefly. (*Fairly* tells how briefly.)

He hit the ball especially hard. (*Especially* tells how hard.)

Ted played rather well. (*Rather* tells how well.)

Practice A

Each sentence contains two adverbs. Write each adverb. Draw a line under the adverb that tells more about the other adverb. The first one is done for you.

1. The frightened child ran extremely quickly.

   <u>extremely</u>, quickly

2. Cyril wants to go to the movies too often.

3. Su Ling cooked the vegetables quite well.

4. Dan answered rather wearily.

5. Ann spoke very happily about her vacation.

6. Kyle lives truly comfortably in that small house.

7. For a Monday, work was going really well.

8. He accepted the new job quite eagerly.

9. She responded so quietly that they did not hear her.

10. Sara worked unusually quickly.

Practice B

Write each sentence. Add an adverb of your own. The new adverb should tell more about the adverb that is given. Use a different adverb in each sentence. The first one is done for you.

11. Someone said the dogs were barking _____ loudly.

    Someone said the dogs were barking very loudly.

12. The writer finished the report _____ fast.

13. Ken read it _____ eagerly.

14. The giant wheel turned _____ slowly.

15. The judges worked _____ carefully.

16. I like to read interesting books _____ often.

17. The first contestant stepped _____ slowly onto the stage.

18. She stared _____ nervously at the audience.

19. She ended the song _____ quickly.

20. **CHALLENGE** Write a sentence of your own using two adverbs. Be sure one adverb tells more about the other adverb.

11·4 ▶ Knowing When to Use Adjectives and Adverbs

Use adjectives to tell more about nouns and pronouns.

▶ **EXAMPLE 1**

The man's voice was loud. (The adjective *loud* tells more about the noun *voice*.)

He was surprised. (The adjective *surprised* tells more about the pronoun *he*.)

Use adverbs to tell more about verbs, adjectives, and other adverbs.

▶ **EXAMPLE 2**

The lightening struck quickly. (The adverb *quickly* tells more about the verb *struck*.)

The sky was very dark. (The adverb *very* tells more about the adjective *dark*.)

It rained quite heavily. (The adverb *quite* tells more about the adverb *heavily*.)

Use the adjective *good* to tell more about a noun or pronoun. Use the adverb *well* to tell more about a verb or verb phrase.

▶ **EXAMPLE 3**

Roger has a good car. (The adjective *good* tells more about the noun *car*.)

He drives it well. (The adverb *well* tells more about the verb *drives*.)

Practice A

Write each sentence. Use the correct word in parentheses. The first one is done for you.

1. It was a (bitter, bitterly) December day.

   It was a bitter December day.

2. Icicles glistened (bright, brightly) on the branches.

3. Several (happy, happily) teenagers climbed up the hill.

4. The hard snow crunched (loud, loudly) under their feet.

5. Miguel jumped onto his (new, newly) sled.

6. His friend ran (swift, swiftly) to join him.

7. The two sledders stared (nervous, nervously) down the hill.

8. They held (tight, tightly) onto the handles of the sled.

9. Miguel and Jon sledded (quick, quickly) down the hill.

10. They (slow, slowly) dragged their sleds back up the hill.

Practice B

Choose between *good* and *well* for each sentence. Then write the word that it tells about. The first one is done for you.

11. They have _____ food there.

    good, food

12. That suit is a _____ choice for your interview.

13. You speak Spanish as _____ as she does.

14. Adam had a _____ feeling about the assignment.

15. Beth played that song _____ on the piano.

16. Spike sees _____ for a dog his age.

17. Lisa has a _____ idea for our project.

18. Zachary read a _____ book this summer.

19. Rodney knows how to swim _____.

20. Sheila's trip to Ireland was a _____ one.

Using Adverbs to Make Comparisons

Adverbs can be used to compare two or more actions. To compare two actions, use an *-er* ending with a few short adverbs. Use *more* or *less* before most adverbs.

EXAMPLE 1

He walks faster than his brother.

He walks more quickly than his brother.

He walks less quickly than his brother.

When you compare more than two actions, use an *-est* ending with a few short adverbs. Use *most* or *least* with longer adverbs.

EXAMPLE 2

She spoke the earliest of all the guest speakers.

She spoke the most thoughtfully of all the guest speakers.

She spoke the least thoughtfully of all the guest speakers.

The forms of the adverb *well* are *well, better,* and *best.* Use *better* when comparing two. Use *best* when comparing more than two.

EXAMPLE 3

He writes well.

He writes better than his friend.

Who writes the best of all?

Practice A

Change each word in parentheses to the correct form of the adverb. Use *more, less, most,* or *least* as needed. The first one is done for you.

1. Tomás worked (hard) than Marty.

   harder

2. A puppy barks (fierce) than a grown dog does.

3. Kyle speaks (slowly) than Lenny.

4. Of all these cut flowers, the orchid will last (long).

5. Ed types the (fast) of all the assistants.

Practice B

Write each sentence. Use the correct form of the adverb *well.*
The first one is done for you.

6. He did _____ on this test than on the last one.

    He did better on this test than on the last one.

7. I can see things _____ close up than far away.

8. Travis danced _____ than Gayle did.

9. He performed _____ at the concert.

10. **CHALLENGE** Write a sentence of your own using one form
of the adverb *well.*

Everyday English

Craig saw a TV commercial describing an allergy medicine. The commercial compared this medicine to other allergy medicines. Read the information given in the commercial, and answer the questions.

1. Which three adverbs compare two actions?

2. Which adverb compares more than two actions?

"Red Alert" allergy medicine works better than other brands. It stops sneezing, watery eyes, and itching faster than the others. It also lasts up to four hours longer. Try "Red Alert", and enjoy the outdoors. "Red Alert" is the allergy medicine that doctors recommend most.

Using Negatives Correctly

A **negative** is a word or phrase that means "no." Some negative words are adverbs.

The words in the box are negatives.

Negatives					
barely	neither	no	none	nothing	no one
hardly	never	nobody	not	nowhere	scarcely

A negative word may change the whole meaning of a sentence. Use only one negative word to make a sentence mean *no* or *not*. Avoid double negatives.

Incorrect: No one never understands how I feel. (double negative)

Correct: No one ever understands how I feel. (one negative)

Hardly anyone ever understands how I feel. (one negative)

Practice

Write each sentence correctly. Use only one negative word. The first one is done for you.

1. No one never orders the supplies in the office.

No one ever orders the supplies in the office.

2. There is scarcely no paper left to put in the copier.

3. Look, there's not nothing left to put in the printer.

4. Barely nobody tells me what supplies we need.

5. I hardly never know that all the supplies are gone.

Using Contractions Correctly

The word *not* can be joined to a verb to form a
contraction. A contraction is a shortened form of a
group of words. An apostrophe takes the place of the
missing letter or letters. Some contractions are shown
in the box.

Verb + Not	Contraction	Verb + Not	Contraction
are + not	aren't	should + not	shouldn't
could + not	couldn't	was + not	wasn't
did + not	didn't	were + not	weren't
do + not	don't	will + not	won't
is + not	isn't	would + not	wouldn't

When you use a contraction with the word *not*, do not
use another negative word in the sentence.

▶ **EXAMPLE**

Incorrect: Bob didn't do nothing.

Correct: Bob didn't do anything.

Correct: Bob did nothing.

Practice

Some of the sentences below have double negatives.
Rewrite these sentences correctly. Write *correct* if the
sentence is correct. The first one is done for you.

1. I can't barely hear you.

   I can barely hear you.

2. Sherry didn't know nothing about the meeting.

3. I often don't work on the weekends.

4. Brad couldn't read nothing without his glasses.

5. Aren't any of you going to the concert?

USING REFERENCES
Thesaurus

A thesaurus is a book of synonyms. It lists words that have similar meanings. It also tells what parts of speech a word is. Sometimes, it lists words with opposite meanings. You can use a thesaurus to make your writing more interesting.

A thesaurus is usually organized like a dictionary. Each word in the thesaurus is called an entry. The entries are arranged in alphabetical order.

Sometimes, an entry refers to other entries. You will see the word *See* or the words *See also* followed by another entry name.

Read the thesaurus entry, and answer the questions below.

> **hardly,** *adv.* scarcely, barely, infrequently, rarely. *See* moderately.

1. What part of speech is *hardly*?

2. What other entry does this entry refer to?

3. How might a thesaurus help you write a more interesting report?

4. **CHALLENGE** Write a sentence using one of the words listed for the entry *hardly*.

Specific Adverbs

Using specific adverbs can make your writing clearer and more interesting.

Read these three sentences. Decide which sentence gives the clearest picture.

▶ **EXAMPLE**

Nina skated.

Nina skated well.

Nina skated quickly and gracefully.

The first sentence has no adverbs. It is hard to picture how Nina is skating. The adverb *well* has been added to the second sentence. However, *well* does not tell much about her skating. It is not a specific adverb. Two specific adverbs have been added to the last sentence. That sentence gives the clearest picture.

Practice A

Write each sentence. Use the more specific adverb. The first one is done for you.

1. That company treats its employees (generously, well).

   That company treats its employees generously.

2. The flowers in the vase were arranged (nicely, beautifully).

3. She sang (badly, horribly).

4. She (slowly, sluggishly) rose out of bed to start her day.

5. The lion roared (loudly, ferociously).

Practice B

Write each sentence. Add a specific adverb of your own. The first one is done for you.

6. He rang the bell _____.

He rang the bell urgently.

7. That couple dances _____.

8. She glared _____ at the noisy child.

9. The committee argued _____.

10. Jack smiled _____.

11. She always speaks so _____.

12. Pilar gazed _____ through the store window.

13. Joanna stood _____ as she gave her speech.

14. **CHALLENGE** I _____ walked to the door, opened it _____, and _____ ran away.

Everyday English

Rolanda wants to make cookies for her family. She found a cookie recipe in a magazine. Read this part of the recipe, and answer the questions below.

1. What are the four specific adverbs?

2. Which adverb is *not* a specific adverb?

3. **CHALLENGE** What specific adverb could replace the adverb *well* in step 2?

1. Gently mix ingredients with a mixer on high speed. Reduce speed to medium. Gradually beat in flour and baking soda. Wrap dough tightly in plastic wrap. Refrigerate 1 hour.

2. Preheat oven to 325°F. Lightly flour a rolling pin. Roll out the dough well. Cut out cookies with a cookie cutter. Place on ungreased baking sheets. Bake 10 minutes.

ENGLISH IN YOUR LIFE
Giving Instructions

Alan Perez is baby-sitting his cousin tonight. His cousin is nine months old. Alan's aunt explained how to care for the baby before she left. She also wrote down the instructions. However, her written instructions contain an error.

Read the instructions, and answer the questions below.

Alan feeds Jonathan.

> Jonathan will be ready for a bottle at 7:30. You can give it to him early if he gets too fussy. Run warm water over the bottle to heat it slightly. Rock him gently after his bottle until he falls asleep. Then lay him in his bed. Do not leave no toys in his bed while he sleeps. Check on him frequently. Call me immediately if you have any problems.

1. Write three adverbs in the instructions.

2. One sentence uses a double negative. Write it correctly.

3. **CRITICAL THINKING** How do adverbs make written instructions clearer?

Writing and Reading

You are baby-sitting a child. You prepared your favorite meal for the child, and the child really liked it. You want to tell the parents how to make the meal. Write instructions for making this meal. Then exchange papers with a partner. Read your partner's note. Notice how your partner used adverbs.

11·8 Writing: Using Specific Adverbs in Sentences

Using specific adverbs in your writing makes verbs, adjectives, and other adverbs clearer and more interesting. You can use the READ, PLAN, WRITE, and CHECK steps to write sentences with specific adverbs.

EXAMPLE

Write two sentences that describe the weather conditions when you woke up this morning. Use specific adverbs.

READ **Do you understand the assignment?**

Rewrite the assignment in your own words.

> *Write two sentences about what the weather was like this morning. Include specific adverbs.*

PLAN **Gather your ideas and organize them.**

Use a spider map to organize your ideas. Write *Weather* in the center circle. On the spokes, write words that describe the weather. Then write a specific adverb that tells more about the word on the spoke.

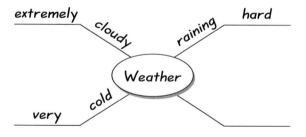

WRITE **Put your ideas into two sentences.**

Write two sentences using the ideas in your spider map.

> *It was raining hard this morning. It was extremely cloudy and very cold.*

CHECK   How can you improve your writing?

Check that your sentences answer the assignment. Make your ideas clearer by changing any general adverbs to specific adverbs.

> It was raining *heavily* this morning. It was *extremely* cloudy and *intensely* cold.

The words in blue type were added. Notice how these specific adverbs give a clearer picture of the weather.

Practice

Complete the writing assignments below. Use a spider map to PLAN your ideas.

1. Write two sentences that describe how you get ready for school. Use specific adverbs.

PLAN
What do you do after you wake up to get ready for school? What tasks do you complete in the morning before you leave for school?

2. Write two sentences that list the first things you do when you get to school. Use specific adverbs.

PLAN
What do you do when you first arrive at school? What events occur before your first class?

Putting It All Together

Write a paragraph that describes your morning routine before your first class in school. You may wish to use the sentences you have written above. Add other sentences that give a clear picture of what you do before school starts.

adverb
contraction
negative

Vocabulary Review

Use a word from the box to complete each sentence.

1. A ____ is a shortened form of a group of words.

2. An ____ tells more about a verb, verb phrase, adjective, or other adverb.

3. A ____ is a word that means "no."

Chapter Quiz

LESSON 11·1

Identifying Adverbs That Tell More About Verbs
Write the adverb in each sentence.

1. The boat's sail blew wildly in the wind.

2. The dancers moved clockwise in a circle.

3. The family moved away from the city.

4. The airplane landed later than expected.

LESSONS 11·2 and 11·3

Identifying Adverbs That Tell More About Adjectives and Adverbs
Write each sentence. Add an adverb of your own. Use a different adverb in each sentence.

5. The elephant is an ____ large animal.

6. Scott has a ____ important job.

7. Jonathan plays the drums ____ well.

LESSON 11·4

Test Tip
Adjectives tell more about nouns and pronouns. Adverbs tell more about verbs, adjectives, and other adverbs.

Choosing Between Adjectives and Adverbs
Write each sentence. Use the correct word in parentheses.

8. This new suit fits (good, well).

9. These cheap shoes fit (poor, poorly).

10. The pitcher made a (good, well) catch.

Using Adverbs to Make Comparisons

Change each word in parentheses to the correct form of the adverb.

11. Mark studied (careful) than Tim did.

12. He laughed the (loud) of anyone in the class.

13. The highway is (fast) than the back streets.

Avoiding Double Negatives

Write each sentence correctly. Use only one negative word.

14. That TV wasn't never watched.

15. They weren't using neither one.

16. Barely no one was at the meeting.

Using Specific Adverbs

Write each sentence. Use the more specific adverb.

17. My elderly grandmother visits (often, monthly).

18. He spoke (passionately, nicely) about the issue.

19. The speech was (badly, terribly) written.

Writing: Using Specific Adverbs in Sentences

Writing Tip
Use a spider map to PLAN what to write. CHECK that your sentences answer the assignment.

20. Write a paragraph that gives students tips on how to be successful on a test. Tell students how to study before a test. Also, tell students what to do during the test. Use specific adverbs.

Group Activity

Work with a group to write instructions for a simple exercise program. The instructions should tell what to do and how, when, and how often to do it. Be sure to include specific adverbs. Then exchange plans with another group. Suggest ways to improve the group's work.

Unit 5 **Review**

Read the passage below to answer questions 1–5. Decide which type of error, if any, appears in each underlined section. Mark the letter for your answer.

From the (1) <u>start of american history,</u> immigrants have come here looking for (2) <u>a better life</u>. By the late 1800s, crossing the Atlantic Ocean (3) <u>was much faster, safer,</u> and cheaper than in (4) <u>earlyer days</u>. Each day, at least one shipload of (5) <u>european immigrants arrived in America</u>.

1. A. Spelling error
   B. Capitalization error
   C. Punctuation error
   D. No error

2. A. Spelling error
   B. Capitalization error
   C. Punctuation error
   D. No error

3. A. Spelling error
   B. Capitalization error
   C. Punctuation error
   D. No error

4. A. Spelling error
   B. Capitalization error
   C. Punctuation error
   D. No error

5. A. Spelling error
   B. Capitalization error
   C. Punctuation error
   D. No error

Read the passage below to answer questions 6–8. Choose the word that belongs in each space. Mark the letter for your answer.

Of all the fruits, which do you like (6) ? I think oranges are (7) than apples. Oranges are better because they have (8) flavor. Don't you agree?

6. A. better
   B. best
   C. good
   D. well

7. A. tastyier
   B. tastyiest
   C. tastier
   D. tastiest

8. A. more
   B. most
   C. less
   D. least

Critical Thinking

Name at least two good things and two bad things about having a part-time job after school.

WRITING Write a paragraph telling what you would and would not like about having a job after school. Use adjectives and adverbs correctly.

Unit 6 ▶ Phrases

Chapter 12 **Prepositions and Prepositional Phrases**

Chapter 13 **Other Phrases**

Billboards are found along many highways and city streets. They advertise services or products. They often contain catchy slogans or phrases. A phrase is a group of words that does not contain both a subject and a verb.

Just like billboards, travel brochures are used to advertise. Notice that the brochure on the right uses both phrases and sentences. Read the brochure, and answer the following questions.

1. What are the complete sentences in the brochure?

2. What is the difference between a sentence and a phrase?

3. Why do you think brochures use both phrases and sentences?

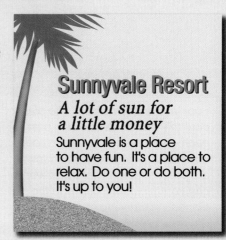

Sunnyvale Resort
A lot of sun for a little money
Sunnyvale is a place to have fun. It's a place to relax. Do one or do both. It's up to you!

Look at the photograph. The planes could fly beside each other, past each other, even toward each other. The words <u>beside,</u> <u>past,</u> and <u>toward</u> are prepositions. What other words can you think of to describe the planes' relationship to each other?

Chapter 12

Prepositions and Prepositional Phrases

Words to Know

preposition	a word that shows how a noun or pronoun relates to another word or group of words in a sentence
prepositional phrase	a group of words that begins with a preposition and ends with a noun or pronoun
object of the preposition	a noun or pronoun at the end of a prepositional phrase

Word-Wheel Project

In the center of a sheet of paper, draw a circle. Inside the circle, write the word *river*. Then draw a spoke leading away from the circle. At the end of the spoke, write a preposition to complete this sentence: *I went ____ the river.* Draw more spokes, and add more prepositions to complete the sentence. When you have finished your word wheel, create another one using a different noun in the center circle.

Learning Objectives

- Identify prepositions.
- Identify prepositional phrases.
- Use pronouns in prepositional phrases.
- Use the correct verb forms after prepositional phrases.
- Use prepositions correctly.
- Write sentences using prepositional phrases.
- Apply knowledge of prepositions to safety instructions and a highway map.

12·1 ▶ What Is a Preposition?

A **preposition** shows how a noun or pronoun is related to another word or group of words in a sentence.

The words in the box are prepositions.

Prepositions			
about	beneath	in	to
above	beside	into	toward
across	besides	like	under
after	between	near	underneath
against	beyond	of	until
along	but	off	unto
amid	by	on	up
among	concerning	onto	upon
around	down	over	with
at	during	past	within
before	except	since	without
behind	for	through	
below	from	throughout	

▶ **EXAMPLE**

The line stretched around the corner.

We waited for an hour.

After the movie, we went home.

Practice A

Write the preposition in each sentence. Some sentences have more than one. The first one is done for you.

1. Bobby Fischer is a legend in chess history.

   in

2. From an early age, he seemed very bright.

3. Bobby Fischer played his first chess game at the age of five.

4. He learned chess with his sister's help.

5. Within a few years, Fischer was playing in tournaments.

6. He traveled around the world playing against champions.

7. He became the youngest grand master in history.

8. He was only 15 years old at the time.

9. During 1972, he became the first American world champion.

10. After three years, Fischer stopped defending his title.

Practice B

Write each sentence. Add a preposition of your own. The first one is done for you.

11. Sidney found her keys _____ the sofa.

　　Sidney found her keys underneath the sofa.

12. She picked up Marta _____ the game.

13. The car broke down _____ warning.

14. Sidney and Marta left the car _____ the field.

15. They had to walk _____ the highway.

16. Several people drove _____ them.

17. The mechanic took them _____ town.

18. The tow truck took the car _____ the garage.

19. The mechanic worked _____ the car's hood.

20. They waited _____ two hours.

21. The car was not ready _____ the next day.

22. CHALLENGE _____ one week, the car broke down again _____ rush hour _____ the way _____ Marta's house.

Practice C

Write the ten prepositions in the paragraph.

Some people find jobs through the classified ads. Classified ads are found in newspapers. Within each ad is a description of the job. The ad also may tell you about the company. Most classified ads are listed in the newspaper by job type. This is very helpful for people who are looking for a job in a certain field.

Everyday English

Benjamin bought a new type of fruit snack. Read the words on the box. Then answer the questions below.

1. What three prepositions are found on the front of the box?

2. CHALLENGE Write another phrase that might be printed on a box of snacks. Use a preposition.

Fruity Chews

Made From Real Fruit Juices

Great Source of Vitamins C and E

FAT FREE

▬▬▬▬▬ Assorted Flavors ▬▬▬▬▬

15 packets in each box

What Is a Prepositional Phrase?

A **prepositional phrase** is a group of words that begins with a preposition and ends with a noun or pronoun. The noun or pronoun at the end of the phrase is the **object of the preposition**. There may be other words between the preposition and the object.

> **EXAMPLE**

He parked across the street.

preposition: across

prepositional phrase: across the street

object of the preposition: street

Practice A

Write the prepositional phrase in each sentence. Draw one line under each preposition. Draw two lines under each object of the preposition. The first one is done for you.

1. The bus rumbled over the bridge.

   over the bridge

2. The Old London Bridge was designed by a priest.

3. The bridge carried people across the Thames River.

4. For thirty years, bridge builders worked.

5. Wooden houses were built on the bridge.

6. It was the only bridge over the Thames.

7. The bridge was important for many reasons.

8. There is a popular song about the bridge.

Practice B

Write each sentence. Add a prepositional phrase from the box. The first one is done for you.

9. The boxes _____ should be put away.

   The boxes on the table should be put away.

10. Someone _____ can help me.

11. _____, I usually eat breakfast.

12. _____, we all went backstage.

13. We ran _____ at the deli.

14. **CHALLENGE** Write a sentence of your own using a prepositional phrase.

After the play
in the store
Before school
on the table
into our friends

Everyday English

Prepositional phrases can be found in all types of writing. Read the Pledge of Allegiance and follow the directions below.

> I pledge allegiance to the flag of the United States of America and to the Republic for which it stands, one Nation under God, indivisible, with liberty and justice for all.

1. What eight prepositional phrases are found in the pledge?

2. Which prepositional phrase has two objects of the preposition?

3. **CHALLENGE** Write a sentence that tells when students might say the Pledge of Allegiance in school. Use a prepositional phrase.

USING REFERENCES
Maps

Maps can help you find where things are located. They also can help you find the best way to get to specific places.

There are several features that help you use a map. A distance scale shows how many miles are represented by a certain amount of space on the map. A compass rose shows which way is north, south, east, and west. Highways are shown as thick black lines. Streets and roads are shown by thin black lines. Bodies of water are shown as blue shaded areas.

Study the map and follow the directions below. Draw a line under each preposition in your sentences.

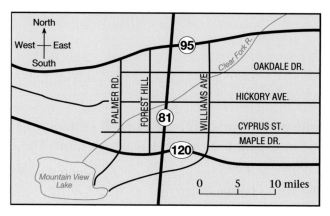

1. Write a sentence that tells which major highways pass over Clear Fork River.

2. Write a sentence that tells where Mountain View Lake is located.

3. **CHALLENGE** Suppose you live on Maple Drive. How would you get to Highway 95?

Pronouns in Prepositional Phrases

The object of a preposition can be a pronoun. The personal pronouns in the box can be used as objects of the preposition.

Remember
A pronoun takes the place of a noun.

Personal Pronouns						
me	you	her	him	it	us	them

▶ **EXAMPLE**

Come with me.

Keep it near you.

The bus went right by her.

I will stand behind him.

The card is under it.

Is that for us?

Cal was with them.

Practice A

Write the prepositional phrase in each sentence. Draw one line under each object of the preposition. The first one is done for you.

1. She stood between them.

   between them

2. Ken walked by them.

3. Jay did the work for me.

4. Susan sang a song about them.

5. Maria ran into them yesterday.

6. My brother often hikes with me.

7. He made a map that we will take with us.

8. Claudia went with him.

9. The story is about her.

10. Victor drove through it.

11. Sandy is somewhere among them.

12. Kara arrived after us.

Practice B

Write each sentence. Add a personal pronoun from the box on page 262. The first one is done for you.

13. Len ran toward _____.

    Len ran toward her.

14. You may go before _____ if you wish.

15. Li hid behind _____ the whole time.

16. I did not see him leave with _____.

17. The two friends vowed that nothing would ever come between _____.

18. I sat beside _____ during the ceremony.

19. This year's family reunion just was not the same without _____.

20. **CHALLENGE** Write a sentence of your own using a prepositional phrase. Use a personal pronoun as the object of the preposition.

COMMUNICATING ON THE JOB
Flight Attendant

Jan Peterson enjoys her job as a flight attendant. She greets passengers and serves food and drinks on the plane. She also explains the safety instructions. These instructions have to be clear. Passengers must understand what to do in an emergency.

Read Jan's safety instructions and answer the questions below.

Jan explains how to use an oxygen mask.

Safety Instructions

In an emergency, a mask may drop down in front of you. The masks on the plane supply oxygen. Slip the strap over your head, and breathe normally. Please help the passengers beside you. Besides oxygen masks, the plane has other safety features. If we land in water, use your seat cushion. It will act like a flotation device.

1. What are the three prepositions in the first sentence?

2. What is the object of the preposition in the fourth sentence?

3. What is the prepositional phrase in the last sentence?

4. **CRITICAL THINKING** How do prepositional phrases make instructions clearer?

Speaking and Listening

Work with a partner to practice reading Jan's safety instructions aloud. Then read the same instructions without the prepositional phrases. Discuss how prepositional phrases improve written and spoken messages.

Using Correct Verb Forms After Prepositional Phrases

Remember that the verb or verb phrase in a sentence agrees with the main noun or pronoun in the subject. A singular noun needs a singular verb. A plural noun needs a plural verb.

Sometimes, a prepositional phrase comes after the main noun in the subject. This prepositional phrase is a part of the subject. The verb or verb phrase still must agree with the main noun or pronoun. The verb does not need to agree with the noun or pronoun in the prepositional phrase.

▶ **EXAMPLE**

The women bowl well.

subject: The women

verb: bowl

The women on the team bowl well.

subject: The women on the team

main noun: women

verb: bowl

Practice A

Write each sentence. Use the correct verb form in parentheses. The first one is done for you.

1. The papers on the table (is, are) mine.

The papers on the table are mine.

2. The jobs at the park (was, were) listed last.

3. The stars of the play (rehearses, rehearse) daily.

4. The man with all the packages (needs, need) help.

5. The members of the audience (clap, claps) loudly.

6. The senators from Ohio (wishes, wish) to speak.

7. The leaders of the other group (agrees, agree) with us.

8. The people of this country (chooses, choose) the President.

9. Our company's best team of engineers (develops, develop) all the new software.

10. His book of paintings (makes, make) a wonderful gift.

Practice B

Write each sentence. Add a present tense verb form of your own. The first one is done for you.

11. The students from Center High School _____ here.

The students from Center High School come here.

12. The reporters on the scene _____ many questions.

13. The people in the airport _____ the planes leave.

14. The packages on the table _____ to Ann.

15. Two supervisors in the company _____ our weekly staff meetings.

16. One of my sisters-in-law _____ very well.

17. His list of possible answers _____ the whole page.

18. The members of the jury _____ to the lawyers.

19. The table near the windows _____ wrapping paper.

20. The papers on this desk _____ very important.

21. The coach of the baseball team _____ laps with the players.

22. **CHALLENGE** The girls on that team _____ better now that the coach of our Olympic champions _____ giving them pointers.

Practice C

Find the four incorrect verb forms in the paragraph below. Write the correct form of each verb. In front of each verb, write its subject.

    For rock climbers, the right kind of shoes make all the difference. Patches of snow and ice is dangerous. Shoes with a rubber sole helps you grip the rocks. Your shoes also should be waterproof. If there are puddles, your feet could get cold and wet. Waterproof shoes help keep your feet dry. The weight of your shoes also are important. Heavy climbing boots may make your legs tired after a while. The lighter the shoes, the better your legs will feel on a long climb.

Everyday English

Jennifer sent an e-mail message to Luke. She used some verbs incorrectly. Read Jennifer's message and answer the following questions.

1. What is the main noun in the first sentence?

2. Rewrite the third sentence using the correct verb form.

3. **CHALLENGE** Why is the fifth sentence incorrect? Rewrite it correctly.

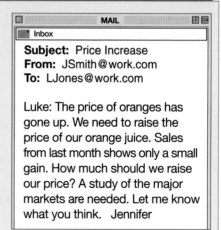

MAIL

Inbox

Subject: Price Increase
From: JSmith@work.com
To: LJones@work.com

Luke: The price of oranges has gone up. We need to raise the price of our orange juice. Sales from last month shows only a small gain. How much should we raise our price? A study of the major markets are needed. Let me know what you think.   Jennifer

12-5 ▶ Using Prepositions Correctly

Some prepositions are often used incorrectly. Avoid this mistake by following a few special rules.

Use *between* when you refer to two people, things, or groups. Use *among* when you refer to more than two people, things, or groups.

The preposition *beside* means "next to." The preposition *besides* means "in addition to" or "except."

▶ **EXAMPLE**

Nick is sitting between his two sisters.

Nick is sitting among all his relatives.

She put the papers beside the book.

Besides paper, she bought envelopes, stamps, and pens.

Practice A

Write the correct preposition for each sentence. The first one is done for you.

1. Our house is (beside, besides) a lake.

   beside

2. (Beside, Besides) Tim, there will be four of us.

3. Larry walked (beside, besides) Anita.

4. Nobody (beside, besides) Mark wants to go.

5. You must choose (between, among) the two.

6. Can anyone (beside, besides) Lee do the job?

7. One pine tree stood (among, between) many elms.

Some of these sentences use prepositions incorrectly. Rewrite these sentences, and add the correct preposition. If a sentence is correct, write *correct*. The first one is done for you.

8. Let's keep this a secret between us three.

Let's keep this a secret among us three.

9. Put the chair besides the table.

10. There will always be a special bond among you and me.

11. I know all of the answers besides that one.

12. I cannot choose between all the desserts.

13. I set my soda besides yours.

14. I walked among the people in the crowd.

Everyday English

Charlie was going to Tyrone's house to study for a test. Tyrone wrote directions to his house. He used some prepositions incorrectly. Read the directions and answer the following questions.

1. What two prepositions are used incorrectly?

2. In which sentence is *besides* used correctly?

Go north on Washington Avenue. I live on the street among Rosewood and Maple. If you get to Maple Street, you have gone too far. Turn right onto Shady Lane. It is the street besides the post office. My house is the two-story house on the right. There are no other two-story houses on this street besides mine.

Prepositional phrases show how words in a sentence are related. You can use the READ, PLAN, WRITE, and CHECK steps to write sentences with prepositional phrases.

▶ **EXAMPLE**

Write two sentences describing the view from your classroom window. Tell where objects are located. Use at least two prepositional phrases.

READ Do you understand the assignment?

Write the assignment. Underline the key words.

Write two sentences <u>describing the view from</u> your <u>classroom window</u>. Tell where objects are located. <u>Use at least two prepositional phrases</u>.

PLAN Gather your ideas and organize them.

Draw a sketch of what you see.

WRITE Put your ideas into a sentence.

Write two sentences that describe the view. Refer to your sketch for ideas.

From my classroom window, I see the library and the deli. I also see the ice cream parlor.

CHECK   How can you improve your writing?

Do your sentences answer the assignment? Add or change information as needed. Be sure to use two prepositional phrases.

From my classroom window, I see the library, the deli, and the ice cream parlor. The library is next to the deli, and the ice cream parlor is behind the school.

The sentence in blue type was added. It contains prepositional phrases that tell where places are located.

Practice

Complete the writing assignments below. Use a sketch to PLAN your ideas.

1. Write two sentences describing the location of your favorite place to eat. Use at least two prepositional phrases.

   PLAN
   Draw a sketch of the area where your favorite place to eat is located.

2. Write two sentences telling how to get from your home to your favorite place to eat. Use at least two prepositional phrases.

   PLAN
   Use your sketch from above to help you write your sentences.

Putting It All Together

Write a paragraph describing some of your favorite places in your neighborhood or town. You may want to use the sentences you have written above. Add other sentences that tell where each place is located.

| object of the preposition |
| preposition |
| prepositional phrase |

Vocabulary Review

Complete each sentence with a term from the box.

1. A ____ is a group of words that begins with a preposition and ends with a noun or pronoun.

2. You can use a ____ to connect a noun or pronoun to other words in a sentence.

3. The noun or pronoun at the end of a prepositional phrase is the ____.

Chapter Quiz

LESSONS 12·1 and 12·2

Identifying Prepositions and Prepositional Phrases
Write the prepositional phrase in each sentence. Draw one line under the preposition.

1. Today, I had a test in math.

2. What did you do to your hair?

3. My brother was lying under his car.

4. I have been standing here for an hour.

5. I have a bicycle with a flat tire.

6. He jumped up and climbed over the fence.

LESSON 12·3

Test Tip
Some personal pronouns are
me, you, him, her, us, them, and *it.*

Using Pronouns in Prepositional Phrases
Write each sentence. Add a personal pronoun of your own.

7. She had brought a book with ____.

8. We were late, but they waited for ____.

9. The car had a sticker on ____.

10. Juan remembered to take his keys with ____.

Using Correct Verb Forms After Prepositional Phrases

Write the correct verb form in parentheses.

11. The bag of groceries (is, are) still in the car.

12. One of the cats (has, have) a short tail.

13. Two students in my school (has, have) chicken pox.

14. The flowers in the vase (is, are) wilted.

15. The cars in the parking lot (is, are) covered with snow.

Using Prepositions Correctly

Write the correct preposition in parentheses.

16. Who (beside, besides) you is coming?

17. Who is sitting (beside, besides) you?

18. Just (between, among) you and me, what is going on?

19. With all of us here, you are (between, among) friends.

Writing: Using Prepositions in Sentences

20. Your principal has asked you to design a flag for your school. Write a paragraph that describes your flag. Tell what it looks like, what symbols you used, and the location of each design feature. Use at least two prepositional phrases.

Writing Tip
Use a sketch to PLAN what you will write. CHECK that you used prepositional phrases correctly.

Group Activity

Work with a group to create a building improvement plan for your school. Tell what you would do to repair, replace, or improve the school building. Be sure to use prepositions correctly. Exchange plans with another group. Suggest ways to improve the other group's plan.

How would you describe the action in this scene? Your description might include a sentence that contains a phrase. Phrases allow you to complete a thought without using both a subject and a verb.

Chapter 13 ▶ Other Phrases

Words to Know

appositive	a noun that follows another noun or pronoun to rename or tell more about it
appositive phrase	a phrase that includes an appositive
participle	a verb form that is used as an adjective
participial phrase	a phrase that begins with a present participle or a past participle
gerund	a verb that ends with *-ing* and is used as a noun
gerund phrase	a phrase that begins with a gerund
infinitive	the word *to* plus the plural form of a verb. Infinitives may be used as nouns, adjectives, or adverbs
infinitive phrase	a phrase that begins with an infinitive

Interview Project

Work with a partner, and interview each other. Find out about your partner's hobbies, outdoor interests, family, and so on. Take notes as you listen. Switch roles. Then use your notes to write a short biography about your partner. Include appositive, participial, gerund, and infinitive phrases.

Learning Objectives

- Identify appositives, and use appositive phrases.
- Identify participles, and use participial phrases.
- Identify gerunds, and use gerund phrases.
- Identify infinitives, and use infinitive phrases.
- Write sentences using phrases.
- Apply knowledge of phrases to a to-do list and a table of contents.

Appositives and Appositive Phrases

An **appositive** is a noun that follows another noun or pronoun. It is used to rename or tell more about it.

An **appositive phrase** is a group of words that includes an appositive.

Appositives and appositive phrases are usually set off from the rest of the sentence by commas.

▶ EXAMPLE

My boss, Mr. Henkins, will be on vacation next week. (appositive)

The Mayville Festival, a celebration of our town's heritage, begins tomorrow. (appositive phrase)

Practice A

Write the appositive or appositive phrase in each sentence. The first one is done for you.

1. Baseball, America's favorite sport, is also popular in Japan.

   America's favorite sport

2. Jeff, an old friend of mine, will be in town tomorrow.

3. My neighbor, Mrs. Karr, asked me to mow her lawn.

4. We are going to Chicago, my hometown.

5. Brandon made spaghetti, my favorite meal.

6. This book, a classic novel, was made into a movie.

7. Michelle, my cousin, works for a law firm in Los Angeles.

Practice B

Write each sentence. Use commas to separate the appositive phrase from the rest of the sentence. The first one is done for you.

8. Andrea a talented artist painted the mural.

> *Andrea, a talented artist, painted the mural.*

9. Alaska the largest state in the United States became a state in 1959.

10. The other movie a comedy about doctors was very funny.

11. You should have spoken to Ms. Hale the manager of the hotel.

12. Nick found that Jay the best player on the team would be his opponent.

Practice C

Combine each pair of sentences. Use an appositive or appositive phrase. The first one is done for you.

13. Dr. Flores moved to a new office.
Dr. Flores is my dentist.

> *Dr. Flores, my dentist, moved to a new office.*

14. Helen Kraft is the actress in this movie.
Helen Kraft won an award for her performance.

15. Have you ever read *Hamlet*?
Hamlet is a play by William Shakespeare.

16. The White House is in Washington, D.C.
Washington, D.C., is our nation's capital.

17. My lucky shirt is not in my closet.
My lucky shirt is the one with the blue stripes.

A **participle** is a verb that is used as an adjective. A **participial phrase** begins with a present participle, such as *running*, or a past participle, such as *seated*. It is also used as an adjective.

Participles and participial phrases give more information about nouns and pronouns. They can appear at the beginning or middle of a sentence.

▶ **EXAMPLE 1**

Remember
A past participle is formed by adding *-d, -ed, -n,* or *-en* to a plural verb form. A present participle is formed by adding *-ing* to a plural verb form.

The storm brought hail and freezing rain. (The participle *freezing* describes *the rain.*)

The cooked turkey smells wonderful. (The participle *cooked* describes the *turkey.*)

Running across the field, the player lost his shoe. (The participial phrase *running across the field* tells more about the *player.*)

Use a participial phrase to combine short, choppy sentences.

Look at the examples below. In each set, the first two sentences are short and choppy. The third sentence uses a participial phrase to combine them. A comma separates the participial phrase from the rest of the sentence.

▶ **EXAMPLE 2**

The car came out of nowhere.

The car tore down the street.

Coming out of nowhere, the car tore down the street.

The boy jumped out of the way.

The boy was not hurt.

Jumping out of the way, the boy was not hurt.

Practice A

Write the participial phrase in each sentence. The first one is done for you.

1. Understanding the problem, I finally found an answer.

   Understanding the problem

2. Arriving late, we walked quietly down the hall.

3. Our friends, having arrived early, already were seated.

4. Arguing calmly, the senator made her point.

5. The choir, singing loudly, filled the hall with music.

6. Washed with care, this sweater will last a long time.

Practice B

Write each sentence. Use a participial phrase from the box. The first one is done for you.

7. _____, she rode the roller coaster.

   Holding on tightly, she rode the roller coaster.

8. _____, Eric changed his answer on the test.

9. _____, the box would not open.

10. The cat, _____, saw the birds.

11. The sweater, _____, fit Tracy perfectly.

12. **CHALLENGE** Write a sentence of your own using a participial phrase.

> looking out the window
> Holding on tightly
> Seeing his mistake
> Glued shut
> knitted with care

Practice C

Combine each pair of sentences. Write the first sentence as a participial phrase. Then add it to the second sentence. Use a comma where it is needed. The first one is done for you.

13. She arrived early.
She also was the first to leave.

Arriving early, she also was the first to leave.

14. I was stalled at the stop sign.
I waited for the tow truck.

15. Stanley looked around the corner.
Stanley noticed the hole in the wall.

16. Hans Christian Andersen began as an actor.
Hans Christian Andersen became a famous storyteller.

17. George felt ill.
George returned home.

Everyday English

Natalie has a new job. She will greet customers at a restaurant. She was given a handbook at a training class. However, the handbook had some mistakes. Read part of the training handbook. Then answer the following questions.

1. Which word is a participle?

2. Which sentence is missing a comma after the participial phrase? Write the sentence correctly.

3. CHALLENGE Use a participial phrase to combine sentences three and four.

Seating Customers

1. Say hello to the customers. Welcome them to the restaurant and invite them to follow you.

2. Walking slowly lead them to an empty table.

3. Hand them each a menu.

4. Point out today's specials.

13-3 ▶ Gerunds and Gerund Phrases

A **gerund** is a verb that ends in *-ing*. However, it is always used as a noun.

A **gerund phrase** begins with a gerund. The phrase includes other words that add to the meaning of the gerund. A gerund phrase is used as a noun.

▶ **EXAMPLE**

Relaxing is important for everybody. (gerund)

Gardening interests many people. (gerund)

My sister relaxes by planting flowers. (gerund phrase)

Growing fruits and vegetables is my hobby. (gerund phrase)

Practice A

Write the gerund in each sentence. The first one is done for you.

1. Volunteering is important.

Volunteering

2. Running can be good exercise.

3. Writing forces you to think.

4. Discoveries can be made by experimenting.

5. You can save time by flying.

6. Sleeping is necessary for good health.

7. You can improve your grades by studying.

8. Some people think cooking is an art.

Practice B

Write each sentence. Add a gerund of your own. The first one is done for you.

9. _____ makes me feel happy.

    Laughing makes me feel happy.

10. _____ can be healthy.

11. I think _____ is the best Olympic event.

12. _____ is better than watching television.

13. I really like _____.

14. _____ is fun.

15. Experts say _____ is great exercise.

16. _____ is a good career choice.

17. _____ takes skill and practice.

18. My favorite pastime is _____.

Practice C

Write the gerund phrase in each sentence. The first one is done for you.

19. Shopping for clothes can take time.

    Shopping for clothes

20. Finding the right size is often a challenge.

21. Trying to find a clerk may be difficult.

22. He took a long time choosing a sweater.

23. Remembering the correct size is easy for Ellie.

24. Ping enjoys choosing presents for his friends.

25. Wrapping the gifts is his favorite part.

26. I prefer presenting the gifts to my friends.

27. She likes knitting sweaters for people.

Practice D

Write each sentence. Use a gerund phrase from the box.
The first one is done for you.

Creating computer graphics	swimming at the shore	Getting a haircut
Learning to ski	Working hard	riding horses
passing the test		

28. _____ will be fun!

Learning to ski will be fun!

29. I always enjoy _____ .

30. _____ can change your looks completely.

31. I think _____ is my favorite memory.

32. _____ seems easy to learn.

33. She knew _____ would be her biggest challenge.

34. _____ is important if you want to succeed.

35. **CHALLENGE** Write a sentence of your own using a
gerund phrase.

USING REFERENCES
Table of Contents

The table of contents of a book is found in the front of the book. It shows you how the book is arranged. It lists the chapters and sections in the book.

The chapter and section titles are listed as main headings and subheadings. The page numbers tell where the chapters or sections begin.

Skim a table of contents to find a certain topic or to get an idea of the information that the book covers. Then go to the page number to find that information.

Look at the table of contents below from a computer book. Then answer the questions that follow.

1. What are the four participles?

2. What are the eight gerund phrases?

3. **CHALLENGE** How are a table of contents and an index similar? How are they different?

Infinitives and Infinitive Phrases

An **infinitive** is made up of the word *to* plus the plural form of a verb.

An **infinitive phrase** begins with an infinitive. Other words in the phrase tell more about the infinitive.

Infinitives and infinitive phrases can be used as nouns, adjectives, or adverbs.

▶ **EXAMPLE**

He likes to draw. (used as a noun)

A bank is the best place to keep your money. (used as an adjective)

Everyone is ready to get on the plane. (used as an adverb)

Practice A

Write the infinitive in each sentence. The first one is done for you.

1. Do you know how to swim?

to swim

2. Kay learned to dive last Wednesday.

3. I want you to listen to this song.

4. You should register to vote today.

5. Armando decided to volunteer for the army.

6. My cousin wants to go to the movies.

7. Julian needs to talk to you later.

8. I will need your help to move this table.

9. To walk to school takes me 30 minutes.

Practice B

Write the infinitive phrase in each sentence. The first one is done for you.

10. Randy needed to find the information.

to find the information

11. Politicians try to persuade people.

12. Grace wanted to succeed in business.

13. It is difficult to know all the answers.

14. A reporter must be able to write quickly.

15. José hurried to catch the train.

16. To guess the answer was impossible.

17. It takes years to become a world-class athlete.

18. CHALLENGE Write a sentence of your own using an infinitive phrase.

Everyday English

Kamal is joining a walkathon to raise money for cancer research. He found out about the walkathon from a flyer he saw in his town library. Read the flyer. Then answer the following questions.

1. What are the five infinitives?

2. What are the five infinitive phrases?

3. CHALLENGE Rewrite the title using an infinitive.

Walking Together
We Can Run Off Cancer!

Do you want to raise money for cancer research?

Please join a walkathon in Smith Park on May 3 at 8:00 A.M.
Things to keep in mind:
• Come early to sign forms.
• Remember to wear comfortable shoes.
• Raise $100 or more to receive a free T- shirt.

ENGLISH IN YOUR LIFE
Creating a To-Do List

Mrs. Garcia is organizing the school talent show. She will also be the show's announcer. She has many things to take care of before the show.

Mrs. Garcia made a to-do list to help her organize her tasks. She put the most important tasks at the top of the list. As she finishes each task, she checks it off her list.

Read the list. Then answer the questions below.

Mrs. Garcia introduces a talent act.

To-Do List

1. ☑ *Make a complete list of all acts.*
2. ☑ *Finalize list to give to printer.*
3. ☐ *Write opening comments.*
4. ☐ *Write notes to introduce each act.*
5. ☐ *Work on memorizing comments and notes.*

Writing and Reading

Think of an event that you need to plan for, such as a party or a trip. Write a to-do list. Use participles, gerunds, and infinitives in your list. Trade lists with a partner. Draw a line under participles, gerunds, and infinitives in your partner's list.

1. What is the gerund phrase?

2. What is the participle in the list?

3. What are the two infinitive phrases in the list?

4. **CRITICAL THINKING** How does a to-do list help you stay organized?

Phrases complete an idea but do not contain both a subject and a verb. You can use the READ, PLAN, WRITE, and CHECK steps to write sentences that contain phrases.

EXAMPLE

Write a sentence that describes two ways in which citizens can be active in government. Then write a sentence that explains why being active in government is important. Use at least one gerund phrase and one infinitive phrase.

READ   Do you understand the assignment?

Write the assignment in your own words.

> *Write a sentence about ways people can be involved in government. Write another sentence that tells why being involved is important. Use a gerund phrase and an infinitive phrase.*

PLAN   Gather your ideas and organize them.

Use an outline like the one below to organize your ideas.

> I. Ways to Be Active
>   A. vote in elections
>   B. write letters
> II. Why Being Active Is Important
>   A. to choose good leaders
>   B. to make our opinions heard

WRITE   Put your ideas into two sentences.

Use the ideas in your outline to write two sentences.

> *People can be active in government by voting in elections and by writing letters to politicians. It is important that we choose good leaders and make our opinions heard.*

How can you improve your writing?

Check that the sentences answer the assignment. Add or change information to make your sentences clearer and easier to read. Make sure phrases are used correctly.

It is important to do *these things so we can choose good leaders and make our opinions heard.*

The words in blue type were added to the second sentence. They answer the part of the assignment that asks you to use at least one infinitive phrase.

Practice

Complete the writing assignments below. Answer the questions under PLAN to make an outline.

1. Write a sentence about a new law that you would like to have passed. Tell why. Use at least one appositive phrase.

   PLAN
   What will go beside Roman numeral I in your outline? What details will you list beneath it?

2. Write a sentence about a law that you would like to eliminate. Tell why. Use at least one participial phrase.

   PLAN
   What will go beside Roman numeral II in your outline? What details will you list beneath it?

Putting It All Together

You have been elected to Congress. What laws would you change? Write a paragraph about a law you want to pass and one you want to eliminate. You may want to use the sentences you have written above. Add other sentences that explain your ideas.

appositive
appositive phrase
gerund
gerund phrase
infinitive
infinitive phrase
participial phrase
participle

Vocabulary Review

Write the vocabulary term that describes the underlined word or words in each sentence.

1. My sister wants <u>to go</u> with us.
2. <u>Walking</u> helps me relax.
3. I nearly forgot <u>to study my notes</u> for the quiz.
4. The <u>experienced</u> trainer taught the dogs a trick.
5. The school, <u>built last year</u>, holds 5,000 students.
6. I bought a shirt in purple, <u>my favorite color</u>.
7. <u>Learning a new language</u> is not easy.
8. My sister, <u>Amanda</u>, picked me up after work.

Chapter Quiz

LESSON 13·1

Identifying Appositive Phrases

Write the appositive phrase in each sentence.

1. This is Mr. Jefferson, my soccer coach.
2. Jamie, my best friend, bought me this CD.
3. I baked brownies, Jerry's favorite dessert.

LESSON 13·2

Test Tip
Use a comma to separate a participial phrase from the rest of the sentence.

Using Participial Phrases to Combine Sentences

Combine each pair of sentences. Write the first sentence as a participial phrase. Then add it to the second sentence.

4. Cal watched the game.
   Cal saw his favorite team lose by a point.
5. Maria walked to the pizza shop.
   Maria considered buying two slices.
6. Cory worked quickly.
   Cory finished the job 15 minutes early.

Identifying Gerund Phrases

Write the gerund phrase in each sentence.

7. Living in South America is Jason's dream.

8. Playing the guitar takes patience.

9. Listening to music relaxes me.

10. Did you do all this cooking for the party?

Identifying Infinitive Phrases

Write the infinitive phrase in each sentence.

11. Pete hoped to be chosen for the team.

12. To gain strength, Jill ran track.

13. Juan decided to take algebra.

14. Anthony hoped to find his book.

Writing Tip
Use an outline to PLAN your writing. CHECK that your paragraph answers the assignment.

Writing: Using Phrases in Sentences

15. Write a paragraph about the kinds of clothing you wear. What do you wear to school? What do you wear on weekends? If you have a job, what do you wear to work? What is your favorite clothing to wear? Use at least one appositive phrase and one participial phrase in your paragraph.

Group Activity

Work with a group to list four things a teenager should consider before taking a part-time job. Write your list items in complete sentences. Use appositive, participial, gerund, and infinitive phrases. Then exchange lists with another group. Suggest ways the group can improve its list.

Unit 6 Review

Read the passage to answer questions 1–5. Choose the word or words that belong in each space. Mark the letter for your answer.

Here is a good office rule to keep in mind. When you talk _(1)_ the phone, keep others in mind. Often, the joining wall _(2)_ two offices can be very thin. If you choose _(3)_ a speakerphone, talk quietly. _(4)_ your voice low, you will be less likely _(5)_ others.

1. A. at
   B. on
   C. under
   D. to

2. A. beside
   B. besides
   C. between
   D. among

3. A. use
   B. to using
   C. using
   D. to use

4. A. By keeping
   B. Keep
   C. To keep
   D. To keeping

5. A. to disturb
   B. disturb
   C. disturbing
   D. to disturbing

Read the passage to answer questions 6–7. Choose the best way to write the passage. Mark the letter for your answer.

If you want a pet, consider adopting one. Pets at an animal shelter need you as much as you need them. (6) Often, a shelter will have the perfect animal for him. (7) Between doing a good deed, you may just find a new friend!

6. A. Often, a shelter will have the perfect animal for I.
   B. Often, a shelter will have the perfect animal for her.
   C. Often, a shelter will have the perfect animal for you.
   D. No error

7. A. Beside doing a good deed, you may just find a new friend!
   B. Besides doing a good deed, you may just find a new friend!
   C. Among doing a good deed, you may just find a new friend!
   D. No error

Critical Thinking

Name a role model that you would like to visit your class. Tell why he or she is a good choice.
WRITING Write a paragraph to convince your teacher that your choice is the best. Be sure to use phrases correctly.

Chapter 14 Simple and Compound Sentences
Chapter 15 Clauses and Complex Sentences

Computers allow people from all over the world to communicate with each other. Varied sentence structures make writing more interesting. In this unit, you will learn how to use different sentence structures to communicate your ideas.

People often use e-mail to communicate with co-workers. E-mail messages may contain memos, letters, or reports.

Look at this e-mail message and answer the following questions.

1. What are the subjects in the second sentence?

2. What is the predicate in the second sentence?

3. What group of words in the last sentence tells *when* Ken will talk to Melissa?

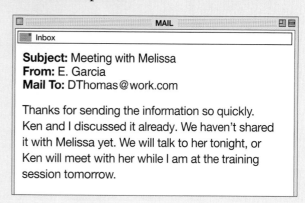

MAIL

Inbox

Subject: Meeting with Melissa
From: E. Garcia
Mail To: DThomas@work.com

Thanks for sending the information so quickly. Ken and I discussed it already. We haven't shared it with Melissa yet. We will talk to her tonight, or Ken will meet with her while I am at the training session tomorrow.

Archaeologists study cultures of the past. This picture shows archaeologists digging up artifacts. Use complete sentences to answer these questions. What object is the woman in the front holding? What is she doing? Now combine the two sentences into one sentence using the word "and." You have just formed a compound sentence.

Chapter 14 ▷ Simple and Compound Sentences

Words to Know

simple sentence	a sentence that expresses a complete thought
compound subject	two or more subjects that have the same predicate
compound predicate	two or more predicates that have the same subject
coordinating conjunction	a word that is used to join words, phrases, or sentences
clause	a group of words that has a subject and predicate and forms part of a sentence
independent clause	a clause that can stand alone as a sentence
compound sentence	a sentence that contains two or more simple sentences, or independent clauses
run-on sentence	two or more sentences that are written as one sentence

Silly Sentence Project

Write five compound sentences in your journal. For example, *Jim runs in the park, and Kim lifts weights in the gym.* Remove some of the nouns and verbs. Replace them with blank lines, such as _____ *runs in the park, and Kim lifts* _____ *in the gym.* Then ask a partner to name nouns. Write them on the blank lines. Read the silly sentences aloud.

Learning Objectives

- Identify simple and compound sentences.
- Identify coordinating conjunctions and independent clauses in compound sentences.
- Use commas and coordinating conjunctions to combine sentences.
- Correct run-on sentences.
- Write compound sentences.
- Apply knowledge of compound sentences to a sports report and a computer grammar checker.

A **simple sentence** expresses one complete thought. It often has one subject and one predicate.

A simple sentence can have a **compound subject**. A compound subject is two or more subjects that share the same predicate. A simple sentence also can have a **compound predicate.** A compound predicate is two or more predicates that share the same subject.

Some simple sentences can have both a compound subject and a compound predicate.

The following are simple sentences. The subjects are in blue type. The verbs in the predicates are underlined.

Remember
A subject tells who or what the sentence is about. A predicate tells what the subject does or is.

▶ **EXAMPLE**

Smoke <u>poured</u> out of the window. (one subject and one predicate)

Smoke and flames <u>poured</u> out of the window. (compound subject)

The men <u>yelled</u> and <u>screamed</u> for help. (compound predicate)

The men and women <u>yelled</u> and <u>screamed</u> for help. (compound subject and compound predicate)

Practice

Write whether each sentence has a compound subject, a compound predicate, or both. The first one is done for you.

1. The wind and waves rocked the boat.

   compound subject

2. The sail and the flag hung in shreds.

3. The waves splashed against and pounded the deck.

4. The captain and passengers trembled and shouted.

5. A boat and a helicopter rescued the passengers.

14·2 Coordinating Conjunctions

Coordinating conjunctions are used to join words, phrases, and sentences. The words in the box are coordinating conjunctions.

Coordinating Conjunctions						
and	but	for	nor	or	so	yet

▶ **EXAMPLE**

Walter and Pauline (joins words)

the black cat or the white dog (joins phrases)

Jon did not go to the movies, but he went to the store. (joins sentences)

Practice

Write each sentence. Draw a line under each coordinating conjunction. The first one is done for you.

1. Ellen or Marie will sing, and Pat will play piano.

Ellen or Marie will sing, and Pat will play piano.

2. Beth went, but Al stayed home.

3. Elizabeth started early, yet she arrived late.

4. His mother and father own a restaurant.

5. Please bring apples or pears for the fruit salad.

6. Mindy could not go, so I went alone.

7. I went to the library, for I thought you were there.

8. My sisters are twins, but they are not identical.

14·3 Compound Sentences

A **clause** is a group of words that has a subject and predicate and forms part of a sentence. A clause that forms a complete sentence is called an **independent clause**.

A **compound sentence** is made up of two or more simple sentences, or independent clauses. Independent clauses are often joined by a coordinating conjunction. So a compound sentence has at least two subjects and two predicates.

The following are compound sentences. The subjects are in blue type. The verbs in the predicates are underlined.

► **EXAMPLE 1**

Tomás <u>was</u> the pitcher, and Claire <u>was</u> the shortstop.

Mike <u>scored</u> two runs, but Andy <u>did</u> not <u>score</u> any.

We <u>could go</u> to the game, or we <u>could watch</u> it on TV.

The following is not a compound sentence. The words after *but* do not form a complete sentence.

► **EXAMPLE 2**

Nora <u>went</u> to the game but <u>did</u> not <u>stay</u>.

Practice A

Read each sentence. If it is a compound sentence, write *Compound*. If it is a simple sentence, write *Simple*. The first one is done for you.

1. One dog ran around the corner, and the other chased him.

   Compound

2. The carpet came, but the curtains did not come.

3. Gordon read the repair manual, but he could not fix the car engine.

Practice

4. The students wrote papers and read them to the class.

5. Brett is studying auto repair, and his sister is studying carpentry.

6. Jim left his wallet in the car, and I found it.

7. You could eat all the salad now, or you could save some of it for lunch tomorrow.

8. I can make dessert or buy it at the store.

9. Sandra called five people, but only one was home.

10. We made a date and agreed to meet at eight o'clock.

11. You made our lunch, but I cleaned up afterward.

12. He fell quite a distance, yet he seems fine.

13. Hanna ate dinner, and Bill went to play soccer.

14. Ray worked on his car and mowed the lawn today.

15. Tomás and Chris went shopping but didn't buy anything.

16. Noah worked on Friday, so Julia could have the day off.

17. Neither Billy nor Keisha went to that party.

18. You should stay home, for you need your rest.

19. So when are you going to Boston and New York?

20. Kelly read a book and went to sleep.

21. Fax the letter to the office, or mail it to my home.

Practice B

Write each sentence. Draw one line under each independent clause. Circle each coordinating conjunction. The first one is done for you.

22. I offered to answer questions, but none were asked.

I offered to answer questions, (but) _none were asked._

23. They packed for days, for it would be a long journey.

24. Nicki painted the walls, and Steve waxed the floor.

25. Purple is my favorite color, yet my car is blue.

26. They told me to report to you, so here I am.

27. Kickboxing is fun, but I like to lift weights.

28. I'm not excited about it, but it will do.

29. Sharon went to the library, and she borrowed a book.

30. Felicia was excited about moving, but she was sad to leave her friends.

Everyday English

Marlene and Rodney wanted to see a movie. They read this movie review in a newspaper. Read the review and follow the directions below.

1. List the three coordinating conjunctions.

2. Write the compound sentence. Draw one line under each independent clause. Circle the coordinating conjunction.

New Release
OFF TRACK ! (110 min., PG-13)
This is one movie you can miss or wait to see on video. The film is about a train that falls off a bridge into a river. Kim Bates plays a passenger, and Al Metcalf plays the train's engineer. Their characters are boring and unpleasant. ★

14·4 Commas in Compound Sentences

Use a comma before the coordinating conjunction in a compound sentence.

EXAMPLE

Montie laughed loudly, but Larry was silent.

I went to the party, and she met me there.

I will go with you, or you can ask Terry to go.

I want to learn to swim, yet I have a fear of the water.

Practice

Write each sentence. Add a comma where it is needed. The first one is done for you.

1. My boss is gone but she left me in charge.

    My boss is gone, but she left me in charge.

2. A ballpoint pen can write on paper or it can write on plastic.

3. Cats are small but they have more bones than we do.

4. The bike broke so we took it back and asked for a refund.

5. Anne is my friend yet I have not seen her in ten years.

6. Danika wore her gloves for it was cold outside.

7. She slept for eight hours yet she was still tired.

8. **CHALLENGE** The salsa tastes great but it is a little spicy so it may upset my stomach.

14·5 Using Coordinating Conjunctions to Combine Sentences

You can form compound sentences by combining two simple sentences. Use a coordinating conjunction and a comma to combine the sentences.

▶ **EXAMPLE**

You can read the book now.

You can listen to the tape.

You can read the book now, or you can listen to the tape.

Jill washed the lettuce.

Mark cut the tomatoes.

Jill washed the lettuce, and Mark cut the tomatoes.

Practice

Combine each pair of sentences. Use a coordinating conjunction and a comma. Draw a line under each coordinating conjunction. The first one is done for you.

1. The librarian looked up the title.
   I found the book on the shelf.

   The librarian looked up the title, <u>and</u> I found the book on the shelf.

2. Mickey asked a question.
   Mary answered him.

3. Mindy wanted a milkshake.
   Tori helped her change her mind.

4. George wanted to have dinner.
   The restaurant was closed.

5. You could study a little every night.
   You could study all weekend.

6. Someone dropped by.
You were not home.

7. Sam examined the car.
Alison filled out the forms.

8. Susan Book really works in a library.
Dale Cook is a chef.

9. The witnesses may have been confused.
They may have been lying.

10. I can read a book about pollution.
I can watch a television program about it.

11. Those speakers are great.
They won't work with my computer.

12. **CHALLENGE** Write a compound sentence of your own. Use a coordinating conjunction and a comma. Draw a line under the coordinating conjunction.

Everyday English

Sheryl is using her computer to make a birthday card for her co-worker Monique. Everyone in the office will sign the card. Read the card and follow the directions below.

1. Combine the first and second sentences. Write the compound sentence you formed.

2. Combine the third and fourth sentences. Write the compound sentence you formed.

3. Combine the sixth and seventh sentences. Write the compound sentence you formed.

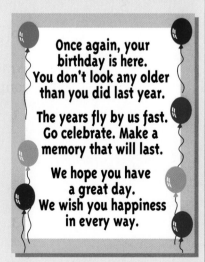

Once again, your birthday is here.
You don't look any older than you did last year.

The years fly by us fast.
Go celebrate. Make a memory that will last.

We hope you have a great day.
We wish you happiness in every way.

14·6 ▶ Avoiding Run-On Sentences

A **run-on sentence** is made up of two or more sentences that are written as one sentence. Some run-on sentences are separated incorrectly by commas. Others have no punctuation at all.

▶ **EXAMPLE 1**

Janis and Sam went to a movie, it was so crowded that they could not get tickets. (incorrect use of comma)

Janis and Sam went to a movie it was so crowded that they could not get tickets. (no punctuation)

One way to correct a run-on sentence is to divide it into two simple sentences. Another way to correct a run-on sentence is to add both a comma and a coordinating conjunction. A third way to correct a run-on sentence is to use a semicolon between the two ideas.

▶ **EXAMPLE 2**

Janis and Sam went to a movie. It was so crowded that they could not get tickets. (two simple sentences)

Janis and Sam went to a movie, but it was so crowded that they could not get tickets. (comma and coordinating conjunction)

Janis and Sam went to a movie; it was so crowded that they could not get tickets. (semicolon)

Practice A

Write each run-on sentence correctly. Use a coordinating conjunction and a comma. The first one is done for you.

1. Jamie is a good pitcher he throws the ball hard.

   Jamie is a good pitcher, and he throws the ball hard.

2. Some people hate roller coasters others like them.

3. The snow fell all night we had school the next day.

4. I have a soccer game I won't be home for dinner.

5. Carmen sewed the costumes Dean built the props.

Practice B

Use a semicolon to correct each run-on sentence. The first one is done for you.

6. White sharks have big appetites they feed on sea lions, tuna, and other sharks.

> *White sharks have big appetites; they feed on sea lions, tuna, and other sharks.*

7. I returned the video a day late I was charged a fee.

8. The Internet is a good place to shop for airline tickets many sites let you name your price.

9. Some states still do not require motorcycle helmets it is dangerous not to use them.

10. Roger missed the plane he should have left earlier.

Everyday English

Miguel and Kevin are at the local batting cages. The batting cage rules contain some run-on sentences. Read the rules, and answer the following questions.

1. Which rules are run-on sentences?

2. Correct each run-on sentence.

Batting Cage Rules

1. A helmet must be worn inside the cage the door must be closed while batting.

2. No children under 12 are allowed in cages.

3. There is a 5-minute limit in cages wait behind the white line for your turn.

Writing Compound Sentences

Good writing contains both simple and compound sentences. You can use the READ, PLAN, WRITE, and CHECK steps to form compound sentences.

▶ **EXAMPLE**

Write a compound sentence about two things that you do well. Then write a compound sentence about two things that you would like to do better. Use a semicolon in one sentence. Use a coordinating conjunction and a comma in the other.

READ   **Do you understand the assignment?**

Write the assignment. Underline the key words.

> Write a <u>compound sentence</u> about <u>two things</u> that you <u>do well</u>. Then write a <u>compound sentence</u> about <u>two things</u> that you would <u>like to do better</u>. Use a semicolon in one sentence. Use a <u>coordinating conjunction</u> and a <u>comma</u> in the other.

PLAN   **Gather your ideas and organize them.**

Create an outline to organize your ideas.

> I. What I Do Well
>   A. I sing fairly well.
>   B. I dance very well.
> II. What I Would Like to Do Better
>   A. I wish I could draw better.
>   B. I want to paint better.

WRITE   **Put your ideas into two sentences.**

Use the ideas in your outline to write two compound sentences.

> I sing fairly well; I dance very well. I wish I could draw better; I want to paint better, too.

CHECK How can you improve your writing?

Check that your sentences answer the assignment.
Make sure that you used the correct punctuation.

*I sing fairly well, and I dance very well. I wish
I could draw better; I want to paint better, too.*

The comma and the conjunction in blue type have
been added. They show the relationship between the
two parts of the sentence.

Practice

Complete the writing assignments below. Use an outline to
PLAN your ideas.

1. Every student in your school will do one hour of volunteer
   work a week. Write a compound sentence about two places
   you can volunteer. Write a second compound sentence
   about the kind of work you can do in each place.

   PLAN
   Where in your community would you like to volunteer?
   What kind of work would you enjoy doing?

2. Write a compound sentence that explains how your work
   will help others. Then write a compound sentence that
   explains how your work will help you.

   PLAN
   How will your volunteer work help someone?
   How will your volunteering help you?

Putting It All Together

Write a paragraph that tells why volunteering is important to
a community. You may wish to use the sentences you wrote
above. Add a sentence that introduces your ideas.

USING REFERENCES
Computer Grammar Checker

A computer grammar checker can help you find errors in your writing. It looks for mistakes in punctuation, capitalization, and subject-verb agreement. It also looks for poor sentence structure.

Sometimes, the grammar checker gives you a possible way to fix the sentence. You may decide to change your sentence to the one shown. If not, you can tell the grammar checker to ignore it.

Other times, an explanation of the problem is shown. You then need to decide how to correct the error yourself.

The grammar checker cannot catch all possible errors. You still must proofread your work.

Look at the computer grammar checker below. Then answer the questions that follow.

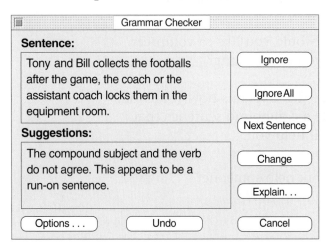

1. How can you correct the subject-verb agreement?

2. What could you do to fix the run-on sentence?

3. **CHALLENGE** Write the run-on sentence correctly.

COMMUNICATING ON THE JOB
Sports Commentator

Wanda Choi works as a sports commentator for a television station. Wanda writes her own reports. Her sentences must be clearly written so that people can understand what she says.

Wanda has tight deadlines, so she writes quickly. Sometimes, she makes mistakes. She corrects her report and rehearses it before the show.

Read her report, and follow the directions below.

Wanda reports on a sporting event.

There were two major upsets last night both local teams won. Chu and Leigh are a winning pair for the Coleman Tigers. The Detroit Bullets played well the team just couldn't beat those Tigers. The Lansing Bears game was a blowout. The Bears' offense and defense were great. The Ann Arbor Rockets didn't stand a chance yet the players held strong. Let's show the tape.

1. The first sentence is a run-on sentence. Use a semicolon to correct it.

2. Add the correct punctuation to the sixth sentence.

3. **CRITICAL THINKING** Why is it important to avoid run-on sentences in speaking, as well as in writing?

Writing and Speaking

Write a short sports report for a local TV station. The report should be about a recent sporting event in your school. Be sure to use some compound sentences. Then present your report to the class.

clause
compound predicate
compound sentence
compound subject
coordinating conjunction
independent clause
run-on sentence
simple sentence

Vocabulary Review

Complete each sentence with a term from the box.

1. A _____ joins words, phrases, or sentences.

2. A _____ is two or more verbs that share the same subject.

3. An _____ is a group of words that can stand alone as a sentence.

4. A _____ is two or more complete sentences that are written as one sentence.

5. A _____ is made up of two or more simple sentences.

6. A _____ is a group of words that has a subject and predicate and forms part of a sentence.

7. A _____ expresses one complete thought.

8. A _____ is two or more subjects that share the same predicate.

Chapter Quiz

LESSON 14-1

Identifying Simple Sentences

Write whether each sentence has a compound subject, a compound predicate, or both.

1. Maggie and I went to the party.

2. Ken shouted and searched for his dog.

3. Sue and Al ate soup and salad for dinner.

4. Sal and Sara waved and yelled for help.

5. The students and the teachers boarded the bus.

LESSONS 14·2 and 14·3

Identifying Coordinating Conjuctions and Independent Clauses

Write each sentence. Draw one line under each independent clause. Circle each coordinating conjunction.

6. Kim and Jack rested, but Joe and Tina took a walk.

7. Either Beth or I will go, so there's room for you.

8. She can walk home, or Josh or I can drive her.

LESSONS 14·4 and 14·5

Test Tip
A comma comes *before* a coordinating conjunction in a compound sentence.

Using Commas and Coordinating Conjunctions

Combine each pair of sentences. Use a coordinating conjunction and a comma.

9. I wanted to go to the mall. It was too late.

10. The volume is too loud. The picture is unclear.

11. I could not stay awake. I took a quick nap.

LESSON 14·6

Correcting Run-On Sentences

Write each run-on sentence correctly.

12. My house is bright pink you will easily see it.

13. The phone rang ten times I finally hung up.

LESSON 14·7

Writing Tip
Use an outline to plan what to write. Check that your paragraph answers the assignment.

Writing Compound Sentences

14. Write a paragraph about your favorite TV show. Tell when it is on, who is in it, and what the show is about. Use at least two compound sentences.

Group Activity

It is Drug Awareness Week at your school. Help spread the message that drugs are harmful. Work with a group to create a song or rap that sends the message. Be sure to use compound sentences. Then perform your song or rap for your class.

How might you describe this photograph? You can use clauses to express your ideas clearly. In this chapter, you will learn about clauses that act as adverbs, adjectives, and nouns. You also will learn how to use clauses to form complex sentences.

Words to Know

dependent clause	a clause that cannot stand alone as a complete sentence
subordinating conjunction	one or more words that begin a dependent clause
complex sentence	a sentence with an independent clause and a dependent clause
adverb clause	a dependent clause that tells more about a verb, an adjective, or another adverb
adjective clause	a dependent clause that tells more about a noun or pronoun
noun clause	a dependent clause that acts as a noun

Police Report Project

You have witnessed an accident in a store parking lot. A driver has dented another vehicle and has driven away. Write a brief police report describing everything you saw. Tell exactly what happened. Give specific details. As you learn more about clauses and complex sentences, revise your report to make it even more specific.

Learning Objectives

- Identify and use subordinating conjunctions and dependent clauses.
- Identify adverb clauses, adjective clauses, and noun clauses in complex sentences.
- Use commas correctly in complex sentences.
- Use adverb clauses and adjective clauses to combine sentences.
- Write complex sentences.
- Apply knowledge of clauses to written directions and a travel article.

Remember
A clause is a group of words that has a subject and a predicate and forms part of a sentence.

A **dependent clause** cannot stand alone as a complete sentence. It does not express a complete thought. Many dependent clauses begin with a **subordinating conjunction**. The subordinating conjunction is part of the dependent clause.

The words in the box are subordinating conjunctions.

Subordinating Conjunctions			
after	because	since	when
although	before	so that	whenever
as	if	than	where
as if	in order that	though	wherever
as long as	once	unless	whether
as though	provided that	until	while

A dependent clause can appear at the beginning or at the end of a sentence.

▶ **EXAMPLE**

Mary lived in this house until she moved last fall.

subordinating conjunction: until

dependent clause: until she moved last fall

While she was unpacking, Mary found an unopened letter.

subordinating conjunction: While

dependent clause: While she was unpacking

Practice A

Write the dependent clause in each sentence. Then underline the subordinating conjunction. The first one is done for you.

1. It has been a long time since I saw you.

<u>since</u> I saw you

2. We finished the work before we left.

3. When we arrived, it was starting to rain.

4. We shall be there provided that you come, too.

5. She took that course because she wanted a better job.

6. Jerri will wait at the house until you get there.

7. While the chicken is cooking, I will make the salad.

8. After the sauce cools, put it in the refrigerator.

9. As long as the sun is out, we can swim.

10. Whenever it snows, school closes.

Practice B

Write each sentence. Add a subordinating conjunction from the box on page 314. The first one is done for you.

11. _____ you sit down, please bring me the paper.

  Before you sit down, please bring me the paper.

12. Tony ate _____ everyone else was served.

13. Sally will baby-sit _____ they return.

14. Rochelle was happy _____ her friends were there.

15. I did not hear the phone ring _____ I was outside.

16. Ms. Hall will help _____ you are willing to try.

17. _____ Kyle answered the phone, the caller hung up.

18. _____ she got her hair cut, her mother went shopping.

15·2 ▸ Adverb Clauses in Complex Sentences

A **complex sentence** is a sentence with an independent clause and a dependent clause.

An independent clause can stand alone as a sentence, but a dependent clause cannot. A dependent clause needs the independent clause to express a complete thought.

▸ **EXAMPLE 1**

Kyla arrived before the doors were open. (complex sentence)

independent clause: Kyla arrived

dependent clause: before the doors were open

subordinating conjunction: before

An **adverb clause** is another term for a dependent clause that begins with a subordinating conjunction. An adverb clause acts as an adverb. It tells more about a verb, an adjective, or another adverb. An adverb clause answers the questions *how*, *why*, *where*, or *when*.

▸ **EXAMPLE 2**

Bryce smiled as if he knew the answer. (tells how)

Because the doors were open, people poured in. (tells why)

Wherever you need to go, I will take you. (tells where)

Please lock the door before you leave. (tells when)

Put a comma after an adverb clause if it comes at the beginning of the sentence. Notice which sentence below has a comma.

▸ **EXAMPLE 3**

He worked hard because he wanted to finish. (end of sentence; no comma)

Because he wanted to finish, he worked hard. (beginning of sentence; comma)

Practice A

Write each complex sentence. Draw one line under each independent clause. Draw two lines under each dependent clause. The first one is done for you.

1. Everyone laughed when you told the story.

Everyone laughed when you told the story.

2. Mr. Gee arrived after the concert began.

3. Hasan walked in while the teacher was speaking.

4. Jackie will not be here today because she is sick.

5. Ralph called me when I got home.

6. Although his job was difficult, Griffin enjoyed it.

7. Whenever I look out my window, I can see your house.

8. Melanie acted as though nothing had happened.

Practice B

Write the adverb clause in each sentence. Then write which question it answers: *how, why, where,* or *when.* The first one is done for you.

9. She willingly travels wherever her job takes her.

wherever her job takes her, where

10. While he was on the phone, his dinner burned.

11. Tracy studied so that she could pass her test.

12. This story picks up where the last one ended.

13. Frank worked as if he owned the company.

(Practice B continues on next page.) ⇨

14. I will not make a decision until I hear from you.

15. Jason acted as though nothing were wrong.

16. The road is icy because it snowed last night.

17. Mallory can draw better than I can.

18. Please wash your hands before you eat dinner.

Practice C

Write each sentence. Add an adverb clause from the box. The first one is done for you.

Since you have been gone	whenever it was in trouble
Because tomorrow is a holiday	As long as he is busy
unless you don't want to go	Before I stepped on stage

19. —————, I have been busy.

> *Since you have been gone, I have been busy.*

20. —————, Kevin doesn't mind being alone.

21. I'll give you the extra ticket —————.

22. —————, I forgot my speech.

23. The dog hid in the basement —————.

24. —————, all the stores will be closed.

25. **CHALLENGE** Write the sentence below using an adverb clause of your own.
—————, you will get an award.

Write each sentence. Add commas where they are needed. The first one is done for you.

26. Because the taxi was late we missed our flight.

   Because the taxi was late, we missed our flight.

27. If you need help ask Ms. Cohen.

28. Until you hear from me please do nothing more.

29. Before I go to the game I must finish my homework.

30. Wherever Sam traveled he met interesting people.

31. When someone visits him his mood always improves.

32. Provided that the weather is good there will be a crowd.

Everyday English

Nolan got his car registration renewal notice in the mail. He needs to read the directions and pay the registration fee. There is a mistake in the notice. Read the notice. Then follow the directions below.

1. Write the two complex sentences.

2. Use your answers above. Draw one line under each adverb clause. Circle the subordinating conjunction.

3. One sentence in the notice is missing a comma after the adverb clause. Write the sentence correctly.

AUTOMOBILE REGISTRATION RENEWAL NOTICE

Destroy this form if you no longer own this automobile.

Send or bring the bottom part of this form along with the correct fee. Write your check or money order to Ohio State DMV. When renewing by mail allow 15 days for processing.

⬇ SEND BOTTOM SECTION WITH PAYMENT ⬇

Using Adverb Clauses to Combine Sentences

You can use adverb clauses to combine sentences. The adverb clause can go at the beginning or at the end of the sentence.

The following sentences can be combined with an adverb clause. A subordinating conjunction is used to form the adverb clause.

▶ **EXAMPLE**

Carlos chose this book for you. You liked it.

Carlos chose this book for you because you liked it.

Because you liked it, Carlos chose this book for you.

Practice A

Combine each pair of sentences. Use an adverb clause. Draw a line under each subordinating conjunction. Remember to use commas as needed. The first one is done for you.

1. Karen saw you.
   She went to San Diego.

   Karen saw you <u>when</u> she went to San Diego.

2. Nancy will pick up the twins.
   She goes to the post office.

3. Someone must have been here.
   We arrived.

4. Stuart wants to be a painter.
   He will take art classes.

5. She finished the cereal.
   Candace went to the store.

6. Keith will stay here.
Mom arrives tomorrow.

7. Amanda calls us.
She is in town.

8. You know the answer.
Please tell us.

9. Jay mopped the floor.
His sister did the dishes.

10. Toshi agreed to help Matt study.
Matt would take her to dinner.

11. I won't tell you.
You promise not to tell anyone else.

12. CHALLENGE Combine the following sentences. Use
adverb clauses.
The final curtain went down. Shannon kept applauding.
We made her leave.

Practice B

Rewrite the paragraph. Use adverb clauses to combine sentences.
The first new sentence is done for you.

I would like to go to cooking school. I can become a
chef. A chef must be very creative. He or she must invent
new dishes. I invent enough new dishes. I might even get
my own cookbook. It makes me a little nervous. I think
about cooking for people I don't even know. Working as a
chef should be fun. It will be challenging!

> *I would like to go to cooking school so that I can
> become a chef.*

15·4 ► Adjective Clauses

Identifying Adjective Clauses

An **adjective clause** is a dependent clause that acts like an adjective in a sentence. An adjective clause tells more about a noun or pronoun.

An adjective clause usually begins with a relative pronoun such as *who* or *which*. But it also may begin with *where* or *when*.

The words in the box are used to begin adjective clauses.

that	where	who	whose
when	which	whom	

► **EXAMPLE**

Susan wanted the dog that was at the pet shop.
(The adjective clause tells more about the noun *dog*.)

I have not talked to anyone who liked the movie.
(The adjective clause tells more about the pronoun *anyone*.)

Practice A

Write the adjective clause in each sentence. The first one is done for you.

1. It was a time when we all worked hard.

   when we all worked hard

2. I saw the man whose address you wanted.

3. The train that left at nine o'clock was delayed.

4. Was it something that I said?

5. Tim talked to the woman who left you the message.

6. This is a house where many families have lived.

7. The show that you like so much is on right now.

8. Everyone who is finished needs to sit quietly.

9. Kelly met the man with whom you had spoken today.

10. You have a teacher who has been at this school for many years.

Practice B

Write each sentence. Add an adjective clause of your own. Begin each adjective clause with *who, which, that, whom, whose, when,* or *where.* The first one is done for you.

11. April 1 is the date _____.

   April 1 is the date when some people play tricks.

12. Earth is a planet _____.

13. Here is the man _____.

14. Those are the people _____.

15. The house _____ is on the next street.

16. Steven is the team member _____.

17. Those are the books _____.

18. The movie _____ was very long.

19. Those are the new skis _____.

20. The key _____ is hanging on the first hook.

Using Commas with Adjective Clauses

Some adjective clauses are not necessary to the meaning of a sentence. The sentence means the same thing without the clause. These adjective clauses are set apart from the rest of the sentence by commas.

▶ **EXAMPLE 1**

Jamie, who can use a computer, works here.
(The adjective clause is not necessary.)

Laura made a key lime pie, which is my favorite.
(The adjective clause is not necessary.)

Other adjective clauses are necessary to the meaning of the sentence. The sentence does not have the same meaning without the clause. Commas are *not* used with clauses that are necessary to the meaning of the sentence.

▶ **EXAMPLE 2**

People who drive too fast are dangerous.
(The adjective clause is necessary.)

I agree with almost everything that he said.
(The adjective clause is necessary.)

Practice

Write each sentence. Underline the adjective clause. Add commas where they are needed. The first one is done for you.

1. The vase which is very beautiful is on the table.

    The vase, <u>which is very beautiful</u>, is on the table.

2. The pears that are in the bag are not ripe yet.

3. The man who works in the grocery store lives in my building.

4. That ring which is made of silver belonged to her grandmother.

5. Juan parked the car which he had just bought in the garage.

6. Scientists who use computers can work quickly.

7. The carpenter who has been working since noon is Jean's neighbor.

8. The weather which has been cold and rainy is expected to improve.

9. Anna's boss whom she had never met attended the meeting with her.

10. The repairperson who fixed my washing machine last week overcharged me.

11. The report which I finished last night will be on your desk in the morning.

Everyday English

Renée had repairs made to her car. Soon afterward, she received a letter and a questionnaire from the car company. The letter contains a mistake. Read the body of the letter. Then follow the directions below.

1. Write the three adjective clauses.

2. CHALLENGE Find the adjective clause that is not necessary to the meaning of the sentence. Write the sentence correctly. Add commas where they are needed.

Dear Ms. Patel,

You recently had your car repaired at our dealership.

We want to keep our customers whose business we value satisfied with our services.

Please fill out the questionnaire. The information that you give us will help us improve our service which is our number one priority.

Thank you.

USING REFERENCES
Periodicals

Periodicals are magazines and journals. Many are written each week or each month. Since they are written often, they generally have more up-to-date information than books.

Periodicals give information on many subjects, such as music, sports, medicine, and travel. They are written to inform and entertain their readers.

Many articles in periodicals use complex sentences. These sentences make the articles interesting. They also give important facts.

Read the following article from a travel magazine. Then follow the directions below.

FIESTA TIME!

Fiesta San Antonio is a popular event that is held each year in San Antonio, Texas. It celebrates the end of the Texas Revolution, which was fought from 1835 to 1836. The Fiesta, which lasts for 10 days, has over 150 events. When you visit Fiesta San Antonio, you will learn first-hand about the history and cultures of San Antonio.

San Antonio ★

1. Write the adverb clause.

2. Write the three adjective clauses.

3. **CHALLENGE** Write a question that could be answered by looking in a periodical. Use an adverb or adjective clause in your question.

Using Adjective Clauses to Combine Sentences

Remember

Adjective clauses begin with *who, whom, whose, which, that, when* or *where.*

▶ **EXAMPLE**

You can use adjective clauses to combine sentences. Always put the adjective clause after the word it describes.

The following sentences can be combined with adjective clauses. The adjective clauses are in blue type.

Harry saw the play. The play was performed on Wednesday.
Harry saw the play that was performed on Wednesday.

The woman left suddenly. Jenny had questioned the woman.
The woman whom Jenny had questioned left suddenly.

My friend will arrive today. My friend lives in Florida.
My friend, who lives in Florida, will arrive today.

Practice

Combine each pair of sentences. Use an adjective clause. Draw a line under the adjective clause. Remember to use commas as needed. The first one is done for you.

1. The players listened to the coach.
   The coach always gave good advice.

   The players listened to the coach, <u>who always gave good advice</u>.

2. A creature lives in the Northwest.
   This creature's name is Bigfoot.

3. Many people have found footprints.
   The footprints supposedly belong to Bigfoot.

4. Toni read the book.
   The book came from the library.

5. The building is being remodeled.
The building is where I work.

6. The two teams played a game.
The game lasted for three hours.

7. Tamara and Mike will take a plane.
The plane leaves at six o'clock.

8. The plane finally took off.
The plane had been at the gate for an hour.

9. My uncle showed us the city.
My uncle has lived in Chicago for 10 years.

10. Molly spent the afternoon at a park.
The park has a beautiful lake.

11. Tomás was playing a violin.
The violin was out of tune.

12. Last year, there was a storm.
The storm dumped a foot of snow on the city.

13. This soap opera has a talented actor.
The actor plays two different roles.

14. The man was on vacation.
I called the man.

15. Rita borrowed the lawn mower.
Chris had rebuilt the lawn mower.

16. CHALLENGE There is a singer.
The singer has a favorite motto.
She uses the motto in every song.

ENGLISH IN YOUR LIFE
Giving Directions

Lauren Jackson is giving a birthday party at a restaurant for her best friend. She included directions with the invitations. Her directions have to be clear so that guests can easily find their way to the restaurant.

Read Lauren's directions carefully. Then follow the directions below.

> Take Route 19 north to Exit 5. Make a left onto Hamilton Street. Go about 3 miles. You will see the Lakeview Shopping Center, which will be on your right. Turn left onto Josey Lane. When the road splits, bear right. Go straight until you see the restaurant on the right. You may need to park across the street. The restaurant's parking lot fills up quickly.

1. Write the two adverb clauses.

2. Write the adjective clause.

3. Combine the last two sentences. Use a subordinating conjunction.

4. **CRITICAL THINKING** How do adverb and adjective clauses make directions easier to follow?

Writing and Reading

Write directions from your school to your home. Give as many specific details as you can, such as street names and landmarks. Be sure to use adverb and adjective clauses. Switch papers with a partner. Read each other's directions. Give suggestions to make the directions easier to follow.

15·6 Noun Clauses

A **noun clause** is a dependent clause that is used as a noun in a sentence.

Noun clauses can be used in a sentence the same way nouns are used. They often answer the questions *who* or *what*.

A noun clause can begin with one of the words in the box.

how	whatever	which	whomever
that	when	who	whose
what	where	whoever	why

▶ **EXAMPLE**

Whatever you saw is gone now.

David explained how he broke his arm.

This is where I go to school.

Give whoever answers the door this package.

You can work with whomever you choose.

Practice A

Write the noun clause in each sentence. The first one is done for you.

1. I shall never know why we went there.

   why we went there

2. She found out whose house you had visited.

3. I do not understand why he is always late.

4. Tell the waiter what you want to order.

5. Whoever answers correctly will be the winner.

6. I can't imagine where you lost your glasses.

7. Noriko always guesses how a story will end.

8. That is not what I said.

9. Whoever called hung up.

10. Why she likes him is obvious to me.

11. **CHALLENGE** Write the two noun clauses in the following sentence.

What you see is what you get.

Practice B

Write each sentence. Use a noun clause from the box.
The first one is done for you.

12. Ben does not understand _____.

Ben does not understand why his team lost.

13. _____ will win the election.

14. The biggest mystery was _____.

15. No one knows _____.

16. _____ is the correct time.

17. I never found out _____.

18. **CHALLENGE** Write the sentence below. Use a noun clause of your own.
Address the envelope to _____.

> why they left so soon
> Whatever that clock says
> why his team lost
> whose jacket this is
> Whoever receives the most votes
> where she went

15·7　Writing Complex Sentences

Complex sentences contain adverb and adjective clauses. Use the READ, PLAN, WRITE, and CHECK steps to write complex sentences.

▶ **EXAMPLE**

You have inherited $5,000. Write two sentences telling what you would do with the money, and why. Include adverb and adjective clauses in your sentences.

READ　**Do you understand the assignment?**

Write the assignment. Draw a line under the key words.

> You have <u>inherited $5,000</u>. Write <u>two sentences</u> telling <u>what you would do with the money</u>, and <u>why</u>. Include <u>adverb and adjective clauses</u> in your sentences.

PLAN　**Gather your ideas and organize them.**

Use a chart to organize your thoughts. Write what you would do with the money in the first column. Then explain why you would do this in the second column.

What I would do	Why
I would buy a stereo.	I do not have one.
I would save the rest.	I want to buy a car next year.

WRITE　**Put your ideas into sentences.**

Write two sentences using the ideas in your chart.

> I would buy a new stereo because I do not have one. Then I would save the rest of the money because I want to buy a car next year.

CHECK   How can you improve your writing?

Make sure your sentences include adverb and adjective clauses. Add more information to better explain your ideas.

> *I would buy a new stereo that I could keep in my room because I do not have one. Then I would save the rest of the money because I want to buy a car next year.*

The adjective clause in blue type was added. It gives more information about the stereo.

Practice

Complete the writing assignments below. Follow the directions to CHECK your sentences.

1. For one day, you can trade places with anyone. Write two sentences telling who it would be, and why. Use adverb and adjective clauses.

   CHECK
   Add information to make your ideas clearer.
   Make sure your sentences are punctuated correctly.

2. What would you do if you traded places with another person? Write two sentences that explain how you would spend the day. Use adverb and adjective clauses.

   CHECK
   Add information to make your ideas clearer.
   Make sure your sentences are punctuated correctly.

Putting It All Together

Write a paragraph that explains how you would spend the day if you could trade places with anyone for one day. You may want to use the sentences that you have written above. Add other sentences to tell what you would do during the day.

Chapter

15 ▶ Review

adjective clause
adverb clause
complex sentence
dependent clause
noun clause
subordinating conjunction

Vocabulary Review

Complete each sentence with a term from the box.

1. A _____ has a subject and verb but cannot stand alone as a complete sentence.

2. A _____ is a dependent clause that acts as a noun in a sentence.

3. A _____ is a sentence with an independent clause and a dependent clause.

4. A _____ is one or more words that begin a dependent clause.

5. An _____ is a dependent clause that tells more about a noun or a pronoun in a sentence.

6. An _____ is a dependent clause that tells more about a verb, an adjective, or an adverb in a sentence.

Chapter Quiz

Using Adverb Clauses in Complex Sentences

Combine each pair of sentences. Use an adverb clause. Draw a line under each subordinating conjunction. Use commas as needed.

1. Sarah did come not back to camp. The sun went down.

2. The trail was dark. She remembered the way back.

3. Sarah had her flashlight. She was not afraid.

4. The others were glad to see her. She finally returned.

5. They had been worried. It was getting late.

6. Sarah agreed to take a buddy. She left camp.

LESSONS 15·1 to 15·3

Test Tip
If a dependent clause comes before an independent clause, it is followed by a comma.

LESSONS 15·4 and 15·5

Test Tip
Words such as *whose, which, when,* and *that* begin adjective clauses.

Using Adjective Clauses in Complex Sentences

Combine each pair of sentences. Use an adjective clause. Draw a line under the adjective clause. Use commas as needed.

7. I wanted the computer. The computer had extra speakers.

8. The salesperson helped me. She told me it was a good buy.

9. My new computer has a great sound! The computer was a real bargain.

10. I bought the computer. The computer was on sale.

LESSON 15·6

Identifying Noun Clauses

Write the noun clause in each sentence.

11. I wonder when the show started.

12. She told me where her office was.

13. What Helen said is the truth.

14. I wish that I had not forgotten my lunch.

LESSON 15·7

Writing Tip
Use a chart to PLAN what you will write. CHECK that your sentences answer the assignment.

Writing Complex Sentences

15. Write a paragraph about a movie you have seen. Tell what the movie was about. Explain whether you liked it. Be sure to include adverb and adjective clauses in your paragraph.

Group Activity

Work with a group to list five rules for using school computers. Write complete sentences. Use adverb and adjective clauses in your sentences. Exchange lists with another group. Check each other's work. Suggest how the group might correct any errors in its list.

Unit 7 **Review**

Read the passage to answer questions 1–4. Choose the word or words that belong in each space. Mark the letter for your answer.

The way we communicate has changed over the years. Faxes and e-mail __(1)__ us to send messages faster than ever before. __(2)__ these ways can save time and money, they limit the meetings __(3)__ keep us connected with others. We must always remember __(4)__ to spend time with others.

1. A. is allowing
   B. allowing
   C. allows
   D. allow

2. A. As if
   B. Whether
   C. While
   D. Before

3. A. who
   B. whom
   C. that
   D. whose

4. A. how important
   B. how important it is
   C. how importantly
   D. how importantly it is

Read the passage to answer questions 5–6. Choose the best way to write the passage. Mark the letter for your answer.

Your attitude can affect your life. (5) A bad outlook can lead to sadness, but a good one can make life happy. (6) Although a good outlook may take time; it is worth it.

5. A. A bad outlook can lead to sadness and a good one can make life happy.
   B. A bad outlook can lead to sadness but a good outlook can make life happy.
   C. A bad outlook can lead to sadness unless a good outlook can make life happy.
   D. No error

6. A. Although a good outlook may take time, but it is worth it.
   B. Although a good outlook may take time, it is worth it.
   C. Although a good outlook may take time. It is worth it.
   D. No error

Critical Thinking
Provide three reasons why getting good grades is important.
WRITING Write a paragraph to convince a classmate that getting good grades is important. Include three reasons. Be sure to use compound and complex sentences.

336

Braille writing machines help the blind to read sentences and paragraphs. These machines use symbols that can be felt with the fingertips. The symbols stand for letters and numbers.

The The   last   game

of the season   was

an   exciting   one.

The box above shows the first sentence of a sports article written in Braille. Read the complete article on the right, and answer the questions.

1. What is the article about?

2. Which sentence best states what the article is about?

Wildcats Win Series

The last game of the season was an exciting one. The Wildcats and the Pirates were tied until the last quarter. Both centers fouled out of the game. In the final six seconds, Wildcats' guard Darren Simon made a shot from half court to win the game!

337

In a speech, a speaker must group related ideas together to organize thoughts. In writing, people use paragraphs to organize information. A paragraph is a group of sentences about the same idea. Name some places where you have seen sentences grouped into paragraphs.

Chapter 16

Parts of the Paragraph

Words to Know

paragraph	three or more sentences that are placed together and relate to the same idea
topic sentence	a sentence that states the main idea of a paragraph
body	the main part of the paragraph. It includes sentences that relate to the main idea.
supporting detail	a sentence that gives more information about the topic sentence
concluding sentence	a sentence that restates the main idea of a paragraph
transitional word	a word that connects one idea or sentence to another

Paragraph Puzzle Project

Write a paragraph that includes a topic sentence, three supporting details, and a concluding sentence. Use transitional words in your paragraph. Copy each sentence in your paragraph onto a separate strip of paper. Mix up the strips. Exchange puzzles with a partner. Arrange the strips of paper so that the sentences form a logical paragraph.

Learning Objectives

- Identify the main idea of a paragraph.
- Identify topic sentences.
- Identify supporting details.
- Identify concluding sentences.
- Identify and use transitional words.
- Write paragraphs.
- Apply knowledge of paragraphs to an e-mail message and a newspaper article.

16·1 ▶ What Is a Paragraph?

Remember A sentence expresses a complete thought. It has a subject and a predicate.

A **paragraph** is a group of sentences that are placed together and relate to the same topic or idea. This topic is called the main idea. It tells what the paragraph is about. All of the sentences in a paragraph must relate to the main idea.

The first line of a paragraph often is indented. It is moved over from the left margin a few spaces to the right. Some paragraphs are not indented. They are separated by blank white spaces.

Read the following paragraph. All of the sentences tell about the highest wind speed ever recorded.

▶ **EXAMPLE**

> The highest wind speed ever recorded was on Mt. Washington in New Hampshire. In 1934, a wind gust of 231 miles per hour (mph) was recorded. This record almost fell in 1997. A wind gust of 236 mph was reported in Guam. However, experts found that the speed was not measured properly. Mt. Washington's record still stands.

Practice A

Read each paragraph. Write the main idea of the paragraph. The first one is done for you.

1. Snowboarding has become a popular sport. It is really popular among young people. Many ski areas have slopes just for snowboarders.

    Snowboarding is a popular sport.

2. No one knows what happened to Amelia Earhart. In 1929, she became the first woman to fly alone across the Atlantic Ocean. In 1937, she took off to fly around the world. Her plane disappeared somewhere over the Pacific Ocean. She was never found.

3. Automated teller machines (ATMs) have changed the way people bank. The first ATM was made in 1978. Before that, people had to cash a check at a store or a bank. ATMs have made it easier for people to get cash.

4. Most earthquakes do not do a lot of damage. About 450 earthquakes each year are too weak to cause any damage. Almost 35 earthquakes a year cause only minor damage. Only about 15 earthquakes each year cause damage to houses, buildings, and roads.

Practice B

Read each group of sentences. Write the sentence that does not belong in the paragraph with the other sentences. The first one is done for you.

5. Camels are able to go without water for a long time.
Camels are capable of drinking large amounts of water.
Desert travelers also use horses.
Camels do not lose any of the water that they drink because they do not sweat.

   Desert travelers also use horses.

6. There are many kinds of berries.
Blueberries, strawberries, and raspberries are the most common.
Oddly, lemons and oranges also are berries.
Orange juice is often served at breakfast.

7. Many people today can work at home.
Computers come in all shapes and sizes.
Computers and fax machines allow people to work at home.
Conference phone calls let you have meetings without being at the office.

(Practice B continues on next page.) ⇨

8. Many people are more afraid of sharks than of lightning.
   They should be more afraid of lightning.
   In a 30-year period, over 3,000 Americans were killed
   by lightning.
   There are 350 different kinds of sharks.
   In the same time period, only 12 Americans were killed
   by sharks.

9. The first bungee jumpers lived hundreds of years ago.
   Long ago, people on a faraway island jumped from
   wooden towers each spring.
   The jumpers tied vines to their ankles to keep them from
   hitting the ground.
   Skydiving also can be a dangerous sport.

10. Some birthstones have special meanings.
    The aquamarine is said to give its wearer courage.
    Jewelry makes a nice birthday gift.
    Some people believe that pearls give wealth or health.

Everyday English

Shana works at a hospital. She writes the monthly newsletter. She wrote a short article about the new parking spaces at the hospital. Read the article, and answer the questions below.

1. What is the main idea of the article?

2. Which sentence does not belong in the article?

3. **CHALLENGE** Write another sentence that supports the main idea of the article.

Monthly Newsletter

As of November 3, Northeast Hospital will have ten new parking spaces. The new parking spaces will be on the east side of the building. Part of the new west wing will be built next month. Only employees of the hospital may use these new spaces.

The **topic sentence** lets the reader know what the paragraph will be about. The main idea of a paragraph is usually stated in the topic sentence. All other sentences in the paragraph should support the topic sentence.

Often, the topic sentence is the first sentence of a paragraph.

EXAMPLE 1

Notice the topic sentence in blue type.

> Mushrooms can be dangerous. People often get poisoned when they pick and eat mushrooms. They think these mushrooms are harmless. The "death cap" mushroom is one of the deadliest. It is found in the woods in the United States. People should be careful when they pick mushrooms.

The topic sentence sometimes sounds better in the middle or at the end of a paragraph.

EXAMPLE 2

Notice where the topic sentence appears in each paragraph below.

> Termites eat wood and paper. They tunnel their way through the woodwork in houses. They snack on books and furniture. Termites are very destructive insects. Some figures show that termites cause as much damage to houses as fires.

> The soldiers had already fought four battles that week. They were tired. They were cold. Many were wounded. A good meal and warm bed were things they could only dream of. Winning this war was going to take a lot more than courage.

Practice A

Write the topic sentence of each paragraph. Remember that the topic sentence does not always come at the beginning of the paragraph. The first one is done for you.

1. Horseshoe crabs may become extinct after 360 million years. Studies show that these animals lived even before the first dinosaurs. Today, they are dying because of the buildings and pollution on beaches. It is hoped that new laws will protect these animals.

   Horseshoe crabs may become extinct after 360 million years.

2. The space mission Neurolab studied nervous systems in outer space. Two thousand mice, crickets, fish, snails, and rats were studied. The seven crew members were also studied. The results may help find ways to treat sleeping problems.

3. All cars and trucks require regular maintenance. You should check the oil level often to make sure it is not too low. It is also important to check the air pressure in your tires frequently. You should make sure that your automobile has enough brake fluid.

4. An average person has about 20 square feet of skin. It weighs an average of 5.6 pounds. The skin is the largest and heaviest human organ. Many people may not even know that the skin is a human organ.

5. E-mail allows you to send and receive messages in only minutes. Postal mail can take days or even weeks to deliver a message. You also can send separate files through e-mail. E-mail is better than postal mail in several ways.

Practice B

Write a topic sentence that connects all of the sentences in each paragraph. The first one is done for you.

6. It used to be unusual to live to be 90. Better diet and medicine have made 90 a more common age. Today, some people even live to be well over 100.

People are living longer than ever.

7. If you can sit down, you can go snow tubing. There are no special skills needed. Just grab the handles and hold on. Also, there is little equipment needed. All you need is a snow tube and warm clothing.

8. Slow music can make you feel sad. Upbeat music can make you feel happy. If you walk while listening to music, a song with a faster beat can make you walk faster. A slow song can make you walk more slowly.

9. Libraries have many books on different topics. There are magazines and newspapers for people to read. Most libraries have computers that you can use. They also have videos, CDs, and tapes that you can check out.

Everyday English

Mike writes for his school paper. He has written about the school's new dress code. Read what Mike has written so far. Then follow the directions below.

1. Write a topic sentence for the paragraph.

2. **CHALLENGE** A title tells the main idea of an article. Write a title for Mike's article.

Next year, students will not be able to wear skirts that do not have sleeves. Also, their shirts must be tucked in at all times. Finally, students cannot wear shorts that are more than four inches above the knee. These changes in the dress code will go into effect at the beginning of the next school year.

16-3 ► Supporting Details

In addition to a topic sentence, all paragraphs must have a **body**. The body is the main part of the paragraph. It includes sentences that relate to the main idea.

The sentences in the body are called **supporting details**. They give more information about the topic sentence.

► **EXAMPLE 1**

Look at the paragraph below. The supporting details are in black type.

> This was a life-and-death situation. Martin was pinned inside his car on Route 41. He was hurt badly. Because it was rush hour, rescue workers had trouble getting through the traffic. The police officers finally arrived. They worked to free him from his crushed car.

The supporting details tell more about the topic sentence. They often answer the questions *who, what, where, when,* or *why.*

► **EXAMPLE 2**

Who was in this situation? Martin

What happened? Martin was pinned inside his car.

Where did it happen? on Route 41

When did it happen? during rush hour

Why was this a life-and-death situation? He was hurt badly.

Practice A

Write each paragraph. Draw a line under each supporting detail. The first one is done for you.

1. It is an advantage for basketball players to be tall. They can easily throw the ball into the hoop. They can catch a ball over the other players' heads.

It is an advantage for basketball players to be tall.
They can easily throw the ball into the hoop. They can
catch a ball over the other players' heads.

2. One kind of South American spider is so big that it eats animals. It eats birds. It also gets big enough to eat lizards. This type of spider can grow so big that one of them could fill a dinner plate.

3. Jupiter is an interesting planet. It has a giant red spot. This red spot is actually a storm. The storm is three times the size of Earth.

Practice B

Read each paragraph. Find the topic sentence. Then write the sentence that does not support the topic sentence. The first one is done for you.

4. The largest pearl in the world weighs 14 pounds. It was found inside a giant clam. The clam was living in the waters off the Philippines. Diamonds are found in mines.

    Diamonds are found in mines.

5. In 1867, the United States bought Alaska from Russia for about $7 million. Many Americans thought it was a foolish purchase. They thought Alaska was a wasteland of ice and snow. However, Alaska is rich in oil, fish, and lumber. Hawaii became a state after Alaska. The purchase of Alaska was a true bargain.

6. Many people confuse alligators with crocodiles. Alligators have a wider, shorter mouth. The mouth of a crocodile is long and narrow. Both animals are reptiles. Snakes are also reptiles. Both animals live in water.

7. **CHALLENGE** Write two supporting details for the following topic sentence: My best friend has two special qualities.

Many paragraphs end with a **concluding sentence**. It tells the reader that the paragraph is ending. The concluding sentence usually does not add new information. It restates the main idea of the paragraph.

▶ **EXAMPLE 1**

Notice the concluding sentence in blue type.

> Shoes take a real beating. Most people take about 9,000 steps each day. In a lifetime, most of us walk more than three times around the Earth. It is no wonder our shoes usually wear out quickly.

The concluding sentence also can summarize the information in a paragraph.

▶ **EXAMPLE 2**

Notice the concluding sentence in blue type.

> Owning a dog is a lot of work. Dogs need to be fed once or twice a day. They also need exercise every day. They should be taken for a walk, or they should be allowed to play outside. They need lots of love and attention. By giving your dog food, exercise, and love, you'll gain a friend for life.

Practice A

Write the concluding sentence for each paragraph. The first one is done for you.

1.   Right and left shoes were not made until the 1800s. For hundreds of years, both shoes in a pair were exactly the same. You could not put the wrong shoe on the wrong foot. Right and left shoes are a fairly new invention.

    Right and left shoes are a fairly new invention.

2. Being prepared for a job interview can help you get a good job. Before the interview, try to learn more about the company. Have several questions in mind to ask during the interview. Think about why you would be a good employee. Finally, make sure you look neat and well-groomed. Preparation for a job interview is very important.

3. Did you know that the potato chip was invented by a Native American chef in 1853? George Crum made French fries for a guest who thought they were too thick. So Crum cut them into very thin slices. These paper-thin potato slices became known as the potato chip. Potato chips have been around for more than 145 years!

Practice B

Each paragraph below is missing a concluding sentence. Write a concluding sentence for each paragraph. The first one is done for you.

4. Advances in medicine have lowered the number of deaths from the flu. Between 1918 and 1919, the flu killed 20 million people. In 1957 and in 1968, the flu hit again. Fewer people died in these years because of better medicine.

   Thanks to new medicine, fewer people now die from the flu.

5. Playing in a marching band takes concentration. You must make sure you are playing the music correctly. At the same time, you must keep marching.

6. The Sahara Desert is the largest desert in the world. It covers the whole width of northern Africa from the Atlantic Ocean to the Red Sea. It stretches over 3 million square miles.

Transitional Words

Many paragraphs use **transitional words** to connect one idea or sentence to another. Transitional words help the sentences flow more smoothly. These words also help organize the paragraph.

A transitional word that comes at the beginning of a sentence is followed by a comma. However, the word *then* is never followed by a comma.

▶ **EXAMPLE**

First, we have to go to the hardware store.

Then we need to fix the shutters.

Next, we must put on the new door.

Finally, we will paint the house.

Some transitional words tell about time. They organize details from beginning to end or first to last.

Transitional Words That Tell About Time			
after	before	later	second
also	finally	next	soon
at last	first	now	then

Other transitional words show how ideas relate to each other. They link sentences together.

Transitional Words That Show Relationship		
although	for this reason	in fact
as a result	however	indeed
even so	in addition	nevertheless
for example	therefore	on the other hand

Practice A

Write the transitional words in each paragraph. The first one is done for you.

1. Everything was still before the storm. Then the clouds rolled in. We saw great flashes of lightning. Next, the rain began to pour. We stayed inside the barn. We knew that we were safe there.

    Then, Next

2. We have a lot to do before our friends come over tomorrow to watch the big game. First, we need to buy chips and dips. Next, we need to bring in our extra chairs from the garage. Then we need to clean the house. We had better get busy!

3. Kevin was not having a good morning. First, his alarm clock did not go off. As a result, he slept too late. Then he couldn't find one of his shoes. He finally found it under his bed. He also forgot to pack his lunch. Kevin hoped that the rest of his day would be better.

Practice B

The following paragraphs do not have any transitional words. Write each paragraph. Add transitional words of your own.

4. During our vacation to the Grand Canyon, we did many fun things. _____, we rode down the canyon on horseback. _____ we camped out in a tent at the bottom of the canyon. We _____ went white-water rafting down the river. It was a very exciting vacation.

5. Great advances have been made in the space program over the last few decades. _____, telescopes and satellites have explored our whole solar system. _____, space stations now allow people to stay in space for months at a time. _____, people may live on other planets or permanently in space stations.

Writing Paragraphs

A good paragraph has a topic sentence, supporting details, and a concluding sentence. It also should contain transitional words. You can use the READ, PLAN, WRITE, and CHECK steps to write paragraphs.

▶ **EXAMPLE**

Your school district wants to start and end the school day 30 minutes earlier. Write a paragraph that explains if you think this is a good or bad idea. Use all three parts of a paragraph and transitional words.

READ   **Do you understand the assignment?**

Summarize the assignment.

> *Write a paragraph that explains if you like the idea of beginning the school day 30 minutes earlier.*

PLAN   **Gather your ideas and organize them.**

Use an outline to organize your ideas.

> *I. I think it is a good idea to start and end the school day earlier.*
>   *A. I get to school early anyway.*
>   *B. I would have more time to do my homework.*
>   *C. I would not have to rush to my job after school.*

WRITE   **Put your ideas into a paragraph.**

Use your outline to write a paragraph.

> *I think it is a good idea to start the school day earlier. I get to school early anyway. I would have more time to do my homework. I would not have to rush to my job after school.*

CHECK   How can you improve your writing?

Make sure the paragraph answers the assignment.
Use transitional words to make your ideas flow.

> *I think it is a good idea to start the
> school day earlier.* First, *I get to school early
> anyway.* Second, *I would have more time to do my
> homework. I* also *would not have to rush to my
> job after school.* <u>For these reasons, changing
> the school day would make my life easier.</u>

The transitional words in blue type were added. They
connect the ideas in the paragraph. A concluding
sentence was also added. It is underlined.

Practice

Create an outline on the good and bad things about being
a teenager. Write your ideas in complete sentences. Use the
questions below to PLAN what you will write.

PLAN
What do you like about being a teenager?
List two good things about being a teenager.
What do you not like about being a teenager?
List two bad things about being a teenager.

Putting It All Together

Write a well-developed paragraph that explains the good and
bad things about being a teenager. Use the outline that you
have created above. Include a topic sentence, supporting details,
and a concluding sentence. Add transitional words to connect
your ideas.

USING REFERENCES
Newspapers

Newspapers contain information about current events. They are written daily to cover the latest news.

A newspaper contains articles with headlines. A headline usually tells the main idea of the article. The article contains paragraphs that explain the headline.

Each paragraph contains a topic sentence and supporting details. Some end with a concluding sentence.

The supporting details answer the questions *who, what, where, when,* and *why.* Try to answer these five questions as you read a newspaper article. They will help you understand the information.

Read the newspaper article. Then answer the questions below.

Town To Get New Water Supply

Soon, residents of Smithtown will be drinking safe water again. Unsafe levels of lead were found in Smithtown's water supply. High levels of lead may cause health problems. As a result, the water company is working to get water from Pensook River. The river water is much safer. The switch should be finished next month. Meanwhile, residents should drink bottled water.

1. What is the topic sentence?

2. Which supporting detail answers the question *why*?

3. What transitional words does the article contain?

4. **CHALLENGE** Why do you think newspapers include headlines?

COMMUNICATING ON THE JOB
Computer Technician

Judy Woo is a computer technician in Boston. She services computers for people and companies. Judy must use clear paragraphs in her writing. This helps her customers follow her directions.

Judy wrote the following e-mail message to a customer. The customer had a problem with the hard drive of his computer.

Read Judy's e-mail. Then answer the questions below.

Judy Woo works at her computer.

Subject: Help for your computer problems
Date: Mon, 28 Nov 2001 10:24:34
From: J_Woo@work.com
To: J_Chambers@work.com
= =

   You can do several things to fix the problem you are having with your hard drive. First, turn the computer off. Then turn it on again. Next, run the scan disk. This will tell you if there are hard-drive problems. If the problem does not go away, I will have to replace the hard drive. After you try these suggestions for fixing your hard drive, let me know what happened.

1. What is the topic sentence of the paragraph?

2. What is the concluding sentence of the paragraph?

3. **CRITICAL THINKING** Why is it important to write clear paragraphs in business e-mail messages?

Writing and Reading
You are going on vacation to a city that you have never been to before. You send an e-mail asking for information about the city's tourist attractions. Write a paragraph telling what information you would like. Then trade paragraphs with a partner. Read your partner's paragraph. Suggest ways to improve your partner's work.

body
concluding sentence
paragraph
supporting detail
topic sentence
transitional word

Vocabulary Review

Complete each sentence with a term from the box.

1. A _____ is a group of sentences that are placed together and relate to the same idea.

2. A _____ restates the topic sentence.

3. A _____ connects one idea or sentence to another.

4. The _____ states the main idea of a paragraph.

5. A _____ gives more information about the topic sentence.

6. The _____ is the main part of the paragraph.

Chapter Quiz

Read Paragraphs A and B. Then answer questions 1–11.

Paragraph A	Paragraph B
The Empire State Building is an amazing structure. It has 6,400 windows and stands 102 stories tall. Its steel frame makes it very strong. For example, only two floors were damaged when a plane crashed into the building in 1945.	Sending e-mail is an easy way to communicate. First, get on-line. Next, type in the name of the person you are writing to. Then you can enter the e-mail address. Now, write your letter. Finally, click on *Send*. Your e-mail is on its way.

LESSON 16·1

Test Tip
The main idea is what the paragraph is mostly about.

Identifying the Main Idea of a Paragraph

1. What is the main idea of Paragraph A?

2. What is the main idea of Paragraph B?

Identifying Topic Sentences and Supporting Details

3. What is the topic sentence of Paragraph A?

4. What is the topic sentence of Paragraph B?

5. Where do you usually find the topic sentence?

6. Write the three supporting details in Paragraph A.

7. Where do you usually find supporting details?

Identifying Concluding Sentences

8. What is the concluding sentence of Paragraph B?

9. Where do you usually find the concluding sentence?

Identifying Transitional Words

10. What transitional word is used in Paragraph A?

11. What transitional words are used in Paragraph B?

Writing Tip
Use an outline to PLAN your ideas. Include at least two supporting details.

Writing a Paragraph

12. Write a paragraph about the state you live in. Tell what special attractions it has, what the area looks like, and what the climate is like. Include the three parts of a paragraph and transitional words.

Group Activity

Work with your group to create a travel brochure for your state. Include a paragraph about your state's major cities, parks, or other interesting sites. Explain when is the best time to visit your state. Decorate your brochure with drawings.

Unit 8 **Review**

Read the passage to answer
questions 1–4. Mark the letter for
your answer.

Jellyfish are very unique animals.
They come in all different sizes. They
can be as small as a pea or larger than
a person. Other kinds of fish also can
be bigger than a person. Jellyfish can
be orange, pink, blue, or other colors.
A jellyfish body looks like a bell or
umbrella. A jellyfish swims by opening
its body and closing it very quickly.
Jellyfish are not like any other animals.

1. The topic sentence is —
   A. A jellyfish body looks like a bell
      or umbrella.
   B. They come in all different sizes.
   C. Other kinds of fish also can be
      bigger than a person.
   D. Jellyfish are very unique
      animals.

2. Another sentence that could go in
   this paragraph would be —
   A. There are many tiny animals in
      the sea.
   B. The name jellyfish comes
      from its jelly-like feel.
   C. An octopus has arms like
      a jellyfish.
   D. Some fish are poisonous.

3. Which sentence does NOT belong
   in the paragraph?
   A. Other kinds of fish also can be
      bigger than a person.
   B. Jellyfish are not like any other
      animals.
   C. Jellyfish can be orange, pink,
      blue, or other colors.
   D. A jellyfish body looks like a bell
      or umbrella.

4. What is the concluding sentence?
   A. A jellyfish swims by opening
      its body and closing it
      very quickly.
   B. Jellyfish are not like any
      other animals.
   C. Other kinds of fish also can be
      bigger than a person.
   D. Jellyfish can be orange, pink,
      blue, or other colors.

Critical Thinking

Your city council wants to set a
curfew for teenagers. Give two
reasons why you agree or disagree.
WRITING Write a letter to your city
council telling if you are for or
against the curfew. Use at least
two supporting details in the body
to explain your opinion.

WRITING PROCESS HANDBOOK

When writers turn words into a paragraph or an essay, they use a set of steps. These steps make up the writing process. The writing process helps you organize your ideas and form them into paragraphs.

The five main steps in the writing process are prewriting, drafting, revising, editing, and publishing.

PREWRITING   Prewriting is the planning stage. This is where you decide what to write about. You gather and organize all of your ideas about your topic.

DRAFTING   In the drafting step, you put your ideas into sentences. Then you build your sentences into paragraphs. You do not have to worry about mistakes in this step. You will find and fix them later.

REVISING   When you revise, you improve your writing. You look for words and phrases that need to be changed. You may decide to add more information or take some information out. You may choose to arrange your ideas in a different way.

EDITING   When you edit, you find and correct any mistakes in spelling, grammar, punctuation, or usage. Then you write a final draft and correct all of the mistakes.

PUBLISHING   There are several ways to publish, or share, your work. One way is to read it to an audience. When reading your work aloud, it is important to use good speaking skills.

PREWRITING
Understand the Assignment

Before you begin to write, you have to plan what to write about. The planning stage of the writing process is called prewriting. The first planning step is to read and understand the assignment.

READ

Do you understand the assignment?
Read the assignment below. Decide exactly what it asks you to do. Underline the key words.

Write a paragraph about your favorite type of music. Explain why you chose this type of music. Provide at least three supporting details for your choice. Present your paragraph to the class.

IDENTIFY

What is the purpose of this writing assignment?
You can write to inform, entertain, persuade, describe, or compare. Look at the assignment again. Write the purpose of this assignment.

The purpose of this assignment is to explain.

Writing Process Activity

READ the assignment below. Copy the assignment, and underline the key words. Then IDENTIFY the purpose.

Write a paragraph about your favorite kind of movie. Choose from the following: action, thrillers, comedies, science fiction, or romances. Explain why you chose this kind of movie. Provide at least three supporting details for your choice. Present your paragraph to the class.

PREWRITING
Choose a Topic

The next step in the prewriting stage is to choose a topic.

BRAINSTORM **List all of your ideas for possible topics to write about.**
When you brainstorm, you think of everything you can about a topic. Do not judge or limit your ideas. Do not correct errors. Use an idea web to put your ideas on paper.

JUDGE **What topics can you cross off your list?**
Check all of your topics against the writing assignment. Cross off any topics that do not relate to the main idea. Cross off any topics that do not interest you.

CHOOSE **Which topic interests you the most?**
Look at the remaining circles in your idea web. Choose the one that interests you the most. Place a star on that circle. This idea is your topic.

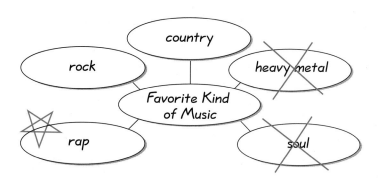

Writing Process Activity

BRAINSTORM ideas for your favorite kind of movie. Then JUDGE your ideas and cross off ones that you do not like. CHOOSE one type of movie to write about.

PREWRITING
Focus the Topic

Check that your topic will work with the assignment. Decide what you want to say about your topic.

CHECK   **Does your topic fit the assignment?**
Can you write about your topic in one paragraph? Is your topic too broad for one paragraph?

FOCUS   **What will be the main idea of your paragraph?**
Make an idea web with the topic you chose in the center circle. Brainstorm ideas that you could write about your topic. Check to be sure each idea relates to the writing assignment.

Your idea web may have many ideas in it. Cross out ones you do not like. Put a star next to your favorite idea. This is the main idea, or the focus, of your paragraph.

Writing Process Activity

CHECK that your topic will work with the writing assignment. Use an idea web to help you FOCUS on the main idea of your paragraph.

PREWRITING
Gather Supporting Details

You need facts to support your main idea. Gather supporting details that can be included in your writing.

PLAN **What will you say about your main idea?**
The assignment tells you to give at least three examples to support your main idea. These examples will be the supporting details.

LIST **What details will you gather?**
Make a list. At the top of the paper, write the topic. Look at your idea web from the previous step. Include the main idea in your list. Then write other ideas that support the topic and the main idea.

You can gather details in several ways, depending on the assignment. You may have to research a topic in the library or on the Internet to find supporting details. For this assignment, you can brainstorm ideas of your own.

> TOPIC: Rap is my favorite kind of music.
>
> MAIN IDEA: I like the sound of it and the messages in the songs.
>
> SUPPORTING DETAILS:
>
> The lyrics tell about real-life situations.
>
> It has a good beat that I can dance to.
>
> The ideas in the songs make me think.

Writing Process Activity

PLAN what you will say about your topic. LIST the details for your paragraph on your favorite kind of movie.

PREWRITING
Organize Details in an Outline

The next step in the prewriting process is to organize your details.

ORGANIZE

How can I organize my ideas?
Create an outline to organize your ideas. An outline shows how your ideas relate to each other.

OUTLINE

What does an outline look like?
Look at the outline on this page. Notice how the information is labeled. The topic comes first and has a Roman numeral. The main idea gets a capital letter. Then each supporting detail is numbered under the main idea.

As you work on longer writing assignments, you add more sections to the outline.

I. Rap is my favorite kind of music.

   A. I like the sound of it and the messages in the songs.

      1. The lyrics tell about real-life situations.

      2. It has a good beat that I can dance to.

      3. The ideas in the songs make me think.

Writing Process Activity
ORGANIZE your ideas about your favorite kind of movie. Use your list of ideas to create an OUTLINE.

DRAFTING
Write the Topic Sentence

You have completed the prewriting process. You are ready to begin drafting. First, you will write a draft of your paragraph. You will revise this draft later. For now, concentrate on getting your ideas into a paragraph.

REVIEW   **What is a topic sentence?**

Most paragraphs begin with a topic sentence. The topic sentence usually contains the main idea. All other sentences in the paragraph should relate to the topic sentence.

DRAFT   **How can I create a topic sentence?**

Look at your list. You have your topic and your main idea. Combine these two ideas to draft a topic sentence.

TOPIC: *Rap is my favorite kind of music.*

MAIN IDEA: *I like the sound of it and the messages in the songs.*

TOPIC SENTENCE: *Rap is my favorite kind of music because I like the sound of it and the messages in the songs.*

Writing Process Activity

REVIEW the definition of a topic sentence. Refer to your outline about your favorite kind of movie. Combine your topic and main idea to DRAFT a topic sentence.

DRAFTING
Write the Body

To start your paragraph, write your topic sentence at the top of your paper. Remember to indent the first line. Now you are ready to draft the body of your paragraph.

REVIEW

What is the body of a paragraph?
The sentences in the body of a paragraph contain supporting details. All of the supporting details should relate to the topic sentence.

DRAFT

How will I draft the details for my paragraph?
Look at your outline. The sentences next to the numbers are supporting details. Write these details after your topic sentence.

Compare the paragraph below to the outline on page 364.

Look at the model paragraph to see how it compares to the outline.

> *Rap is my favorite kind of music because I like the sound of it and the messages in the songs. The lyrics tell about real-life situations. It has a good beat that I can dance to. The ideas in the songs make me think.*

Writing Process Activity
REVIEW what you should include in the body of your paragraph about your favorite kind of movie. DRAFT your supporting details after your topic sentence.

DRAFTING
Write a Conclusion

Now it is time to draft a conclusion for your paragraph.

REVIEW   **What is the concluding sentence?**
Most paragraphs end with a concluding sentence. This sentence tells the reader that you are finished writing about this idea.

DECIDE   **How should this paragraph end?**
The concluding sentence can sum up the paragraph. It also can restate the main idea in different words. Think about how you want to end your paragraph.

DRAFT   **End your paragraph with a good conclusion.**
Draft a concluding sentence for your paragraph.

Look at the model concluding sentence. It sums up the information in the paragraph.

 CONCLUDING SENTENCE: I like rap music the best because I can relate to it.

Writing Process Activity

REVIEW what the concluding sentence of a paragraph should do. DECIDE how you want to conclude your paragraph about your favorite kind of movie. DRAFT your concluding sentence.

REVISING
Improve Your Draft

You have a complete draft of your paragraph. Now you are ready to revise it. When you revise, you rewrite your first draft. You work to improve your writing.

REREAD

Does the paragraph answer the assignment?
Reread the entire paragraph. Make sure it addresses all parts of the assignment.

ADD

How can you make the sentences flow better?
Transitional words help the reader move from one idea to the next. Look at the transitional words below.

also	finally	furthermore
next	in addition	therefore
first	for example	on the other hand

REVISE

How can you use transitional words in your revision?
Look at the body of the paragraph. The transitional words appear in blue type.

> Rap is my favorite kind of music because I like the sound of it and the messages in the songs. For example, the lyrics tell about real-life situations. In addition, it has a good beat that I can dance to. The ideas in the songs make me think. I like rap music the best because I can relate to it.

Writing Process Activity

REREAD your paragraph about your favorite kind of movie. ADD transitional words as you REVISE it.

REVISING
Check Your Draft

A checklist can help you as you revise your paragraph.

CHECK

How can you improve your paragraph?
Ask yourself each question in the checklist below.

- ✓ Does my paragraph address all parts of the assignment?
- ✓ Does the topic sentence contain the main idea?
- ✓ How can I organize my supporting details more clearly?
- ✓ What transitional words can I add?
- ✓ How can I make my concluding sentence stronger?

EVALUATE

In what ways is the revision better?
Compare the paragraph below to the draft on page 368. What changes do you notice? In what ways has it been improved?

> Rap is my favorite kind of music because I like the sound of it and the messages in the songs. For example, it has a good beat that my friends and I can dance to. In addition, the lyrics tell about real-life situations. Finally, the ideas in the songs make me think about important issues. I like rap music because I can relate to it better than other types of music.

Writing Process Activity

Use the checklist to improve your paragraph about your favorite kind of movie. EVALUATE your revision.

EDITING
Find and Correct Errors

Now that you have revised your paragraph, you are ready to check it for errors in grammar, spelling, and mechanics. This is called editing. Use the checklist below.

CHECK

Are there errors in your paragraph?
- ✓ Do all the sentences begin with a capital letter?
- ✓ Do all the sentences end with the correct punctuation mark?
- ✓ Do all the sentences have a subject and a predicate?
- ✓ Are commas and coordinating conjunctions used correctly?
- ✓ Are any words missing?
- ✓ Are there any spelling mistakes?

PROOFREAD

How can you mark errors in your paragraph?
Use proofreaders' marks to make your corrections.

∧ Insert letters or words here.

≡ Capitalize this letter.

/ Make this letter lowercase.

_ℓ Delete or replace this.

For example, it has a good B̶eat that my friends and I can dance to. in addition, the lyrics tell about *real-life situations. Finally, the ideas in the songs songs make me think about important issues.*

REVISE

Create a final draft.
Rewrite your paragraph on a clean sheet of paper. Make sure your paragraph is neat and easy to read.

Writing Process Activity

CHECK your paragraph for errors. PROOFREAD it, then REVISE it correctly and neatly.

PUBLISHING
Share Your Work with Others

There are several ways to share your work with others. One way is to give a computer presentation. Another way is to display your work on a bulletin board. One of the most common ways to present your work is to read it to an audience.

The following tips can help you become a better public speaker.

REVIEW

Are you familiar with your material?
Before you speak in public, make sure you are well prepared. Be very familiar with what you have written.

PRACTICE

Have you read the material aloud?
Practice reading your paragraph aloud. The checklist below can help you become a better public speaker.

- ✓ Speak loudly and clearly.
- ✓ Pause after commas and periods.
- ✓ Do not rush. Pace yourself.
- ✓ Stress certain words to add meaning to your sentences.
- ✓ Make eye contact with your audience.
- ✓ Use appropriate facial expressions and gestures.

PRESENT

Are you ready to present your work?
Take deep breaths before you present your work. Relax. When presenting, remember to use the strategies that you practiced.

Writing Process Activity

REVIEW your paragraph, PRACTICE reading it, and PRESENT it to the class. You now have completed your writing assignment on your favorite kind of movie.

Extra Practice Chapter 1

LESSON 1·1 *pages 4–5*
Rewrite each fragment as a sentence.

1. Went to math class.

2. The class right before lunch.

3. Never been hungrier.

4. Until the bell rang.

LESSON 1·2 *pages 6–7*
For each sentence, write what kind of sentence it is. Write
declarative, interrogative, imperative, **or** *exclamatory.*

1. I got the job!

2. Who else applied for it?

3. Find out and let me know.

4. I will start working Monday.

5. Where will you work?

6. Call me tonight.

LESSON 1·3 *pages 8–10*
**Rewrite each sentence. Use capital letters and correct
end punctuation.**

1. did you bring your lunch

2. let me see it, please

3. that was the scariest movie I ever saw

LESSON 1·5 *pages 14–16*
**Rewrite each interrogative sentence as a declarative sentence.
Draw one line under the subject. Draw two lines under the
predicate.**

1. Did you hear the alarm this morning?

2. Will this software run on your computer?

3. Are those jeans on sale?

LESSON 1·7 *pages 18–19*
Write a paragraph about your favorite outdoor activity. Explain why you
enjoy the activity. Be sure each sentence has a subject and a predicate.
Use correct capitalization and punctuation. Use the READ, PLAN, WRITE,
and CHECK steps to help you write your paragraph.

Extra Practice Chapter 2

LESSONS 2·1 to 2·4 *pages 26–35*
Write each sentence. Use a comma where it is needed to make the sentence easier to understand.

1. After studying Shawn called Kyle.

2. Kyle do you want to see a movie?

3. Kyle however doesn't like movies.

4. Your choice for lunch is pizza hamburgers or tacos.

5. Courtney Beth and Hannah made a picnic lunch.

6. The new high school will open on September 3 2005 if we are lucky.

7. It was built to look like a famous school in Albany New York.

8. I will fly to Atlanta Georgia for the next meeting.

9. There were many celebrations on December 31 1999.

LESSON 2·6 *pages 38–41*
Write each sentence. Use quotation marks, commas, periods, question marks, or exclamation points where they are needed.

1. Juan asked What time is it

2. I'll be home soon Matrice said.

3. I left my camera on the bus Cole exclaimed.

4. Will you wait for me she asked.

5. I have decided announced Kathy not to go to the game.

6. Didn't he say The test will be tomorrow

LESSON 2·8 *pages 48–49*
Write a paragraph that describes today's weather where you live. In one sentence, use at least three words to describe the current weather. Then tell the time, date, and location of your observation. Be sure to use commas correctly in your sentences. Use the READ, PLAN, WRITE, and CHECK steps to help you write your paragraph.

Extra Practice Chapter 3

LESSONS 3·1 and 3·2 *pages 56–59*
**Write the nouns in each sentence. Then underline the
compound nouns.**

1. My sister-in-law lives in a small town.

2. Did your uncle go to Los Angeles yet?

3. Did Joanne park the car on Cherry Lane?

4. His German shepherd chased the ball for two blocks.

LESSON 3·3 *pages 60–61*
Write the proper nouns in each sentence.

1. Scientists explored a cave in Virginia.

2. Martin Luther King, Jr., started college at fifteen.

3. Uncle Alex is in charge of the new youth group.

4. Jordan has gym class every Tuesday and Thursday.

LESSON 3·4 *pages 63–66*
**Write each sentence correctly. Capitalize the proper nouns
and the abbreviations of proper nouns.**

1. Please write to mrs. myra sol in brooklyn, new york.

2. Our teacher, mr. hill, suggested that we read *the miracle worker.*

3. Mt. rainier is south of seattle.

4. My mother just saw dr. lee on march 4.

LESSON 3·5 *pages 68–69*
Write a paragraph about your favorite store. What is the name of
the store? Where is it located? Why do you like it? Be sure to
capitalize all the proper nouns. Use the READ, PLAN, WRITE, and
CHECK steps to help you write your paragraph.

Extra Practice Chapter 4

LESSON 4·1 *pages 74–76*
Write the nouns in each sentence. If a noun is singular, write *S* after it. If a noun is plural, write *P* after it.

1. Can Kevin drive your car?

2. Last week we rode bikes to the park.

3. Those papers are on my desk.

4. Sue planted flowers in her garden.

LESSON 4·2 *pages 77–82*
Write the plural form of each singular noun.

1. porch

2. tooth

3. berry

4. scarf

LESSON 4·3 *pages 83–85*
Change the noun in parentheses to its possessive form.

1. My family ate dinner at (Helen) house.

2. Several (students) books were found in the hall.

3. My (brother) phone number was changed.

LESSON 4·4 *pages 87–88*
Write the nouns in each sentence. If the noun is concrete, write *C* after it. If the noun is abstract, write *A* after it.

1. The girl wrote her thoughts in her diary.

2. The witness swore to tell the truth.

3. Fire is a danger to children.

LESSON 4·5 *pages 90–91*
Write a paragraph telling how people can be good citizens. Use different noun forms in your sentences. Use the READ, PLAN, WRITE, and CHECK steps to help you write your paragraph.

Extra Practice Chapter 5

LESSON 5·1 *pages 98–102*
Write the personal pronoun and antecedent in each sentence.

1. Sheila typed the notes and gave them to Pam.

2. As soon as Ken got home, he called Scott.

3. After the car is repaired, Pablo will pick it up.

LESSON 5·2 *pages 103–104*
Write each sentence. Add a reflexive pronoun of your own.

1. They do not plan to keep all the money for _____.

2. I am proud of _____ for finishing my report early.

3. Have you ordered a sandwich for _____?

LESSON 5·3 *pages 105–107*
Write the correct pronoun in each sentence.

1. What happened to (our, ours) tickets?

2. This report looks like (my, mine).

3. She brought (her, hers) umbrella in case it rained.

LESSON 5·4 *pages 108–109*
Write the indefinite pronouns in each sentence.

1. Nobody can do everything well.

2. Few, if any, could have thought this would have happened.

3. I would be grateful for anything anybody could do to help.

LESSON 5·5 *pages 110–111*
Write a paragraph about your family. Who are the members of your family? What does each family member like to do in his or her spare time? What do you do as a family? Include pronouns in your sentences. Use the READ, PLAN, WRITE, and CHECK steps to help you write your paragraph.

Extra Practice Chapter 6

LESSON 6·1 *pages 118–120*
Write each sentence. Add the correct interrogative pronoun.

1. _____ are you making for dinner?

2. For _____ is the last slice of pizza?

3. _____ one of the twins is older?

4. _____ will help me wash the dishes?

5. _____ name is on the envelope?

LESSON 6·2 *pages 121–122*
Write the demonstrative pronoun in each sentence.

1. Both shirts are nice, but this is the one I really want.

2. Please bring that over here.

3. I have read two of those.

4. Are these the shoes you are going to wear?

5. Which of these did Juan choose?

LESSON 6·3 *pages 123–125*
Write each sentence. Add the correct relative pronoun.

1. This homework, _____ seemed hard, is not taking me long to do.

2. It is great having a friend _____ is a good listener.

3. The person _____ name is drawn will be the winner.

4. I saw Celia _____ I met last week.

5. I chose the topic _____ most interested me.

LESSON 6·4 *pages 128–129*
You have the chance to meet anyone who ever lived. Write a
paragraph about the one person you would like to meet and why.
Be sure to include pronouns in your sentences. Use the READ,
PLAN, WRITE, and CHECK steps to help you write your paragraph.

Extra Practice Chapter 7

LESSONS 7·1 to 7·3 *pages 136–143*
Write the verb or verbs in each sentence. Then write whether each is a linking verb or an action verb.

1. Your idea sounds great.

2. The basketball player rebounded and made a goal.

3. The fire engine rushes past traffic.

4. The players looked upset when they heard the news.

5. The security guard checks the building carefully.

LESSON 7·5 *pages 145–150*
Write each sentence. Use the correct form of the verb in parentheses.

1. Either the cats or the dog (scare, scares) the birds away.

2. Some workers (train, trains) on the job.

3. Everyone (want, wants) to win the contest.

4. The United Nations (hope, hopes) for a peaceful resolution.

5. Almost three fourths of Earth (are, is) covered by water.

LESSONS 7·6 and 7·7 *pages 151–156*
Write the past tense verb form in each sentence.

1. He (speak) angrily at the meeting yesterday.

2. Picasso (be) an artist.

3. A local restaurant (donate) the team uniforms that we (wear).

4. The bell (ring), and the students (leave) the classroom.

5. His career (take) off after his first public performance.

LESSON 7·8 *pages 158–159*
Write a paragraph comparing cold weather activities to warm weather activities. Include at least one linking verb, one present tense verb, and one past tense verb. Use the READ, PLAN, WRITE, and CHECK steps to help you write your paragraph.

Extra Practice Chapter 8

LESSONS 8·1 to 8·4 *pages 164–171*
Write the verb phrase in each sentence.

1. That mechanic has repaired our truck.

2. I was watching the basketball team.

3. Did you see the movie?

4. We must decide quickly.

5. The show is not beginning on time.

6. I am making a birthday cake for my dad.

7. Sam could play his guitar.

8. Jonathan should perform his magic act.

LESSON 8·6 *pages 174–175*
Write the verb phrase in each sentence. Then write whether the action takes place in the *present*, *past*, or *future*.

1. Ricardo and Amy will race on Saturday.

2. My brother and I had explored a cave.

3. I will talk to you later.

4. Martie is enjoying that book.

5. Dena had eaten the pie.

LESSON 8·8 *pages 180–181*
Write a paragraph about an event in your life that you would like to do over. Describe what you did in the past and what you might do differently now. Explain why you would like to have another chance to change this event. Use verb phrases in some of your sentences. Use the READ, PLAN, WRITE, and CHECK steps to help you write your paragraph.

Extra Practice Chapter 9

LESSONS 9·2 and 9·3 *pages 190–196*
Write each sentence. Draw one line under the direct object.
Draw two lines under the indirect object.

1. Rikki bought me a present.

2. Jennie showed Betsy the pictures.

3. Harry gave the kitten milk.

4. Ms. Chow handed my sister the prize.

LESSON 9·4 *pages 198–199*
Write each sentence. Draw one line under the direct object.
Draw two lines under the object complement.

1. I find that book interesting.

2. That gift made Jessica happy.

3. Jeremy found the machine useful.

4. Carmen found the box empty in the cupboard.

LESSON 9·5 *pages 200–201*
Write each sentence. Draw one line under each linking verb.
Draw two lines under each predicate nominative.

1. We are students.

2. He will be a good teacher.

3. Mike Thompson is our family doctor.

4. She was my coach last year.

LESSON 9·6 *pages 202–203*
Write a paragraph about what you would like to do this summer.
Tell what your plans are and who will be included in them. Be
sure to use at least one direct object, indirect object, and predicate
nominative in your paragraph. Use the READ, PLAN, WRITE, and
CHECK steps to help you write your paragraph.

Extra Practice Chapter 10

LESSON 10·1 *page 210*
Write the adjectives in each sentence. Each sentence has more than one.

1. Whitney and Nicole bought new red cars.

2. Gina baked banana bread for the breakfast meeting.

3. That clothing store sells great shoes too.

4. You have two phone messages from Mr. Duncan.

LESSON 10·3 *pages 213–214*
Write the adjectives in each sentence. Then write the subject it describes. Do not write the articles.

1. Kevin seems upset and worried.

2. Vermont is cool and beautiful in the autumn.

3. The leaves became dry and yellow.

4. The painting is old and valuable.

LESSON 10·5 *pages 217–220*
Write the correct form of the adjective for each sentence.

1. Today was the (long) day of the year.

2. Sheila found it (easy) to tell the truth than to lie.

3. My new job is (good) than my last one.

4. Boxing is one of the (dangerous) sports.

5. Running one mile is (difficult) than running five miles.

LESSON 10·8 *pages 226–227*
Write a paragraph comparing your two favorite foods. Tell how these foods are the same and how they are different. Be sure to use at least two comparative adjectives in your sentences. Use the READ, PLAN, WRITE, and CHECK steps to help you write your paragraph.

Extra Practice Chapter 11

LESSON 11·2 *pages 234–235*

Write the adverb in each sentence. Beside each adverb, write the adjective it tells more about.

1. Matt was really happy about his new car.

2. The sun is very bright today.

3. Tyler played a fairly good game.

LESSON 11·4 *pages 238–239*

Write each sentence. Use the correct word in parentheses.

1. The horse jumped (quick, quickly) over the gate.

2. You are a (kind, kindly) person to bring me flowers.

3. The students in our class work (good, well) together.

LESSON 11·5 *pages 240–241*

Change each word in parentheses to the correct form of the adverb. You may need to use *more, less, most,* or *least*.

1. I like oranges (good) than apples.

2. Thomas studies (often) than his friend Keri.

3. I sang the (loud) of everybody in the chorus.

LESSON 11·6 *pages 242–243*

Write each sentence correctly. Use one negative word.

1. There is scarcely no one here.

2. Isn't nobody going to the party?

3. Don't neither of you like strawberries?

LESSON 11·8 *pages 248–249*

You have been invited to dinner at your friend's house. Write a paragraph about how you will use good manners. Include specific adverbs. Use the READ, PLAN, WRITE, and CHECK steps to help you write your paragraph.

Extra Practice Chapter 12

LESSON 12·2 *pages 259–260*
Write the prepositional phrases in each sentence. Draw one line under each preposition. Draw two lines under each object of the preposition.

1. Some of my friends were waiting across the street.

2. After the game, we stopped by Pizza Palace.

3. Jaime ate three slices of pizza in fifteen minutes.

4. We drove over the bridge and past the lake.

LESSON 12·3 *pages 262–263*
Write each sentence. Add a personal pronoun of your own.

1. You go ahead. I'll be right behind _____.

2. Have you seen my other shoe? I am looking for _____.

3. It's mom's birthday, so I bought a present for _____.

4. Everyone besides _____ has answered a question.

LESSON 12·4 *pages 265–267*
Write each sentence. Use the correct verb form in parentheses.

1. One of my friends (was, were) in the baseball game.

2. Members of this group (is, are) meeting on Monday night.

3. A backpack with wide straps (makes, make) hiking easier.

4. The road beyond these trees (become, becomes) very narrow.

LESSON 12·6 *pages 270–271*
Write a paragraph giving safe-driving tips. Tell what things drivers can do to keep safe. Be sure to use prepositional phrases in your sentences. Use the READ, PLAN, WRITE, and CHECK steps to help you write your paragraph.

Extra Practice Chapter 13

LESSON 13·2 *pages 278–280*
Write the participial phrase in each sentence.

1. Walking to school, Jenna saw a car accident.

2. Searching for my glasses, I found my missing glove.

3. Bruce, covered with snow, changed the flat tire.

4. The students, waiting for the end of class, did their homework.

LESSON 13·3 *pages 281–283*
Write the gerund phrase in each sentence.

1. Playing basketball in the park is what I'll be doing tomorrow.

2. I do not like cleaning my room.

3. Reading a newspaper every day is a good habit.

4. Many people fear giving speeches.

LESSON 13·4 *pages 285–287*
Write the infinitive phrase in each sentence.

1. I ran to answer the phone.

2. When you answer the phone, it's important to speak clearly.

3. Ask if the caller would like to leave a message.

4. To finish my book report is my goal for today.

LESSON 13·5 *pages 288–289*
Write a paragraph that tells about things you want to achieve. Explain what you would gain or learn by accomplishing one of your goals. Use at least one gerund phrase, participial phrase, and infinitive phrase in your sentences. Use the READ, PLAN, WRITE, and CHECK steps to help you write your paragraph.

Extra Practice Chapter 14

LESSON 14·1 *page 296*
Write whether each sentence has a compound subject, a compound predicate, or both.

1. You might sleep too late and miss your bus.

2. David, Nick, and Chris all want to go to college.

3. Carol and Frank wish they could fly to Detroit and visit their cousins.

LESSON 14·5 *pages 302–303*
Combine each pair of sentences. Use a coordinating conjunction and a comma. Draw a line under each coordinating conjunction.

1. It was a very hot day. The waves were too rough for swimming.

2. Raymond was still asleep when we called. We went to Don's house.

3. The lights aren't working. The phone isn't working either.

LESSON 14·6 *pages 304–305*
Write each run-on sentence correctly. Use a coordinating conjunction and a comma.

1. Will and Molly go bowling often they bought their own bowling shoes.

2. I only read the poem once I know it by heart.

3. I will write the speech you can make all the charts.

LESSON 14·7 *pages 306–307*
You want to enter your school talent show. What two things can you do in the talent show? What are two ways that you can prepare? Write a paragraph that answers these questions. Use at least two compound sentences. Use the READ, PLAN, WRITE, and CHECK steps to help you write your paragraph.

Extra Practice Chapter 15

LESSON 15·2 *pages 316–319*
Write each complex sentence. Draw one line under
each independent clause. Draw two lines under each
dependent clause.

1. Because I studied, I did well on the test.

2. You chop the onions while I beat the eggs.

3. Wait at the corner until your brother gets here.

4. Before I leave my house to pick you up, I'll call you.

LESSON 15·5 *pages 327–328*
Combine each pair of sentences. Use an adjective clause.
Draw a line under the adjective clause. Remember to use
commas as needed.

1. Ricky bought the table. Leroy made the table.

2. Nicolas won the race. Nicolas was the youngest runner.

3. The man is talking to the police. The man's truck was stolen.

LESSON 15·6 *pages 330–331*
Write the noun clause in each sentence.

1. What I told you yesterday is no longer true.

2. I can't remember where I parked the car.

3. Give this book to whomever you wish.

LESSON 15·7 *pages 332–333*
You can invent any type of machine that you want. Write a
paragraph that tells what machine you want to invent and why.
Tell what the machine does, what you would call it, and who
might use it. Be sure to use adverb and adjective clauses in your
sentences. Use the READ, PLAN, WRITE, and CHECK steps to help
you write your paragraph.

Extra Practice Chapter 16

LESSONS 16·2 and 16·3 *pages 343–347*
Write the topic sentence of each paragraph. Then write the sentence that does not support the topic sentence.

1. Habitat for Humanity is a group that builds houses for people who need them. The costs are low because people volunteer to do the work. The homeowners also help build their own houses. There are many organizations that feed the hungry. Many people give their time and money to this cause.

2. Many games and sports we play today came from other countries. For example, chess began in India. Pickup-sticks came from China. Football was invented in the United States. The Dutch brought bowling. The French gave us tennis.

LESSON 16·4 *pages 348–349*
Write a concluding sentence for each paragraph.

1. The Internet is a useful tool. It has information about current events. You can learn about many topics on the Internet. You can buy and sell products on-line. You can also communicate with others around the world.

2. It is important to protect yourself from the sun. To prevent sunburn, you should use sunscreen with at least a 15 SPF. SPF stands for sun protection factor. When you go to the beach, you should wear a hat. It is also a good idea to wear sunglasses to protect your eyes.

LESSON 16·6 *pages 352–353*
Write a paragraph describing your dream house. Tell where it would be located and what it would look like. Be sure to use a topic sentence, supporting details, transitional words, and a concluding sentence. Use the READ, PLAN, WRITE, and CHECK steps to help you write your paragraph.

CHAPTER SUMMARY
Chapter 1: Sentences

LESSON 1·1 **What Is a Sentence** *pages 4–5*

A sentence is a group of words that expresses a complete thought. Every sentence begins with a capital letter and ends with a punctuation mark. Every sentence has a subject and a predicate. The subject tells who or what the sentence is about. The predicate tells what the subject does or is.

José swims every day in the summer.

Subject: José   **Predicate:** swims every day in the summer.

LESSONS 1·2 to 1·3 **Four Kinds of Sentences** *pages 6–10*

There are four types of sentences. A declarative sentence tells what someone or something does or is. An interrogative sentence asks a question. An imperative sentence gives a command or makes a request. An exclamatory sentence shows strong feeling.

Type	Example	End Punctuation
Declarative	José swam in the ocean yesterday.	period
Interrogative	Did you ever swim in the ocean?	question mark
Imperative	Watch out for the jellyfish!	period or exclamation point
Exclamatory	What a beautiful day it is!	exclamation point

LESSONS 1·4 to 1·6 **Subjects and Predicates** *pages 11–17*

In most sentences, the subject comes before the predicate. In many interrogative sentences, part of the predicate comes before the subject. In most imperative sentences, the subject is not written or spoken. It is understood to be *you*.

In each example below, the subject is in blue type.

Declarative: Jeremy sings in the band.

Interrogative: Does he sing well?

Imperative: Call me if you need a drummer. (Subject is You.)

CHAPTER SUMMARY
Chapter 2: **Punctuation**

LESSONS 2·1 to 2·4   Using Commas   *pages 26–35*

A comma shows a short pause between words. The examples
below show how commas are used in sentences.

> Getting dressed, I straightened my tie. (after an introductory phrase)

> Lyle, I think, is going to the party with us. (to set off words that interrupt the
> flow of a sentence)

> Steven, what time are you going? (to set off a person called by name)

> We will bring the soda, cake, and gifts. (between items in a series)

> January 1, 2000, is an important day to celebrate. (one comma between
> the day of the month and the year, and one comma after the year)

> Miami, Florida, is a fun city to visit. (one comma between the city and the
> state or country, and one comma after the state or country)

LESSON 2·5 Punctuating Interjections   *pages 36–37*

An interjection is a word or group of words that expresses
emotion. A comma or an exclamation point follows.

> Yes, I finished my homework.   Hurray! I did great on this test.

LESSON 2·6 Capitalizing and Punctuating   *pages 38–41*
Direct Quotations

A direct quotation tells the exact words a person said. Use
quotation marks at the start and end of a direct quotation.
Capitalize the first word in a quotation. Use commas to set off
the quotation from who is speaking.

> "Lee," said Beth, "we won."   Lee shouted, "That's great!"

LESSON 2·7 Using Colons, Semicolons, and Hyphens   *pages 43–46*

A colon is used to begin a series. A semicolon is used to join
two related sentences. A hyphen is used in the numbers
twenty-one through *ninety-nine* and some compound words.

> I made the following food: rolls, salad, and pie. (colon begins a series)

> The movie was sold out; we went to dinner instead. (semicolon joins related sentences.)

> twenty-nine (hyphen in a compound number)

CHAPTER SUMMARY
Chapter 3: Common and Proper Nouns

LESSONS 3·1 and 3·2 Nouns and Compound Nouns   *pages 56–59*

A noun names a person, place, thing, event, or idea.
A compound noun is a group of words that names a person,
place, thing, event, or idea.

	Person	Place	Thing	Event	Idea
Noun	girl	Florida	book	concert	kindness
Compound Noun	teenager	North Dakota	notebook	dinner dance	right-of-way

LESSON 3·3 Common and Proper Nouns   *pages 60–61*

A common noun is the name of *any* person, place, thing,
event, or idea. A proper noun is the name of a *particular*
person, place, thing, event, or idea.

	Person	Place	Thing	Event	Idea
Common Noun	adult	city	month	parade	culture
Proper Noun	Ed Jones	Boston	May	Labor Day Parade	Hispanic

LESSON 3·4 Capitalizing Proper Nouns   *pages 63–66*

Every important word in a proper noun begins with a capital
letter. Capitalize the names of the parts of the country.
Capitalize each important word in a title.

A shortened form of a noun is an abbreviation. Abbreviations
of proper nouns begin with a capital letter. Most abbreviations
end with a period. In abbreviations of states in the United
States, capitalize both letters and do not place a period at
the end.

Arizona is in the Southwest. (part of the United States)

Our class is reading Pride and Prejudice. (book title)

Tuscon, AZ, is where Mimi lives. (abbreviation of Arizona)

Mr. Garcia is her favorite teacher. (abbreviation of Mister)

CHAPTER SUMMARY
Chapter 4: Noun Forms

LESSON 4·1 Singular, Plural, and Collective Nouns   *pages 74–76*

A singular noun names one person, place, thing, event, or idea. A plural noun names more than one person, place, thing, event, or idea. A collective noun names a group of persons, places, things, or animals that act as one unit.

Singular Noun	Plural Noun	Collective Noun
bicycle	houses	team
computer	lamps	herd
dog	shovels	committee

LESSON 4·2 Spelling Plural Nouns Correctly   *pages 77–82*

To form the plural of nouns that end with *x, s, z, ch,* or *sh,* add –*es* to the end of the word

box (singular)	boxes (plural)
bus (singular)	buses (plural)
buzz (singular)	buzzes (plural)
ranch (singular)	ranches (plural)
wish (singular)	wishes (plural)

To form the plural of nouns that end with a *y*, add -*s* to the end of the word. To make the plural form of nouns that end with a consonant and a *y*, change the *y* to *i* and add -*es*.

play (singular)	plays (plural)
penny (singular)	pennies (plural)

For some singular nouns that end with *f, ff,* or *fe,* form the plural by adding -*s*. For others that end with *f, ff,* or *fe,* change the *f* to *v* and add -*es*. Listen to the sound before the -*s* to see if it is an *f* sound or a *v* sound.

cuff (singular)	cuffs (plural)
wolf (singular)	wolves (plural)
knife (singular)	knives (plural)

(Chapter 4 Summary continues on next page.) ⇨

To form some plurals of nouns that end with a vowel, add -*s*. For the nouns that end with a consonant and an *o*, form the plural by adding -*es*. Some nouns that end with a consonant and *o* refer to music. Make these nouns plural by adding -*s*.

    rodeo (singular)   rodeos (plural)

    hero (singular)   heroes (plural)

    solo (singular)   solos (plural)

Some plural nouns do not end with -*s*. These irregular nouns become plural by changing other letters in the word.

    child (singular)   children (plural)

    man (singular)   men (plural)

Some nouns are the same in the singular and plural forms.

    data (singular)   data (plural)

    sheep (singular)   sheep (plural)

LESSON 4·3 Possessive Nouns
pages 83–85

A possessive noun shows ownership or relationship. To form the possessive of most singular nouns, add an apostrophe and -*s*. To form the possessive of most plural nouns that end with *s*, add an apostrophe. To form the possessive of plural nouns that do not end with *s*, add an apostrophe and -*s*.

    dog (singular)   dog's (singular possessive)

    teachers (plural ending with –s)   teachers' (plural possessive)

    women (plural not ending with –s)   women's (plural possessive)

LESSON 4·4 Concrete and Abstract Nouns
pages 87–88

A concrete noun names something you can see, hear, touch, smell, or taste. An abstract noun names an idea, quality, or feeling.

    soldier (concrete noun)   courage (abstract noun)

    teacher (concrete noun)   knowledge (abstract noun)

    parent (concrete noun)   love (abstract noun)

CHAPTER SUMMARY
Chapter 5: Pronouns and Antecedents

LESSON 5·1 Personal Pronouns and Antecedents   *pages 98–102*

A pronoun takes the place of one or more nouns. A personal pronoun identifies the speaker, the person spoken to, or the person or thing spoken about. An antecedent is a noun or group of nouns that a pronoun refers to or stands for. An antecedent and a pronoun must be the same in number and person.

Jo washed the car and waxed it.

Singular antecedent: car   **Singular pronoun:** it

Ty and Sid said they helped.

Plural antecedent: Ty and Sid   **Plural pronoun:** they

Lynn cooks food she likes.

Feminine antecedent: Lynn   **Feminine pronoun:** she

Al calls when he can.

Masculine antecedent: Al   **Masculine pronoun:** he

LESSON 5·2 Reflexive Pronouns   *pages 103–104*

A reflexive pronoun refers back to a noun or pronoun already named in the sentence. A reflexive pronoun adds new information or gives extra importance to the word it refers to.

Ed did this himself. (new information)

Ed himself did this. (extra importance)

LESSON 5·3 Possessive Pronouns   *pages 105–107*

A possessive pronoun shows ownership or relationship.

This is Monique's desk. (possessive noun)

This is her desk. (possessive pronoun)

LESSON 5·4 Indefinite Pronouns   *pages 108–109*

An indefinite pronoun takes the place of a noun that is not identified in the sentence.

Everybody was quiet.

CHAPTER SUMMARY
Chapter 6: Pronouns That Ask and Point

LESSON 6·1 Interrogative Pronouns   *pages 118–120*

An interrogative pronoun is used to ask a question. *Who, whom, whose, what,* and *which* are interrogative pronouns.

> I wonder who will be at the party. (Who refers to a person that is the subject of the sentence.)

> From whom did you receive that gift? (Whom refers to a person that is not the subject of the sentence.)

> Whose car is parked in my parking spot? (Whose asks about ownership or relationship.)

> Let me know what I need to bring. (What refers to people, places, things, events, and ideas.)

> I don't know which of these I like the best! (Which is used when there is a choice between two or more people, places, things, events, or ideas.)

LESSON 6·2 Demonstrative Pronouns   *pages 121–122*

A demonstrative pronoun points out one or more nouns. *This, that, these,* and *those* are demonstrative pronouns. *This* and *that* refer to singular nouns or pronouns. *These* and *those* refer to plural nouns or pronouns. *This* and *these* refer to nouns or pronouns that are close by. *That* and *those* refer to nouns or pronouns that are farther away.

> I gave you this. (singular, close by)

> That is my gift. (singular, farther away)

> These are my pens. (plural, close by)

> Those are Lu's friends. (plural, farther away)

LESSON 6·3 Relative Pronouns   *pages 124–126*

A relative pronoun connects a noun or pronoun with a group of words that tells more about it. This noun or pronoun is the antecedent of the relative pronoun. *Who, whom, whose, that,* and *which* are relative pronouns. *Who* and *whom* refer to a person or people. *Whose* shows ownership or relationship. *That* and *which* refer to places or things.

> The man who is on the phone is George's brother.

> **Pronoun:** who   **Antecedent:** man

CHAPTER SUMMARY
Chapter 7: Verb Forms

LESSON 7·1 What Is a Verb?   *pages 136–138*

Every sentence must have at least one verb. A verb expresses
an action or a state of being.

> The player catches the ball with a glove. (expresses action)

> He is the shortstop on the team. (expresses a state of being)

LESSONS 7·2 and 7·3 Action and Linking Verbs   *pages 139–143*

An action verb expresses physical or mental action. A linking
verb expresses what is or what seems to be. It links the subject
of a sentence with a word that describes it.

> We tasted the food. (action verb)

> The food tasted hot and spicy. (linking verb)

LESSON 7·4 Present Tense Verb Forms   *page 144*

The present tense shows action or being that is happening
now. The present tense can also show repeated action.

> Seth plays the guitar in a band. (action happening now)

> Seth plays the guitar in a band every Saturday night. (repeated action)

LESSON 7·5 Subject – Verb Agreement   *pages 145–150*

Use singular verbs with singular subjects. Most singular forms
of verbs end with -s. Use plural verbs with plural subjects. The
plural forms of verbs usually do not end with -s.

> Leroy speaks at the meeting. (singular subject, singular verb)

> The students sit in class. (plural subject, plural verb)

LESSONS 7·6 and 7·7 Past Tense Verb Forms   *pages 151–156*

Past tense verb forms show action or being that has already
happened. Many past tense verb forms are made by adding -d
or -ed to the plural verb form. Some verbs form the past tense
in other ways. These are irregular verbs.

> I work hard. (present tense)   I worked hard. (past tense, add -ed)

> I drink milk. (present tense)   I drank milk. (irregular, past tense)

CHAPTER SUMMARY
Chapter 8: Verb Phrases

LESSON 8·1 Verb Phrases with *To Be*   *pages 164–165*

A verb phrase is made up of a main verb and one or more
helping verbs. A verb phrase tells what happens or what is.

Sentence:	Amani is reading.
Verb phrase:	is reading
Helping verb:	is
Main verb:	reading

Am, are, is, was, and *were* are forms of the helping verb
to be. The main verb that follows the helping verb *to be* is
called the present participle. It shows continuing action and
ends with *–ing.*

I am talking with Mark.

She is driving tomorrow.

LESSON 8·2 Verb Phrases with *To Have*   *pages 166–167*

Have, has, and *had* are forms of the helping verb *to have.*
The main verb that follows the helping verb *to have* is called
the past participle. It shows completed action and ends with
-d, -ed, -n, or *-en.*

I have talked with Mark.

She has spoken with Emily.

We had gone to the movies.

LESSON 8·3 Verb Phrases with *To Do*   *pages 168–169*

A form of *to do* can be used as a helping verb in a verb phrase.
It is used in interrogative sentences and with *not.*
It is also used for emphasis. *Do* and *does* are present tense
forms of the verb *to do. Did* is the past tense form.

Do you like movies? (The verb phrase *do like* is used as a question.)

Sharon does not like movies? (The verb phrase *does like* is used with *not.*)

I do like movies. (The verb phrase *do like* is used for emphasis.)

LESSON 8·4 Other Helping Verbs

pages 170–171

The helping verbs *can, could, may, might, must, should*, and *would* are followed by a plural verb form.

He can dance. (The verb phrase is *can dance.*)

Mary might play. (The verb phrase is *might play.*)

Angie should perform. (The verb phrase is *should perform.*)

LESSON 8·5 Verb Phrases and *Not*

pages 172–173

The word *not* usually comes between the words in a verb phrase. It is not part of the verb phrase.

They have not eaten. (The verb phrase is *have eaten.*)

Paula could not finish the entire meal. (The verb phrase is *could finish.*)

LESSON 8·6 Future Tense

pages 174–175

The future tense shows action or being that will take place in the future. To form the future tense, use the helping verb *will* or *shall* and a plural verb form. Use *shall* only if the subject of the sentence is *I* or *we*.

Tomorrow, Louis will apply for a job at the video store. (The future tense verb phrase is *will apply.*)

I shall start training for the race next week. (The future tense verb phrase is *shall start.*)

LESSON 8·7 Active and Passive Voice

pages 177–178

If the subject *does* the action in a sentence, then the verb is in the active voice. If the action is *done to* the subject, then the verb is in the passive voice.

Jo bought a gift. (active voice)

A gift was bought by Jo. (passive voice)

Gina read a story. (active voice)

A story was read by Gina. (passive voice)

CHAPTER SUMMARY
Chapter 9: Verbs and Sentence Patterns

LESSON 9·1 Simple Subjects and Simple Predicates   *pages 186–187*

The simple subject is the main noun or pronoun in the subject of a sentence. The simple predicate is the main verb or verb phrase in the predicate of a sentence.

The large truck moved slowly up the hill.

Subject: The large truck   **Simple subject:** truck

Predicate: moved slowly up the hill   **Simple predicate:** moved

LESSONS 9·2 and 9·3 Direct and Indirect Objects   *pages 190–196*

A direct object is a noun or pronoun that receives the action of a verb. A direct object comes after the verb.

An indirect object is a noun or pronoun that tells *to whom* or *for whom* an action is done. An indirect object never comes after the word *for* or *to*.

Kurt gave his sister a birthday card.

Direct object: card   **Indirect object:** sister

LESSON 9·4 Object Complements   *pages 198–199*

An object complement is a noun or adjective that follows a direct object. An object complement renames or tells more about the direct object.

The class elected Dwayne secretary.

Direct object: Dwayne   **Object complement:** secretary

LESSON 9·5 Predicate Nominatives   *pages 200–201*

A predicate nominative is a noun or pronoun that renames, describes, or identifies the simple subject. The predicate nominative always follows a linking verb or verb phrase.

Ned was the last student to leave.

Simple subject: Ned

Linking verb: was

Predicate nominative: student

CHAPTER SUMMARY
Chapter 10: Adjectives

LESSON 10·1 What Is an Adjective?
page 210

An adjective is a word that describes a noun or pronoun. Adjectives usually tell *what kind*, *which one*, or *how many*.

> I want a used car. (tells what kind)
>
> This car is for sale. (tells which one)
>
> Several cars are for sale. (tells how many)

LESSON 10·2 Articles
pages 211–212

An article comes before the noun it describes. *The, a*, and *an* are articles. *The* refers to a specific noun. It is used with both singular and plural nouns.

> The student opened his locker and took out his books.

A and *an* refer to any one of a group of things. Use *a* and *an* with singular nouns. Use *a* when the word that follows it begins with a consonant. Use *an* when the word that follows it begins with a vowel or sounds as if it begins with a vowel.

> Al eats a bagel for breakfast. (*Bagel* begins with a consonant.)
>
> Ed has an egg and toast. (*Egg* begins with a vowel.)
>
> He eats an hour before he exercises. (*Hour* begins with a vowel sound.)

LESSON 10·3 Predicate Adjectives
pages 213–214

A predicate adjective comes after a form of the verb *to be* or another linking verb. It tells about the subject of the sentence.

> The shirt is red.
>
> The house was dark.

LESSON 10·4 Proper Adjectives
pages 215–216

A proper adjective refers to the name of a particular person, place, thing, event, or idea. Proper adjectives always begin with capital letters.

> I like Greek food.
>
> I bought an African doll.

(Chapter 10 Summary continues on next page.) ⇨

LESSON 10·5 **Comparative Adjectives** *pages 217–220*

Adjectives that compare two items are called comparative adjectives. They often end in –*er*. Adjectives that compare three or more items are called superlative adjectives. They often end in –*est*.

> I am taller than you. (comparative)

> She is the tallest one in the group. (superlative)

Many adjectives have three or more syllables. Use *more* or *less* before these adjectives to compare two items. Use *most* or *least* before these adjectives to compare three or more items. Use *more, most, less,* and *least* before some adjectives that have two syllables.

> This roller coaster is more thrilling than that one. (comparative)

> That book is the least informative of all. (superlative)

The forms of the adjective *good* are *good, better,* and *best.* The forms of the adjective *bad* are *bad, worse,* and *worst.* Use *better* and *worse* to compare two items. Use *best* and *worst* to compare three or more items.

> This CD is better than the other one. (comparative)

> This is the worst movie I have ever seen. (superlative)

LESSON 10·6 **Spelling Adjectives Correctly** *pages 222–223*

Some one-syllable adjectives end with a vowel followed by a consonant. Double the final consonant before you add -*er* or-*est.* Some adjectives end with a consonant followed by a *y.* Change the *y* to *i* before you add -*er* or -*est.*

mad	madder (comparative)	maddest (superlative)
happy	happier (comparative)	happiest (superlative)

LESSON 10·7 **Specific Adjectives** *page 224*

Use specific adjectives to make your writing clearer.

> The hungry athletes ate a large meal. (less specific)

> The famished athletes ate a five-course meal. (more specific)

CHAPTER SUMMARY
Chapter 11: Adverbs

LESSON 11·1 What Is an Adverb? *pages 232–233*

An adverb is a word that tells more about a verb, a verb phrase, an adjective, or another adverb. An adverb tells *how, where, when,* or *how many times* an action takes place.

> Vincent played the guitar loudly. (tells how the guitar was played)
>
> Anika brings her flute everywhere. (tells where the flute is brought)
>
> Kim practiced the piano today. (tells when the piano was practiced)
>
> Luis danced once. (tells how many times Luis danced)

LESSONS 11·2 and 11·3 Adverbs That Describe Adjectives and Other Adverbs *pages 234–237*

Some adverbs tell more about adjectives or other adverbs. These adverbs tell *to what degree.*

> Ted has an extremely powerful voice. (tells more about the adjective *powerful*)
>
> Ted sang very well. (tells more about the adverb *well*)

LESSON 11·4 Knowing When to Use Adjectives and Adverbs *pages 238–239*

Use adjectives to tell more about nouns and pronouns. Use adverbs to tell more about verbs, adjectives, and other adverbs. The word *good* is an adjective. The word *well* is an adverb.

> Don's car is fast. (The adjective *fast* tells more about the noun *car.*)
>
> We drove slowly. (The adverb *slowly* tells more about the verb *drove.*)
>
> Sam has a good job. (The adjective *good* tells more about the noun *job.*)
>
> Bridget paints well. (The adverb *well* tells more about the verb *paints.*)

(Chapter 11 Summary continues on next page.) ⇨

LESSON 11·5 **Using Adverbs to Make Comparisons** *pages 240–241*

To compare two actions, add *-er* to the end of the adverb, or use *more* or *less* before the adverb. To compare more than two actions, add *-est* to the end of the adverb, or use *most* or *least* before the adverb.

> Kelly sews slower than Christine.

> Kelly sews more carefully than Christine.

The forms of the adverb *well* are *well*, *better*, and *best*. Use *better* when comparing two adverbs. Use *best* when comparing more than two adverbs.

> He draws well.

> He draws better than his friend.

> He draws the best of all the students in class.

LESSON 11·6 **Avoiding Double Negatives** *pages 242–243*

A negative is a word or phrase that means "no." Use only one negative word to make a sentence mean "no" or "not."

> Incorrect: Nobody never listens to me.

> Correct: Nobody ever listens to me.

The word *not* can be joined to a verb to form a contraction. A contraction is a shortened form of two or more words. An apostrophe takes the place of the missing letters. When you use a contraction with the word *not,* do not use another negative word in the sentence.

> Incorrect: Terry wouldn't say nothing.

> Correct: Terry wouldn't say anything.

LESSON 11·7 **Specific Adverbs** *pages 245–246*

Use specific adverbs to make your writing clearer.

> Jordan pitched well. (less specific)

> Jordan pitched rapidly and skillfully. (more specific)

CHAPTER SUMMARY
Chapter 12: Prepositions and Prepositional Phrases

LESSONS 12·1 to 12·3 Prepositions and   *pages 256–263*
Prepositional Phrases

A preposition shows how a noun or pronoun is related to another word or group of words in a sentence. A prepositional phrase is a group of words that begins with a preposition and ends with a noun or pronoun. The noun or pronoun at the end of the phrase is called the object of the preposition.

Keisha swam in the pool.

Preposition: in

Prepositional phrase: in the pool

Object of the preposition: pool

LESSON 12·4 Verb Forms After Prepositional Phrases   *pages 265–267*

Sometimes, a prepositional phrase comes between the main noun or pronoun in the subject and the verb of the sentence. The verb must agree with the main noun.

The books on the shelf are old.

Complete subject: The books on the shelf

Main noun: books (plural)

Object of the preposition: shelf (singular)

Verb: are (plural; agrees with main noun)

LESSON 12·5 Using Prepositions Correctly   *pages 268–269*

Use *between* to refer to two people, things, or groups.
Use *among* to refer to more than two people, things, or groups.

Gerald stood between John and Mindy. (refers to two people)

Andrew stood among the students in class. (refers to a group)

Use *beside* when you mean "next to." Use *besides* when you mean "in addition to" or "except."

Jill put the glass beside the newspaper. (means *next to*)

Besides the newspaper, she bought milk and bread.
(means *in addition to*)

CHAPTER SUMMARY
Chapter 13: Other Phrases

LESSON 13·1 Appositives and Appositive Phrases   *pages 276–277*

An appositive is a noun that follows another noun or pronoun and renames it or tells more about it. An appositive phrase is a group of words that includes an appositive.

> My sister Melanie can drive us to work tomorrow. (appositive)

> Chicago, my favorite city, will be our next stop. (appositive phrase)

LESSON 13·2 Participles and Participial Phrases   *pages 278–280*

A participle is a verb form that is used as an adjective. A participial phrase begins with a participle and gives more information about a noun or pronoun.

> The baked muffins smell delicious. (*Baked* is a participle that describes *muffins.*)

> Talking softly, Mia told me the news. (*Talking softly* is a participial phrase that tells more about *Mia.*)

LESSON 13·3 Gerunds and Gerund Phrases   *pages 281–283*

A gerund is a verb that ends in *-ing*. It is always used as a noun. A gerund phrase begins with a gerund. The phrase includes one or more words that add to the meaning of the gerund.

> Swimming is great exercise. (gerund)

> Swimming in very cold water can be dangerous. (gerund phrase)

LESSON 13·4 Infinitives and Infinitive Phrases   *pages 285–286*

An infinitive is made up of the word *to* plus the plural form of a verb. An infinitive phrase begins with an infinitive. Infinitive phrases are used as nouns, adjectives, or adverbs.

> He likes to jog. (used as a noun)

> Taking vitamins is a good way to stay healthy. (used as an adjective)

> Bob wants to work here. (used as an adverb)

CHAPTER SUMMARY
Chapter 14: Simple and Compound Sentences

LESSON 14·1 Simple Sentences *page 296*

A simple sentence expresses a complete thought. A simple sentence can have a compound subject, a compound predicate, or both. A compound subject is two or more subjects that share the same predicate. A compound predicate is two or more predicates that share the same subject. The subjects in the simple sentences below are shown in blue type. The predicates are underlined.

> The dog ran around the park. (one subject and one predicate)

> Jill ate and danced at the party. (one subject and compound predicate)

> Paul and Eli work at the mall. (compound subject and one predicate)

> The students and teachers clapped and cheered for the team. (compound subject and compound predicate)

LESSON 14·2 Coordinating Conjunctions *page 297*

Coordinating conjunctions are used to join words, phrases, or sentences. The words in the chart are coordinating conjunctions.

Coordinating Conjunctions					
and	but	for	nor	or	so

LESSON 14·3 Compound Sentences *pages 298–300*

A clause is a group of words that has a subject and a predicate and forms part of a sentence. A clause that forms a complete sentence is called an independent clause.

A compound sentence is made up of at least two independent clauses. A coordinating conjunction often joins independent clauses, words, and phrases. A compound sentence has at least two subjects and two predicates. The subjects in the compound sentences below are shown in blue type. The predicates are underlined.

> Sue is the president, and Tom is the vice-president. (two subjects and two predicates)

(Chapter 14 Summary continues on next page.) ⇨

LESSON 14·4 Commas in Compound Sentences

page 301

Use a comma before the coordinating conjunction in a compound sentence.

Lisa made the salad, and Eric baked the rolls.

I want to go fishing, but I have to work.

You can go to the movies, or you can go to the mall.

LESSON 14·5 Using Coordinating Conjunctions to Combine Sentences

pages 302–303

You can form compound sentences by combining two simple sentences. Use a coordinating conjunction and a comma to combine the sentences.

We are going skiing. (simple sentence)

You can stay here. (simple sentence)

We are going skiing, but you can stay here. (compound sentence)

LESSON 14·6 Avoiding Run-On Sentences

pages 304–305

A run-on sentence is made up of two or more sentences that are written incorrectly as one sentence. There are three ways to correct a run-on sentence: divide it into two simple sentences, add a comma and a coordinating conjunction, or use a semicolon between the two ideas.

Incorrect: I went home, no one was there. (run-on sentence)

Correct: I went home. No one was there. (two simple sentences)

Correct: I went home, but no one was there. (comma and coordinating conjunction)

Correct: I went home; no one was there. (semicolon)

CHAPTER SUMMARY
Chapter 15: Clauses and Complex Sentences

LESSON 15·1 Subordinating Conjunctions *pages 314–315*

A dependent clause cannot stand alone as a complete sentence. Many dependent clauses begin with a subordinating conjunction. The subordinating conjunction is part of the dependent clause.

> I'll call you when I'm finished studying.
>
> **Dependent clause:** when I'm finished studying
>
> **Subordinating conjunction:** when

LESSONS 15.2 and 15.3 Adverb Clauses *pages 316–321*

A complex sentence is a sentence with an independent clause and a dependent clause. An adverb clause is a dependent clause that tells more about a verb, an adjective, or another adverb. It begins with a subordinating conjunction. An adverb clause answers the questions *how, why, where,* or *when.*

> **Complex sentence:** Vicky went to work after school was over.
>
> **Adverb clause:** after school was over
>
> **Subordinating conjunction:** after

LESSONS 15·4 and 15·5 Adjective Clauses *pages 322–328*

An adjective clause is a dependent clause that tells more about a noun or pronoun. When an adjective clause is not necessary to the meaning of a sentence, it is separated from the rest of the sentence by commas.

> My chili, which won first prize, is very spicy. (The adjective clause is not necessary; it is separated by commas.)
>
> I made the chili that has the peppers in it. (The adjective clause is necessary; there are no commas.)

LESSON 15·6 Noun Clauses *pages 330–331*

A noun clause is a dependent clause that is used as a noun.

> This is where I work during the summer.

CHAPTER SUMMARY
Chapter 16 Parts of the Paragraph

LESSON 16·1 What Is a Paragraph?   *pages 340–342*

A paragraph is a group of sentences that are placed together
and relate to the same topic. This topic is called the main idea.

> Knowing what to do in an emergency can save a life. For example, if
> someone you know has been bitten by a poisonous snake, you must act
> quickly. First, stay calm. Second, tell the victim not to move. The poison
> can move through the body quickly if the victim moves. Finally, call an
> ambulance or take the victim to the hospital. By following these steps,
> you can help someone in an emergency.

Main idea: knowing what to do in emergencies

LESSON 16·2 The Topic Sentence   *pages 343–345*

The main idea of a paragraph is usually stated in the topic
sentence. The topic sentence is usually the first sentence of a
paragraph. It also can be in the middle or end of a paragraph.
The topic sentence is underlined in the paragraph below.

> <u>Knowing what to do in an emergency can save a life.</u> For example, if
> someone you know has been bitten by a poisonous snake, you must act
> quickly. First, stay calm. Second, tell the victim not to move. The poison
> can move through the body quickly if the victim moves. Finally, call an
> ambulance or take the victim to the hospital. By following these steps,
> you can help someone in an emergency.

LESSON 16·3 Supporting Details   *pages 346–347*

The body is the main part of the paragraph. It includes
sentences called supporting details that relate to the main
idea. Supporting details give information about the topic
sentence. The supporting details often answer the questions
who, *what*, *where*, *when*, and *why*. The supporting details are
underlined in the paragraph below.

> Knowing what to do in an emergency can save a life. <u>For example, if
> someone you know has been bitten by a poisonous snake, you must act
> quickly. First, stay calm. Second, tell the victim not to move. The poison
> can move through the body quickly if the victim moves. Finally, call an
> ambulance or take the victim to the hospital.</u> By following these steps,
> you can help someone in an emergency.

LESSON 16·4 The Concluding Sentence   *pages 348–349*

Many paragraphs end with a concluding sentence. The concluding sentence restates the main idea or summarizes the information in a paragraph. It usually does not add new information. The concluding sentence is underlined in the paragraph below.

> Knowing what to do in an emergency can save a life. For example, if someone you know has been bitten by a poisonous snake, you must act quickly. First, stay calm. Second, tell the victim not to move. The poison can move through the body quickly if the victim moves. Finally, call an ambulance or take the victim to the hospital. <u>By following these steps, you can help someone in an emergency.</u>

LESSON 16·5 Transitional Words   *pages 350–351*

Many paragraphs use transitional words to connect one idea or sentence to another. Transitional words help the paragraph flow more smoothly. They also help organize the paragraph. Look at the chart to find some transitional words.

Transitional Words About Time		Transitional Words About Relationships	
after	before	as a result	for example
finally	first	however	therefore
next	second	in fact	nevertheless

The transitional words are in blue type in the paragraph below.

> Knowing what to do in an emergency can save a life. For example, if someone you know has been bitten by a poisonous snake, you must act quickly. First, stay calm. Second, tell the victim not to move. The poison can move through the body quickly if the victim moves. Finally, call an ambulance or take the victim to the hospital. By following these steps, you can help someone in an emergency.

Glossary

abbreviation   a shortened form of a word

abstract noun   a noun that names an idea, quality, or feeling

action verb   a word that expresses physical or mental action

active voice   the verb form that shows the action is done *by* the subject of a sentence

adjective   a word that describes a noun or a pronoun

adjective clause   a dependent clause that tells more about a noun or pronoun

adverb   a word that tells more about a verb, verb phrase, adjective, or another adverb

adverb clause   a dependent clause that tells more about a verb, an adjective, or another adverb

antecedent   the noun or nouns that the pronoun refers to or stands for

apostrophe [']   a punctuation mark used with possessive nouns to show ownership or relationship

appositive   a noun that follows another noun or pronoun to rename or tell more about it

appositive phrase   a phrase that includes an appositive

articles   a special group of adjectives that includes the words *a*, *an*, and *the*

body   the main part of the paragraph. It includes sentences that relate to the main idea.

clause   a group of words that has a subject and predicate and forms part of a sentence

collective noun   a noun that names a group of people, things, or animals that act as a unit

colon [:]   introduces a series of items

comma [,]   shows a short pause between words or groups of words

common noun   a word that names any person, place, thing, event, or idea

comparative adjective   an adjective that compares two people, places, things, events, or ideas

complex sentence   a sentence with an independent clause and a dependent clause

compound noun   a group of words that names a person, place, thing, event, or idea

compound predicate   two or more predicates that have the same subject

compound sentence   a sentence that contains two or more simple sentences, or independent clauses

compound subject   two or more subjects that have the same predicate

concluding sentence   a sentence that restates the main idea of a paragraph

concrete noun   a noun that names something that can be seen, heard, touched, smelled, or tasted

contraction   a shortened form of a group of words in which an apostrophe takes the place of the missing letter or letters

coordinating conjunction   a word that is used to join words, phrases, or sentences

declarative sentence   a sentence that tells what someone or something is or does

demonstrative pronoun   a pronoun that points out one or more nouns

dependent clause   a clause that cannot stand alone as a complete sentence

direct object   a noun or pronoun that receives the action of a verb

exclamatory sentence   a sentence that shows strong feeling

fragment   a group of words that does not express a complete thought

future tense   the verb form that shows action in the future

gerund   a verb that ends with *-ing* and is used as a noun

gerund phrase   a phrase that begins with a gerund. Gerund phrases are used as nouns.

helping verb   the verb in a verb phrase that helps the main verb tell what happens or what is

hyphen [-]   used between parts of compound numbers, fractions, and some compound words

imperative sentence   a sentence that gives a command or makes a request

indefinite pronoun   a pronoun that does not replace a particular noun. The antecedent often is not known.

independent clause   a clause that can stand alone as a sentence

indirect object   a noun or pronoun to whom or for whom an action is done

infinitive   the word *to* plus the plural form of a verb. Infinitives may be used as nouns, adjectives, or adverbs.

infinitive phrase   a phrase that begins with an infinitive

interjection   a word or group of words that expresses emotion and is followed by an exclamation point or a comma

interrogative pronoun   a pronoun that is used to ask a question

interrogative sentence   a sentence that asks a question

irregular verb   a word that does not form its past by adding *-d* or *-ed*

linking verb   a verb that expresses what is or what seems to be

main verb   the verb in a verb phrase that tells what happens or what is

negative   a word or phrase that means "no," such as *not*

noun   a word that names a person, place, thing, event, or idea

noun clause   a dependent clause that acts as a noun

object complement   a word that follows the direct object and refers to it

object of the preposition   a noun or pronoun at the end of a prepositional phrase

paragraph   three or more sentences that are placed together and relate to the same idea

participial phrase   a phrase that begins with a present participle or a past participle. Participial phrases are used as adjectives.

participle   a verb form that is used as an adjective

passive voice   the verb form that shows the action is done *to* the subject of a sentence

past participle   a verb form that shows completed action

past tense   a verb form that shows action or being in the past

personal pronoun   a pronoun that identifies the speaker, the person spoken to, or the person or thing spoken about

plural noun   a noun that names more than one person, place, thing, event, or idea

possessive noun   a noun that shows ownership or relationship

possessive pronoun   a pronoun that shows ownership or relationship

predicate   the part of a sentence that tells what the subject does or is

predicate adjective   an adjective that comes after a linking verb and tells about the subject of the sentence

predicate nominative   a noun or pronoun that follows a linking verb or verb phrase and renames the simple subject

preposition   a word that shows how a noun or pronoun relates to another word or group of words in a sentence

prepositional phrase   a group of words that begins with a preposition and ends with a noun or pronoun

present participle   a verb form that shows continuing action

present tense   a verb form that shows action or being at the present time

pronoun   a word that takes the place of one or more nouns

proper adjective   an adjective that refers to the name of a particular person, place, thing, event, or idea

proper noun   a word that names a particular person, place, thing, event, or idea

quotation marks [" "]   show the beginning and end of someone's exact words

reflexive pronoun   a pronoun that refers to a noun or pronoun already named

relative pronoun   a pronoun that connects a noun or pronoun with a group of words that tells more about it

run-on sentence   two or more sentences that are written incorrectly as one sentence

semicolon [;]   joins two closely related sentences

sentence   a group of words that expresses a complete thought

simple predicate   the main verb or verb phrase of a sentence

simple sentence   a sentence that expresses a complete thought

simple subject   the subject noun or pronoun of a sentence

singular noun   a noun that names one person, place, thing, event, or idea

subject   the part of a sentence that tells who or what the sentence is about

subordinating conjunction   one or more words that begin a dependent clause

superlative adjective   an adjective that compares three or more people, places, things, events, or ideas

supporting detail   a sentence that gives more information about the topic sentence of a paragraph

tense   the time of the action or being expressed by a verb

topic sentence   a sentence that states the main idea of a paragraph

transitional word   a word that connects one idea or sentence to another

verb   a word that expresses action or a state of being

verb phrase   a phrase made up of one or more helping verbs and a main verb

Index

A

Abbreviations
  defined, 55, 64
  of proper nouns, 64
Abstract nouns
  v. concrete nouns, 87–88
  defined, 73, 87
Action verbs, 139–140
  defined, 135, 139
  irregular, 135, 154–156
  past tense verb forms, 135, 151–152
  present tense verb forms, 135, 144–145
Active voice, 163, 177–178
Addresses, capital letters in, 63–64
Adjective clauses, 322–328
  combining sentences with, 327–328
  defined, 313, 322
  list of words used to begin, 322
  relative pronouns in, 322–323
  using commas with, 324, 327–328
Adjectives, 208–229
  v. adverbs, 238–239
  articles, 209, 211–212
  comparative, 209, 217–220
  defined, 209, 210
  after linking verbs, 213–214
  before nouns, 210–212
  predicate, 209, 213–214
  proper, 209, 215–216
  specific, 224
  spelling correctly, 222–223
  superlative, 209, 217–220
  writing with, 226–227
Adverb clauses
  combining sentences with, 320–321
  commas with introductory, 316–319
  in complex sentences, 316–319
  defined, 313, 316
  subordinating conjunctions in, 320–321

Adverbs, 230–251
  v. adjectives, 238–239
  avoiding double negatives, 231, 242–243
  defined, 231, 232
  specific, 245–246
  that tell about adjectives, 234–235
  that tell about other adverbs, 236–237
  using to make comparisons, 240–241
  writing with specific, 248–249
Agreement
  of pronoun and antecedent, 101–102
  of subject and verb, 145–150, 265–267
Almanac, 179
Antecedents
  agreement with, 101–102
  defined, 97, 100
  of indefinite pronouns, 108
Apostrophes
  in contractions, 243
  defined, 73, 83
  with possessive nouns, 83–85
Appositive phrases
  combining sentences with, 277
  commas with, 276–277
  defined, 275, 276
Appositives
  combining sentences with, 277
  commas with, 276–277
  defined, 275, 276
Articles, 211–212
  defined, 209, 211

B

To be
  forms of, 141
  as a helping verb, 165
  as a linking verb, 141–143
  verb phrases with, 164–165
Biographical reference book, 113
Body, 346–347
  of paragraph, defined, 339, 346
Book of quotations, 42

Q

Question marks
    as end marks, 6–7, 8–10
    in direct quotations, 38–39
Quotation marks
    in direct quotations, 38–39
    defined, 25, 38
Quotations
    punctuation with, 38–39
    use of, 38–41

R

References
    almanac, 179
    biographical reference book, 113
    book of quotations, 42
    computer grammar checker, 308
    computer spelling checker, 86
    dictionary, 157
    encyclopedia, 21
    index, 189
    Internet search engine, 123
    library catalogs, 67
    maps, 261
    newspapers, 354
    periodicals, 326
    phone book, 221
    table of contents, 284
    thesaurus, 244
Reflexive pronouns, 103–104
    defined, 97, 103
    lists of, 103
Relative pronouns, 124–126
    in adjective clauses, 322–323
    defined, 117, 124
    list of, 124
Résumé, 153
Run-on sentences, 304–305
    defined, 295, 304

S

Semicolons, 44–45
    defined, 25, 44
Sentence patterns, verbs and, 184–205
    writing with, 202–203

Sentences, 2–23
    capitalization at the beginning of, 8–10
    combining, *See* Combining sentences
    complete, 18–19
    complex, 313, 316–319
    compound, 295, 298–303
    declarative, 3, 6–7, 8, 11–13
    defined, 3, 4
    end punctuation in, 8–10
    exclamatory, 3, 6–7, 8
    v. fragments, 3, 4–5
    imperative, 3, 6–7, 8, 17
    interrogative, 3, 6–7, 8, 14–16
    patterns, verbs and, 184–205
    predicate of, 3, 4–5
    run-on, 295, 304–305
    simple, 295, 296
    subject of, 3, 4–5
    writing in complete, 18–19
Simple predicates, 186–188
    defined 185, 186
Simple sentences
    defined, 295, 296
Simple subjects, 186–188
    defined, 185, 186
Singular
    nouns, 73, 74–75
    pronouns, 101–102, 103–104, 105–106,
        108–109
Specific adverbs, 245–246
Spelling
    adjectives, 222–223
    plural nouns, 77–82
Subject of a sentence, 4–5
    agreement with verb, 145, 150
    compound, 295, 296
    in declarative sentences, 11–13
    defined, 3, 4
    in imperative sentences, 17
    in interrogative sentences, 14–16
    in prepositional phrases, 265–267
    simple, 185, 186–188

Photo Credits

Cover: *library:* Adam Woolfitt/CORBIS, *telephone:* Ken Davies/Masterfile, *newspaper:* PhotoDisc, Inc., *Dictionary:* PhotoEdit, *pencil, mouse and mousepad:* Stefano Carbini. The Stock Market 1; Peter Beck, The Stock Market 2; Seth Resnick, Stock Boston 21; Hiroyuki Matsumoto 24; David Young-Wolff, Photo Edit 47; Corbis/Adam Woolfit 53; David Young-Wolff, Photo Edit 54; Amy C. Etra, Photo Edit 67; David Young-Wolff, Photo Edit 72; Bob Daemmrich, Stock Boston 89; United Nations, FPG 95; Janet Hohoda Rogers, Photo Researchers 96; Myrleen Ferguson, Photo Edit 112; Steve Dunwell, The Image Bank 113; Tom Wurl, Stock Boston 116; Prentice Hall, Inc. 123; Mark Richards, Photo Edit 133 (T); Photo Researchers, Inc. 133 (B); Ron Chapple, FPG International 134; Prentice Hall, Inc. 157; Corbis/Kelly-Mooney Photography 162; Tony Freeman, Photo Edit 176; Tom Stewart, The Stock Market 184; Jay Schlegel Photography, The Stock Market 207; Corbis/Wolfgang Kaehler 208; Photo Researchers 225; Dean Abramson, Stock Boston 230; Jeffrey Myers, FPG 247; Joseph Sohm, ChromoSohm Inc./Corbis 253; Index Stock International 254; Jeff Greenberg, Photo Edit 264; Corbis/Richard Hamilton Smith 274; Tom Prettyman, Photo Edit 287; Wayne R. Bilenduke, Tony Stone Images 293; PNI Sovfoto, Eastfoto 294; David Young-Wolff, Photo Edit 309; NASA, Photo Edit 312; Bob Daemmrich, Stock Boston 337; PNI, Bob Daemmrich, Stock Boston 338; David Young-Wolff, Photo Edit 355.